MEDIEVAL CANON LAW

THE MEDIEVAL WORLD
Editor: David Bates

Already published

. . . .

MEDIEVAL CANON LAW

James A. Brundage

LONGMAN
London and New York

Longman Group Limited,
Longman House, Burnt Mill,
Harlow, Essex CM20 2JE, England
and Associated Companies throughout the world.

*Published in the United States of America
by Longman Publishing, New York*

© Longman Group Limited 1995

First published 1995

ISBN 0 582 09357 0 CSD
ISBN 0 582 09356 2 PPR

British Library Cataloguing-in-Publication Data

A catalogue record for this book is
available from the British Library

Library of Congress Cataloging-in-Publication Data

Brundage, James A.
Medieval canon law / James A. Brundage.
p. cm. – (Medieval world)
Includes bibliographical references and index.
ISBN 0-582-09357-0. – ISBN 0-582-09356-2
1. Canon law–History. 2. Law, Medieval. I. Title. II Series.
LAW
262.9–dc20   94-33506
                                                  CIP

Set by 7p in 11/12pt Baskerville
Produced by Longman Singapore Publishers (Pte) Ltd.
Printed in Singapore

For Kris, at long last

CONTENTS

. . . . .

EDITOR'S PREFACE

The dominance of the church within medieval European society is an obvious truism to all interested in the development of the civilisation of western Europe and the history of Christianity. The mechanisms by which this dominace was sustained and by which the church contributed to the organisation and development of this society are therefore subjects of profound importance to all who wish to understand not just medieval Europe, but also its impact on a wider world. At the heart of this dominance was the system of canon law which is the subject of this book. Its ramifications were far-reaching since, in the same way that the church's authority reached into the furthest recesses of society, so too did canon law evolve rules which attempted to deal with all the situations that confronted it. The history of canon law is therefore of central importance, not just to the history of the church itself, but for an historical understanding of themes as diverse and basic as sexual behaviour, marriage, commerce and the family.

James Brundage's book is an extremely welcome addition to the Medieval World series for several reasons. Chief of these is that this very important topic has no accessible treatment in English. For this reason alone, *Medieval Canon Law* will be an invaluable guide to all interested in the medieval period. A system of law is inevitably a very complex subject. Canon law, which was applied over many centuries and was for a long time the subject of intensive academic study, is no exception. James Brundage's book is remarkable because, while it does not shirk these complexities, it also surveys the subject with remarkable lucidity; readers are left in no doubt about the difficulties and importance of the subject while they are guided smoothly and assuredly through its various aspects. Professor Brundage's book takes us through the entire medieval history of canon law, from its beginnings in the early Christian centuries to the fully-fledged system of courts and decretals of the later Middle Ages. Successive chapters deal with origins and development, the era of Gratian, the application of canon law to government and society, procedure and jurisprudence. In conclusion, Professor Brundage reflects on the wider historical importance of canon law and its modern relevance: his conclusion that canon law 'constituted a fundamental force in the creation of some of the elemental ideas and institutions that continue to this day to characterize Western societies' is both apt and thought-provoking. The book ends with two necessary appendices on technicalities and people, that is, on methods of citation and on the biographies of the main canon lawyers, which will be indispensable to all who wish to take the subject further.

James Brundage's extensive experience and outstanding publications in the field of medieval canon law and its application within medieval society make him the ideal author to write this book for the Medieval World series. He is the author of distinguished books which deal with Canon Law and the Crusader and with Canon Law and Sex and Marriage. His achievement both in distilling this vast range of experience into an accessible general study and in explaining the structure of legal and scholarly activity which underpins all writings on canon law will be of great importance to all interested in the European Middle Ages and its wider significance.

David Bates

. . . . .

AUTHOR'S PREFACE

This book attempts to sketch the broad outlines of the development of the canon law of the Western church from its beginnings to the end of the Middle Ages, which, in this context at least, means until the commencement of the Protestant Reformation in the early sixteenth century. Growing numbers of medievalists during the second half of the twentieth century have come to realize that canon law formed a crucial component of medieval life and thought. Its rules affected the lives and actions of practically everyone, its enforcement mechanisms were increasingly able to reach into everyday affairs at all social levels, from peasant villages to royal households, and the ideas debated in the canon law schools constituted an influential and pervasive element in medieval intellectual life. The records of contentious matters that came before canonical courts as well as the archives of ecclesiastical administrators who applied (or failed to apply) canonical rules make up a very large fraction of the evidence that survives from the Middle Ages.

Serious study of medieval canon law quickly becomes highly technical. '[Law] schools make tough law', observed Frederic William Maitland, and as usual he was right on the mark.[1] Canon law was extremely tough indeed, not only in the sense that it that it was institutionally strong and sturdy, but also in the sense that it was difficult and technical. Medievalists have usually preferred to shy away from its

---

1. Frederic William Maitland, *English law and the Renaissance*, Reid Lecture for 1901 (Cambridge, 1901), repr. in *Selected historical essays of F. W. Maitland*, ed. Helen M. Cam (Boston, 1957), p.144.

technical mysteries. I have tried in this book to avoid most technical details. I should, however, alert readers that canonical waters, although alluring, can also be treacherous and warn historians that they must be prepared to steer carefully when they embark on investigations that may bring them into the vicinity of canonical shoals.

I have incurred numerous debts in the course of writing this book. David Bates suggested the project to me during a chance encounter in the British Library tea room and I want to say here how glad I am that he did – it is a book that has long needed doing. Andrew MacLennan and his staff at Longman have been both courteous and helpful throughout the process of bringing it to fruition. I am grateful as well for the institutional support I have consistently received from the University of Kansas, especially from its libraries and their staffs. I owe many debts to Kenneth Pennington, and not least among them is my gratitude, not only for reading the book in manuscript, but also for numerous suggestions that have improved it. I am likewise grateful to Charles Donahue, Jr, for suggesting additional improvements and for saving me from some imprudent generalizations. Any faults that remain are mine alone.

LIST OF ABBREVIATIONS

The system of legal citations used in this book is explained in Appendix I.

Clem. *Constitutiones Clementinae.* In *Corpus iuris canonici.* See Appendix.

COD *Conciliorum oecumenicorum decreta.* Eds G. Alberigo, P. P. Joannou, C. Leonardi, P. Prodi, and H. Jedin. Basel, 1962.

Cod. *Codex Iustinianus.* In *Corpus iuris civilis.* See Appendix.

DDC *Dictionnaire de droit canonique.* Ed. R. Naz. 7 vols Paris, 1935–65.

DMA *Dictionary of the Middle Ages.* Joseph R. Strayer, editor-in-chief. 13 vols New York, 1982–89.

Dig. *Digestum.* In *Corpus iuris civilis.* See Appendix.

Extrav. comm. *Extravagantes communes.* In *Corpus iuris canonici.* See Appendix.

Glos. ord. *Glossa ordinaria.* See Appendix.

Gratian *Decretum Gratiani.* In *Corpus iuris canonici.* See Appendix.

Inst.	*Institutiones Iustiniani.* In *Corpus iuris civilis.* See Appendix.
L ed	United States Reports, Lawyers' edition.
Le Bras, Lefebvre, and Rambaud	Gabriel Le Bras, Charles Lefebvre, and Jacqueline Rambaud, *L'âge classique, 1140–1378: Sources et théorie du droit.* Histoire du droit et des institutions de l'église en occident, vol. 7. Paris, 1965.
MGH	*Monumenta Germaniae Historica inde ab anno Christi quingentesimo usque ad annum millesimum et quingentesimum.* Hannover, Leipzig, Berlin, Munich, etc. [imprint varies], 1828– [in progress].
MIC	*Monumenta iuris canonici.* Vatican City, etc. [imprint varies], 1965– [in progress] *Corpus collectionum* (1973– ; 7 vols to date) *Corpus glossatorum* (1969– ; 3 vols to date) *Subsidia* (1965– ; 9 vols to date).
Nov.	*Novellae leges.* In *Corpus iuris civilis.* See Appendix.
PL	*Patrologiae cursus completus ... series Latina.* Ed. J.-P. Migne. 221 vols Paris, 1844–64.
S Ct	Supreme Court Reports.
Schulte, QL	Johann Friedrich von Schulte, *Geschichte der Quellen und Literatur des canonischen Rechts.* 3 vols Stuttgart, 1875–7; repr. Granz, 1956.
U.S.	United States Reports.
VI	*Liber sextus.* In *Corpus iuris canonici.* See Appendix.
X	*Liber extra (Decretales Gregorii IX).* In *Corpus iuris canonici.* See Appendix.

. . . . .

INTRODUCTION

Most of the records that survive from the European Middle Ages are legal documents. They include such things as charters, registers, writs, contracts, wills, court rolls, tax records, and other written instruments of civil administration. They also include ecclesiastical legal documents, such as the canons of councils and synods, collections of church law, the act books and cause papers of ecclesiastical courts, bishops' registers, mandates, memoranda, formularies, monastic cartularies, and numerous other artifacts of ecclesiastical administration. Likewise the chronicles, annals, and other narrative sources upon which historians also rely are typically filled with accounts of lawsuits and other legal actions that arise from property disputes, treaties, crimes, and the punishment of malefactors, not to mention domestic matters, such as marriages, dowries, divorces, and the disposition of estates. All of these had profound legal consequences and were governed by legal rules, many of them highly technical. Even medieval poets on occasion employed the language of the law to describe the legal consequences of love and marriage, betrayal and perjury, adultery and rape, death and mourning.[1]

Some grasp of medieval laws and legal conventions is accordingly essential for the study of almost any facet of

1. Christopher Brooke, *The medieval ideal of marriage* (Oxford, 1989) contains numerous examples; see also Henry Ansgar Kelly, *Love and marriage in the age of Chaucer* (Ithaca, NY, 1975) and Kathryn Gravdal, *Ravishing maidens: Writing rape in medieval French literature and law* (Philadelphia, 1991).

medieval life. But which laws? Medieval laws came in abundant variety. Multiple legal systems coexisted and overlapped within the same town or region, each with its own complex rules and conventions as well as its own system of courts that applied them. Manorial law, feudal law, municipal law, royal law, maritime law, merchant law, Roman law, and canon law all nestled cheek by jowl with each other in medieval communities. Each claimed its special areas of competence, to be sure, but jurisdictional claims frequently competed with one another and disputes over jurisdictional questions erupted with lamentable regularity.

Worldly-wise and canny litigants, however, could find ways to manipulate this competition for jurisdiction to their own advantage. Multiple courts and legal systems gave individuals and institutions the opportunity to take their lawsuits to the jurisdiction that seemed most likely to produce the result that they wanted in the shortest time and at the least expense. This does not mean, of course, that all medieval litigants acted rationally, any more than their modern counterparts do. But the situation certainly furnished clear-headed parties with ample opportunity either to stretch out or abbreviate the settlement of their legal claims, depending upon what best suited their interests.

To penetrate the mists of the legal documents that survive from any of the multiple jurisdictions that flourished in the Middle Ages requires some knowledge of the subtleties and conventions of the legal language and procedures peculiar to that jurisdiction. In legal records, as historians have occasionally learned to their sorrow, things are seldom what they seem. The words 'By force and arms' (*vi et armis*) in English common law documents, for example, do not necessarily mean that the trespass of which the petitioner complains involved either weapons or physical coercion – at least not in any ordinary meaning of these terms. *Vi et armis* was simply a technical formula necessary to bring the matter under royal jurisdiction. Similarly the 'clerics' who appear in ecclesiastical documents were not always religious professionals, while some full-time religious professionals, such as nuns or members of military religious orders, for example, were technically not 'clerics' at all. Likewise, a 'libel' (*libellus*) in canon law need not be defamatory, nor does it mean a 'little book', which is another possible definition – in legal records, however, the term refers to the formal petition for redress necessary to initiate an action before a canonical judge. The terminology of legal documents is often baffling to the uninitiated, and people have complained about this for centuries.[2]

Canon law occupied a unique niche among the legal systems that flourished in the high and later Middle Ages. While most legal systems were confined to a particular region or locality, canon law emerged as a working and often quite effective international law. With relatively few exceptions, the same canonical rules applied everywhere in Latin Christendom. Canonists were often highly mobile in a society where both geographical and occupational mobility were uncommon. Men trained in the law schools of Bologna and other recognized centres of canonistic learning could and did practise their craft virtually anywhere. They turn up in the records in an amazing variety of roles – as bishops or archdeacons, as royal judges or ambassadors, as advocates and proctors, as professors and podestà.

Canon law was also remarkable because, at least in principle, its rules applied equally to everyone, regardless of gender, class, or social standing. Thus dynastic alliances between royalty at the upper end of the social scale and peasant marriages at its lower end were both subject to the same body of canonical marriage rules. This does not mean, of course, that in practice canonical courts treated princes and ploughmen with even-handed impartiality. The canonical legal system, like any other, often – perhaps too often – fell short of its ideals. What was remarkable, however, was that impartial equality was a canonical ideal at all.

This book aims to provide an introduction to medieval

---

2. John of Salisbury, *Policraticus, sive de nugis curialium* 5.19, ed. C. C. J. Webb, 2 vols (Oxford, 1909), i, pp.350–1; cf. E. K. Rand, 'Ioannes Saresberiensis sillabizat', *Speculum* 1 (1926) 447–8. For a slightly more recent version of the same complaint, see Jonathan Swift, *Gulliver's Travels*, pt 4, ch. 4.

canon law. It seeks to provide an orientation to the subject and some sense both of what it dealt with and how readers may pursue these matters further, as time and interest dictate. It is not designed as a textbook that will systematically lay bare all the mysteries of the law or supply detailed answers about how the law applied to specific situations and problems. That is the function of many of the books and articles mentioned in the footnotes and others listed in the select bibliography. It also needs to be said here that many important questions about how canon law operated in medieval society cannot now be answered with great certainty. The history of canon law has not yet been written, in part because the evidence is so plentiful and in part because too few modern scholars have yet sifted through, digested, and published large and important parts of the surviving evidence.[3]

The mass of available material is enormous and the problems – legal, theological, ecclesiological, and palaeographical – that it presents are formidable. At the same time, however, canonical records, documents, commentaries, and glosses can reveal a great deal about how medieval institutions worked, about how medieval people of all sorts thought and acted, and about the delicate relationship between law and society in the Middle Ages. Beyond that, the study of medieval canon law has already shown important and previously unsuspected linkages between the medieval church's legal system and the development of some of the most basic institutions of modern constitutional government. Both canonical public law, which treats the relationship between governments and their subjects, and canonical private law, which deals with the ways in which private persons managed their affairs, can tell us much about the sources of our own institutions and societies, as well as about the vanished world of medieval Christendom, out of which the world we see around us ultimately grew.

3.   Charles Donahue, Jr, *Why the history of canon law is not written*, Selden Society lecture, 1984 (London, 1986).

Chapter 1

LAW IN THE EARLY CHRISTIAN CHURCH

Christians have from the beginning felt ambivalent about the proper role of law in religious life. Jesus expressed grave reservations about the Mosaic law as a source of spiritual guidance and enlightenment, although he denied that he wished to abolish the law.[1] The ambivalence was even more marked in St Paul's letters. Some Pauline passages strongly hinted that law was an altogether inappropriate mechanism for defining the spiritual goals of Christian believers, although elsewhere Paul described the Law of Moses as sacred, just, and good.[2]

Despite the evident reservations of its founder and early teachers about the place of law in Christian life, the church soon began to develop its own legal system, for its leaders quickly discovered that a viable community not only needed goodwill and fraternal love, but also required some rules and regulations for the orderly conduct of its business, to define the functions of its officers, and to govern relationships among its members.

Collections of such regulations for the use of church authorities appeared quite early in Christianity's history. The earliest surviving handbook of church law, the *Didache* or *Doctrine of the Twelve Apostles*, dates from the end of the first or the beginning of the second century. This brief

---

1. Thus, for example, Matt. 5:17–20 and Matt. 23:23. See generally Stephan Kuttner, 'Reflections on Gospel and Law in the History of the Church', in *Liber amicorum Monseigneur Onclin*, Bibliotheca ephemeridum theologicorum Lovaniensium, vol. 42 (Gembloux, 1976), pp.199–209, reprinted with original pagination in Kuttner's *Studies in the history of medieval canon law* (London, 1990).
2. Thus cf. Rom. 7:12 with Rom. 10:4, Gal. 3:10–13, and Col. 2:14.

work – it is scarcely more than pamphlet-size – consists of a series of moral precepts, followed by prescriptions for the conduct of liturgical services and a handful of rules about church governance. The *Didache* was soon followed by more ample expositions of the basic rules that governed conduct in early Christian communities. The second-century *Pastor* of Hermas seems more like an apocalypse than a lawbook. It consists of five 'visions' or revelations, a dozen rules of conduct, and ten parables on eschatological themes. The *Traditio apostolica*, ascribed to Hippolytus, appeared early in the third century. Its author, whoever he may have been, claims that his book transmits the genuine doctrine of the apostles and warns that deviation from that tradition will lead to doctrinal error and heretical beliefs. While the subject matter of the *Traditio apostolica* is chiefly liturgical, it also contains valuable information about the organization and structure of the third-century church. The *Didascalia apostolorum* (which dates from the mid-third century) incorporates much of the material in the *Traditio apostolica*, but adds further information about such matters as the Christian community's responsibility for widows and orphans, Jewish-Christian relations, and rules on fasting and penance, as well as liturgical matters.[3]

Christian communities throughout the Roman Empire struggled for generations to survive in a hostile environment. Jewish communities rejected Christian claims about the Messiahship of Jesus, deplored the conversion of Jews to the new faith, and were scandalized by the failure of those converts to continue observing the prescriptions of Mosaic law. Many Gentiles were equally unwelcoming to the new religion, but for different reasons. Pagan intellectuals dismissed Christian claims to have received divine revelations as irrational, while government authorities suspected Christians of criminal, perhaps even treasonous, conspiracies. Ordinary people found the abstemious habits

---

3. A recent and reliable guide to these and other early writings on canon law is Jean Gaudemet, *Les sources du droit de l'église en Occident du IIe au VIIe siècle* (Paris, 1985). A briefer introduction in English to early canonical materials may also be found in Roger L. Reynolds's article, 'Law, Canon: To Gratian', in the *Dictionary of the Middle Ages*, 13 vols (New York, 1989; cited hereafter as DMA), vii, 395–413.

of Christians peculiar and resented their rejection of the social bonding involved in the celebration of the civic festivals of the pagan religious calendar.

Because Christians constituted a small, close-knit, secretive group who habitually kept to themselves and shunned intimate contact with the surrounding society, hostility towards them soon hardened into open persecution. This began as early as the reign of Nero (54–68), who found the Christians convenient scapegoats for the great fire at Rome in 64 CE and for other civic discontents. Persecution continued sporadically until the abdication of the emperor Diocletian (284–305), who made the liquidation of Christianity one of the major goals in his programme of imperial renewal.

Under these circumstances, it is scarcely surprising that the law of the Christian church during the first three centuries of its existence was directed chiefly towards maintaining discipline among church members and concentrated on the internal concerns of the group. Since it was difficult for persecuted Christian communities to hold and administer property openly and since they could expect scant help from public authorities in maintaining their joint interests against outsiders, Christian law during these centuries concerned itself largely with such internal matters as the order of worship, relationships among members of the community, and the rights and obligations assigned to different subgroups among the members. Rules governing these issues seem to have been formulated by bishops and other community leaders, and presumably represented some sort of group consensus about appropriate behavioural norms.

The period of persecution ended with the accession to power of Constantine I, who ruled between 311 and 337. Constantine and his successors[4] transformed the relationship between the Christian church and the Roman government. They not only embraced Christianity themselves, but made it a pillar of the Roman official establishment. In that process the church became virtually an organ of imperial government, enriched by privileges,

4. With the glaring exception of the emperor Julian the Apostate (361–3).

favours, and public funds, but also used as an arm of imperial administration. These developments entailed substantial changes in the rules that operated within the church and inevitably altered relationships between its officials and its members.[5]

From Constantine's time onward church councils, in which large numbers of bishops came together to work out common policies, emerged as an increasingly important feature in the governance of the Christian world and the canons and decrees of these bodies soon became the principal sources of church law.

Church councils, as well as smaller regional assemblies of the clergy and leading laymen, often known as synods, thus emerged as legislative bodies and became the source of new law, doctrinal pronouncements, and spiritual guidance. Councils and synods, in addition, often functioned as courts, for they listened to complaints about deviant belief and conduct and rendered decisions on important contested matters within Christian communities.

At the same time the church began to develop an organizational structure whose main features still endure to the present day in catholic Christianity. That structure is hierarchical, that is, authority and responsibility within the organization are distributed unequally among functionaries according to their rank or position.[6] Thus, priests and

5. For further details on what follows see especially Jean Gaudemet, *L'église dans l'empire romain (IVe–Ve siècles)*, Histoire du droit et des institutions de l'église en Occident, vol. 3, 2nd edn (Paris, 1989).
6. This hierarchical system emerged as a new stage in the organizational development of the Christian church. Prior to the fourth century, the structure of the church was far simpler and is better described as collegial, rather than hierarchical. Christianity in that early period was concentrated largely in cities and the entire community of the faithful in each city formed a single unit (usually referred to simply as the church of, say, Ephesus, or Alexandria, or whatever the city's name might be), over which a bishop presided. The bishop was chosen by the members of the local church and he appointed subordinate ministers, such as priests and deacons, to assist him. The bishop, however, remained the sole pastor of all the Christians within his city and was not formally responsible to any higher authority outside of it. The church adopted the principle of subordination of authority in the fourth century as a consequence of its integration into the administrative system of the Empire, which was already organized as a hierarchical structure. For a fuller

other ministers among the lower clergy enjoy limited authority over the laity within a small geographical region that came ultimately to be known as a parish. Parish priests are responsible to a bishop, who supervises a larger region, called a diocese. The bishop has the right to impose rules on his priests and to discipline or remove those who fail to obey them. The bishop, in turn, is subordinate to a metropolitan or archbishop, whose authority extends throughout a still larger region, called a province, which includes several dioceses. Each bishop must answer to his metropolitan for the conduct of the priests and laypersons within his diocese and the metropolitan has the authority to prescribe rules that the bishops subordinate to him must follow. Metropolitans, in their turn, are responsible to even higher authorities, the patriarchs, who may supervise church affairs in several different kingdoms. By the late fourth century the First Council of Constantinople (381) recognized the bishops of Alexandria, Antioch, Constantinople, Jerusalem, and Rome as patriarchs.[7] Among these five patriarchs (collectively called the pentarchy), the bishops of Rome not only claimed patriarchal authority throughout the Western Empire, but also asserted that they possessed a preeminent authority over the other patriarchs, a claim that made the Eastern patriarchs uneasy, but which they hesitated to disavow.

These fourth-century structural developments established long-term patterns of thought and action that not only endured throughout the Middle Ages, but have also lasted into modern times. The new organizational scheme inevitably gave increased scope and prominence to church

6. (*continued*)
   sketch of these developments, as well as the extensive literature on the subject, see Michael A. Fahey, 'The catholicity of the church in the New Testament and in the early patristic period', *The Jurist* 52 (1992), 44–70.
7. 1 Constantinople c. 2–3, in *Conciliorum oecumenicorum decreta*, ed. Giuseppe Alberigo et al., 2nd edn (Basel, 1962; cited hereafter as COD), pp.27–8. Each patriarch presided over councils and synods of bishops, exercised judicial power, and had the right to consecrate the bishops and metropolitans within his region; Justinian, Nov. 123.3. This and the other legal citations that follow are explained in Appendix I below.

law. Such a complex system of hierarchical authority and responsibility virtually demanded elaborate regulations to define the powers and obligations of officials at each level of the structure.

By the fifth century, moreover, partly in consequence of the claims to special authority that they had begun to assert over the other bishops of the Christian world, the bishops of Rome commenced to take a more prominent role as makers of ecclesiastical law. Papal decretals, or letters, in which the Roman bishops not only stated their decisions on issues that had been appealed to them but also set forth general rules for determining similar controversies, accordingly began to figure with increasing prominence in canonical collections.

Those collections themselves grew in number, size, and complexity from the fourth century onward. Thus, for example, the so-called *Constitutiones apostolicae*, compiled in Syria or Palestine, probably about 380, is far longer than the *Didascalia* and other early collections. Organized systematically in eight books, the *Constitutiones apostolicae* drew upon a wide array of sources – the scriptures, apocryphal literature, creeds, conciliar canons, and church histories – to articulate a detailed scheme of the obligations and prerogatives of various groups within the Christian fold. Other major canonical collections of this period included the *Statuta ecclesiae antiqua*, a fifth-century collection of decrees drawn from Gallic and Spanish councils, which was particularly rich in disciplinary regulations for clergy and laity alike. The *Dionysiana*, compiled by a Scythian monk, Dionysius Exiguus, probably in the first half of the sixth century, was notably better organized and more systematic than its predecessors. Dionysius included both papal decisions, or decretals, and conciliar canons in his collection and arranged his materials in chronological order. He questioned the authenticity of the so-called apostolic canons and some other traditional material and therefore chose to omit them from his work. A lengthy seventh-century collection known as the *Hispana* was long regarded as an authoritative canonical collection. It comprised a great mass of canons, drawn not only from the early Greek councils, but also from North Africa, Gaul, and especially from Spain, where

10

conciliar legislation was both extensive and important. In addition, the *Hispana* included numerous papal decretals, from Pope Damasus I (366–84) to Gregory I (590–604). The canonical material in the *Hispana* was reworked several times. The earliest version was known as the *Collectio hispana chronologica*, because it presented its conciliar canons and papal decretals in chronological order. During the second half of the seventh century some unknown editor or editors reorganized this material into subject categories to create a revised version of the collection that is known as the *Collectio hispana systematica*. The *Hispana systematica* provided its users with more convenient access to the canons than most other early collections had done and that no doubt accounted, at least in part, for its long-continued popularity.

The canons (the word comes from the Greek κανοων meaning a rule) during the first five centuries defined norms for the religious life of members of early Christian communities. Canons regulated such matters as the structure of the liturgical calendar, which governed the annual rhythm of Christian life, established forms and ceremonies for performing the Eucharist, baptism, and other liturgical functions, prescribed the details for observance of fasting seasons and the celebration of feasts, and provided for the distribution of charitable offerings to widows and other disadvantaged members of the communities. Above all, the early canons defined the key elements of mainstream Christian doctrine and drew increasingly sharp lines between authentic Christians and others, whom they labelled heretics, apostates, and unbelievers. In addition, canon law in the early church sought to enumerate the powers and qualifications of bishops and other clerics, to define their obligations, and to provide for disciplinary measures to curb those who exceeded their authority or failed to measure up to the high standards of conduct expected of the clergy. From the fourth century onward, as monasticism became an increasingly prominent feature of Christian religious life and practice, canon law also needed to take account of the status of monks and nuns. Likewise, since Christian communities after Constantine's time soon became large property holders, the canons prescribed rules for the management and use of the church's material goods.

From the reign of Constantine, moreover, the Christian emperors explicitly recognized the jurisdictional authority of bishops and other church officers over issues that involved doctrine and morals and gave their decisions the force of public law.[8] Bishops, in consequence, established their own courts, the *audientia episcopalis*, in order to adjudicate matters that fell under their authority. Canon law thus came to be vested with coercive power, as well as moral authority, and the ecclesiastical hierarchy became in effect an arm of the judicial apparatus of Roman government.

The judicial functions of bishops in the early stages of this development mainly involved arbitration. Bishops typically sought to reconcile the antagonists in disputes and to resolve conflicts by mediating between the parties, rather than imposing judgments from on high. In some situations, however, canonical judges felt obliged to penalize members of the church either for heinous moral lapses or for serious deviations from mainstream teachings and doctrine. Arianism, Manichaeanism, Donatism, Pelagianism, and other sectarian movements during the fourth and fifth centuries challenged the authority of orthodox leaders and in consequence the *audientia episcopalis* and other church tribunals, particularly councils and synods, asserted a penal jurisdiction over deviations from the Christian faith to combat the threat of heresy.

Since canon law in the fourth and fifth centuries had barely begun to develop its own distinctive rules governing evidence and procedure in contentious matters, episcopal courts by and large adapted for their own purposes the norms current in Roman civil law. The details of this adaptation, however, are obscure and the scraps of information that survive do not present a coherent picture. The ecclesiastical courts of this early period appear in general to have enjoyed great latitude in determining the standards of proof that they would demand and the scanty surviving sources give the impression that procedures varied considerably between different regions and perhaps even between different judges in the same region.

8. Cod. Theod. 1.27.1–2.

Early canonical collections, such as those mentioned above, included material on a wide variety of substantive issues that concerned the leaders of Christian communities. Prominent among the problems that they dealt with were Christian marriage and family law, Christian attitudes towards slavery, military service, and economic activities, relations between Christians and their non-Christian neighbours, and the preservation of beliefs and practices that church authorities regarded as essential.

The canons were from the outset concerned with regulating marriage and family relationships, a topic already conspicuous in the letters of St Paul,[9] and subsequent writers about the rules governing Christian life almost invariably dealt with it. Christian subjects of the Roman Empire contracted marriage in much the same way as other Romans did, although from quite an early period they supplemented the observances customary among pagans with Christian rituals and blessings. Christian communities, however, conceived of the nature and consequences of marriage in quite different terms than their pagan contemporaries did. Christians, for one thing, strongly discouraged marriage across religious lines and imposed sanctions, often quite severe ones, upon those who sought to marry adherents of other religions. For another, Christian law came to interpret matrimonial consent rather differently than did civil marriage law. Most Christian teachers believed that consent to marriage involved a permanent commitment that, once given, could not subsequently be revoked; whereas pagan Roman lawyers conceived of marital consent as an on-going process, and marriage continued, in consequence, so long as the parties continued to consent to the union, but terminated once one party withdrew consent. Like contemporary pagan law, early Christian law required that parents, as well as the parties, consent to a prospective marriage; but unlike pagans, Christians did not reserve the right of consent solely to the male head of household, but rather expected that couples should seek the agreement of all those

---

9. For example, 1 Cor. 7:1–9, 26–36; Eph. 5:3–4; Gal. 5:16–21.

charged with the care and supervision of the young before entering into a marital union.[10]

Christian law concerning slavery also departed in important ways from the norms common among pagan Romans. No Christian authorities condemned the practice of slavery outright, to be sure; they commonly accepted the institution as a necessary and inevitable social institution. It was not unusual for Christian churches and the clergy, as well as laymen, to possess slaves of their own and to employ them to perform the many kinds of routine labour for which the technology of late antiquity provided no satisfactory alternative energy sources. At the same time, however, Christian religious teachers, like some of their pagan counterparts, particularly among the Stoics, affirmed that slavery was unnatural, and that in an ideal world all human beings ought to be free. Since this present terrestrial world was far from ideal, however, both the law and the practice of early Christian communities sought to limit the exploitation of slaves, rather than to abolish an institution so central to the society and economy of their age. Christian law, although it did not attack the institution of slavery, did insist that Christians must treat their slaves humanely and admonished owners to make every effort to provide for the religious needs of their slaves. The canons, unlike Roman civil law, recognized the capacity of slaves to marry legitimately and attempted to preserve the integrity of slave families by restricting the rights of owners to separate married slaves from their spouses and children.[11]

The canons of the early church were also much concerned with issues involving military service and, more generally, the restrictions that Christian society ought to place on violence. The question of whether Christians could serve in the Roman army troubled several early church fathers, as did related questions about the circumstances under which it was proper for a Christian to use force to defend himself, his family, or his community

---

10. Susan Treggiari, *Roman marriage: Iusti coniuges from the time of Cicero to the time of Ulpian* (Oxford, 1991); Gaudemet, *L'église dans l'Empire Romain*, pp.515–54.
11. *Ibid.*, pp.563–7; Miguel Falcão, *Las prohibiciones matrimoniales de caracter social en el Imperio Romano* (Pamplona, 1976).

from aggressors. During the period of religious persecution prior to Constantine, Christians debated whether it was lawful for them to resist the persecutors, while after Constantine the focus shifted to questions about the circumstances under which a Christian government might wage war and whether Christians should participate in the execution of criminals condemned by Roman courts.[12]

Economic conduct, like the morality of violence and physical conflict, was another concern that early church authorities addressed. The canons from quite early on forbade priests and bishops to take interest when they loaned money.[13] Authoritative Christian writers in the fourth and fifth centuries, such as St Jerome (ca. 331–419/20), St Ambrose (ca. 340–97), and St Augustine (354–430), argued that the laity, as well as the clergy, should refrain from taking interest, which Augustine described as no better than legalized robbery. By the fifth century the Roman bishops had come around to this view as well and Pope St Leo I (ca. 400–61) made the ban on interest-taking a cornerstone of the church's economic policy. As an institution of growing wealth and power, the church was increasingly in a position to regulate trade and business practices and canon law prescribed norms for profits and prices, which it demanded that Christian merchants obey.[14]

Church authorities in the Christian Empire became increasingly anxious to insulate members of their flock from Jews and pagans who remained outside the fold.

---

12. Adolf von Harnack, *Militia Christi: The Christian religion and the military in the first three centuries*, trans. David McInnes Gracie (Philadelphia, 1981); John Helgeland, 'The early church and war: The sociology of idolatry', and Louis J. Swift, 'Search the Scriptures: Patristic exegesis and the *Ius belli*', in *Peace in a nuclear age*, ed. Charles J. Reid, Jr (Washington, D.C., 1986), pp.34–68.

13. 1 Nicaea (325) c. 17, in COD, p.13.

14. John T. Gilchrist, *The church and economic activity in the Middle Ages* (New York, 1969), pp.48–52, 104–18; Kenneth S. Cahn, 'The Roman and Frankish roots of the just price of medieval canon law', *Studies in medieval and renaissance history* 6 (1969), 1–52; John W. Baldwin, *Medieval theories of the just price: Romanists, canonists and theologians in the twelfth and thirteenth centuries*, Transactions of the American Philosophical Society, new ser. 49, pt 4 (Philadelphia, 1959).

Hence canon law showed growing concern during the fifth and sixth centuries about limiting even casual contacts with unbelievers. Canons of councils and local synods forbade the faithful to dine with non-Christians, to dance with them, or to share the baths with them, much less to participate, even passively, in circumcisions and other non-Christian religious observances. Christians were not to accept the ministrations of Jewish physicians or to call Jews as witnesses in lawsuits. No pagan or Jew was to exercise authority over Christians as a judge or magistrate, and non-Christians were restrained from buying or keeping Christian slaves. Christian parents, moreover, were encouraged to see to it that their children were taught exclusively by Christian teachers. Christian teachers, in turn, were warned repeatedly to beware of the harmful consequences of having their pupils study pagan literature and philosophy save under strict supervision, lest they imbibe ideas and attitudes that might inhibit proper spiritual development. All of these restrictions on contacts between Christians and those who did not share their religious beliefs sought in part to preserve religious orthodoxy from contamination by alien beliefs and ideas and also to foster the dissemination of Christian beliefs and ideas among the faithful.

It was not sufficient, in the eyes of many church authorities, simply to isolate Christians from non-believers. Church policy, with the backing of government authority, sought in addition to penalize Christians who rejected beliefs and practices that the church's leaders regarded as central. As early as 380 the emperor Theodosius described as 'demented and insane' those who rejected the tenets of faith defined by the bishops of Rome and Alexandria and warned menacingly that anyone who persisted in erroneous beliefs would be subject to imperial retribution.[15] In 386 Theodosius spelled out the meaning of this last phrase more bluntly. He decreed that 'authors of sedition and disturbers of the peace of the Church' must 'pay the penalty of high treason with their life and blood'.[16]

---

15. Cod. Theod. 16.1.2.1.
16. Cod. Theod. 16.1.4.

Deviance from approved Christian doctrine or disobedience to the behavioural standards set by the bishops was now a capital crime.

Thus in the course of about three generations Christianity had been transformed from the religion of a small, persecuted minority on the fringes of Roman society into the official religion of the Roman Empire. At the beginning of the fourth century the church's canons had dealt largely with the church's order of worship, its moral aspirations, and the partition of responsibilities among the leadership of a sect whose very existence was precarious. By the century's end the canons had become part of the law of the land, bishops had been vested with judicial authority to enforce them, and flouting them, at least in public, was rapidly becoming hazardous to life and fortune.

Together with the fourth-century transformation of church organization and law came changes in religious beliefs and practices that have also endured over the centuries. By the end of the fourth century the Christian church was much different, and in particular far more legalistic, than it had been a hundred years before. Canon law had begun to emerge as not only an important element of Christian religious life, but also as an autonomous legal system complementary to the legal system of late Roman government.

Chapter 2

CANON LAW IN THE EARLY MIDDLE AGES

The Christian Empire early in the fifth century began to face a rapid series of grave political crises. Although Roman governments had weathered innumerable earlier emergencies during a turbulent history that stretched back more than a millennium, the fifth-century invasions inflicted irreversible wounds. The Empire in the West failed to survive.[1] The crises of the fifth and sixth centuries centred upon the successful invasion of the Western Empire by Germanic peoples, who subsequently settled in and secured political control of the whole region that we now describe as Western Europe. The new ethnic and political order in the West inevitably altered the relationship between ecclesiastical institutions and civil governments, as Germanic kingdoms began to replace the political and legal structures of the old Western Empire. Those changes, in turn, shaped the subsequent development of the church's own institutional structures and its legal system.

Non-Roman peoples from northern and central Europe had begun to make inroads into imperial territory during the fourth century and before the year 400 a few groups had already settled in some of the less densely populated provinces of the Empire. Although the initial settlements represented more-or-less peaceable accommodation between the perennial Roman need for military manpower

---

1. The Eastern half of the Roman Empire, however, survived the loss of its Western twin and continued not merely to exist but even to flourish for another thousand years. After the sixth century the surviving East Roman state is usually referred to as the Byzantine Empire.

and the settlers' desire to enjoy the benefits of the Roman lifestyle, the situation deteriorated sharply after 400. Attacks soon grew in number and frequency, to the point where the invaders finally overwhelmed Roman defences. By the fifth century's close Roman rule had ended for practical purposes nearly everywhere west of the Adriatic Sea.[2]

We conventionally lump the invaders together as 'Germans', although not all of them were by any means 'Germanic' in language, dress, customs, habits, or appearance. Common usage also describes them as 'barbarians', despite the fact that not a few of them knew Latin and were by Roman standards tolerably 'civilized'.

The political and social changes of the fifth century inevitably altered the relationship between church and government in the West. The Western church accordingly had to adapt its canon law to the new situation. Among the rulers of the new Germanic kingdoms that replaced Roman government few were Christians and those Germans who had been converted before the invasions (mainly Visigoths and Ostrogoths) had embraced the Arian, rather than the catholic, version of the new faith. Thus during the early stages of Germanic settlement the church no longer enjoyed the patronage of the new political rulers and some regions, notably Ostrogothic Italy and Visigothic Spain, experienced episodes of sharp hostility between the Germanic monarchs and the catholic hierarchy. Even when Germanic kings finally converted to catholic Christianity – as all of them eventually did – the new rulers proved less willing than Constantine and his successors had been to allocate generous political and judicial powers to the clergy. A warrior elite dominated the Germanic kingdoms and its members were inclined to retain political power in their own hands, rather than to share it with priests and bishops.

To complicate matters further, Germanic rulers regarded law as an attribute of personality, rather than of territory –

2. On the Germanic invasions see generally E. A. Thompson, *Romans and barbarians: The decline of the Western Empire* (Madison, 1982); J. M. Wallace-Hadrill, *The barbarian West, 400–1000* (London, 1952) and *The long-haired kings* (New York, 1962); Walter Goffart, *Barbarians and Romans, A.D. 418–584: The techniques of accommodation* (Princeton, 1980); and Lucien Musset, *The Germanic invasions* (Pittsburgh, 1975).

that is, they assumed that a legal tradition formed an inalienable part of each individual's ethnic heritage, and accordingly that everyone should be governed by the norms of the legal system into which he or she was born. Thus in the Germanic kingdoms persons of Roman heritage remained subject to Roman law, while Burgundians were judged by Burgundian law, Visigoths by Visigothic law, Franks by Frankish law, and so forth.[3] Germanic rulers, accordingly, tended to regard canon law as simply one further kind of personal law, applicable to those born into catholic families, but irrelevant to Arians, pagans, or Jews. Even after their own conversion to catholic Christianity, Germanic kings continued to be cautious about delegating extensive jurisdiction, even over internal ecclesiastical problems, to church courts or using the coercive powers of government to enforce the rulings of bishops or other prelates.

Still, the rulers of barbarian Europe often respected the technical competence of the Christian clergy as administrators and in addition recognized the authority that the clergy exercised over their flocks. Once they themselves had decided to embrace Catholicism, Germanic kings often employed clerics in their own households as administrative assistants, advisers, and political functionaries. When they found it advisable to put the customary tribal laws of their own peoples into written form – a development that normally followed not long after religious conversion – Germanic rulers typically delegated the technical task of redacting oral traditions in written form to clerical members of their entourage.[4] It is perhaps not surprising, in view of this, that early Germanic laws on the

3. Simeon L. Guterman, *The principle of the personality of law in the Germanic kingdoms of Western Europe from the fifth to the eleventh century* (New York, 1990).
4. Germanic rulers began to publish written versions of their laws late in the fifth century, beginning with the Visigothic laws, whose earliest redaction dates before 484 and the Burgundian laws of King Gundobald (ca. 480–516). The most comprehensive guide to this process is Rudolf Buchner, *Die Rechtsquellen*, a supplementary volume to Wilhelm Wattenbach and Wilhelm Levison, *Deutschlands Geschichtsquellen im Mittelalter: Vorzeit und Karolinger*, 3 vols (Weimar, 1952–57).

Continent were written in Latin and frequently incorporated provisions to protect the clergy, churches, and church property.[5]

The period of Germanic migration and settlement coincided with the growth in numbers and importance of monastic communities in Western Europe. Christian monasticism first appeared during the third century in the eastern Mediterranean, above all in Egypt and Syria. Monks, nuns, and hermits emerged in the West in the mid-fourth century and large-scale growth in monasticism commenced there during the fifth and sixth centuries. Early monasteries in Europe adopted customs and practices current in the East. After the mid-sixth century, however, a distinctively Western style of monastic life, following the prescriptions of the *Rule* of St Benedict of Nursia (d. ca. 547), began to emerge and quickly became the dominant form of monasticism in Europe.[6]

Benedictines thought of their monasteries as self-sufficient agricultural communities, isolated so far as possible from contact with worldly society. Benedict's *Rule* prescribed a balanced regimen in which the monk's daily routine centred on periods of formal community worship, physical labour, and individual meditation and prayer. Each monastic house constituted an autonomous, self-governing community, headed by an abbot whom the monks elected for life. Under the abbot, and responsible to him, subordinate officials bore responsibility for organizing and managing the spiritual and material resources of the group.

Although bishops in principle retained the right, indeed the obligation, to supervise the monastic communities within their dioceses, monasteries commonly preferred to look after themselves and sought to regulate their own

5. For example, *The laws of the Salian Franks*, trans. Katherine Fischer Drew (Philadelphia, 1991), pp.157, 163; *The laws of the Alamans and Bavarians*, trans. Theodore John Rivers (Philadelphia, 1977), pp.70–71, 119–22; Laws of Aethelberht, c. 1, in *The laws of the earliest English kings*, ed. and trans. F. L. Attenborough (Cambridge, 1922), p.4.
6. The literature on the history of monasticism is very large; for a guide to discussions of individual topics see Giles Constable, *Medieval monasticism: A select bibliography* (Toronto, 1976).

members and their internal affairs with as little reference as possible to episcopal authority. Indeed monastic communities often resented what they regarded as interference by bishops and resisted efforts to impose controls upon their independence. Tension over these issues was common everywhere and presented thorny problems that early medieval canon law attempted, with only partial success, to resolve.

Ordinary Christians commonly regarded monks and nuns with mixed feelings. Most people accorded them a degree of awe and respect as holy people whose prayers were especially valuable and pleasing to God. But this veneration was often mixed with envy and resentment as well. Monks and nuns constituted a self-designated spiritual elite and their sense of moral superiority to the general run of mankind was not uncommonly tinged with arrogance, even scorn, for those who were unable to attain the level of discipline and self-denial that the monastic life entailed.

Nonetheless, as the numbers of monasteries grew, so also did their wealth and power. Each recruit customarily bestowed all of his or her worldly goods on the community at the time of admission; the families of community members frequently made additional gifts to support the institution; pious people, as well as many who had not been notably pious earlier in their lives, often left part of their worldly goods to monasteries in the hope that the prayers of the community would intercede for them with God after death. Even when these individual gifts were relatively modest, they could readily mount up over the course of generations into substantial accumulations of wealth and property. And as the riches of monastic houses increased, temptations for abuse likewise grew in attractiveness and frequency. Church councils, popes, and kings regularly attempted to repress the more flagrant kinds of abuses as they appeared and successive collections of canon law featured ever greater varieties of measures designed to maintain and regulate monastic discipline.

The absence of any single, universally agreed-upon formulation of the content of the canon law sharply limited its effectiveness during these centuries. The problem did not arise from a shortage of law; if anything, there was too much of it – conciliar canons, synodal decrees, papal decisions, and the dicta of the church fathers provided a luxuriant abundance of rules and regulations. But the wealth of canons included numerous rules that were contradictory, obsolete, or unworkable. The canons presented a maze of conflicts and inconsistencies, too numerous and too difficult for most priests or bishops to master. To discover just what rules were supposed to govern a particular situation at a specific time and in a specific place – say, for example, the validity of a marriage between third cousins twice removed, or the fraction of the parochial tithe that a pastor was required to remit to his bishop – might demand lengthy research in a well-stocked library. But well-stocked libraries were rare, while time and inclination to use them were probably even rarer. In consequence enforcement or application of canonical rules tended to be haphazard or lacking altogether.

Canon law in the Germanic kingdoms inevitably reflected the isolationism and particularism that typified the new political order that followed the invasion and settlement of Germanic peoples in the West. The church within each region tended to frame its own canons, to develop its own practices, and to pay less heed to Roman leadership than had been usual when imperial government still prevailed. Local councils and synods in each region of the old empire accordingly adopted their own rules about fasts, holy days, liturgy, and the like, with scant reference to practices elsewhere. The power of metropolitans increased, while that of the Western patriarch at Rome diminished.

Germanic kings, too, almost as soon as they accepted baptism, liked to cast themselves in the role of protectors of the church and in consequence to claim a degree of control over the church within their realms. Thus the kings of Visigothic Spain, for example, almost immediately after renouncing Arianism and adopting the catholic faith of the majority of their subjects, began to describe themselves as the heads of Christian society. They proceeded to implement that description by presiding over synods, appointing bishops, executing heretics, and punishing offences against Christian morality as they understood it. The canonical jurisdiction of bishops was largely restricted to settling disputes among the clergy and supervising the treatment of slaves and freedmen, while royal courts dealt with a wide range of matters that earlier would have come before the episcopal *audientia*.[7] Similar expansion of royal power and contraction of canonical jurisdiction occurred elsewhere as well, in Frankish Gaul, in Italy under the Lombards, in the Anglo-Saxon kingdoms of Britain, and in the newly converted regions east of the Rhine.

The new, inward-looking character of canon law in the seventh, eighth, and ninth centuries is strikingly evident in the penitentials that became so numerous and influential during those centuries. The penitentials were handbooks that provided guidance for priests who heard confessions. Prior to the sixth century, the church normally forgave sins in formal public ceremonies, during which the repentant sinner had to make a public confession of wrongdoing. The penitent was then obliged to perform openly certain public acts of expiation before he or she could be reconciled with the church and readmitted to communion. Since public penance could be performed only once in a lifetime, many Christians understandably chose to postpone repentance until late in life.[8]

The practice of public penance began to be displaced late in the sixth century by private rites of confession and reconciliation in which the penitent confessed and received forgiveness in secret. The efficacy of absolution was contingent upon performance of individual acts of expiation that the confessor tailored to suit the circumstances and the offences that the penitent had committed. The penances were usually private, as was confession. Private penance, moreover, unlike public penance, could be repeated as often as necessary.

---

7. P. D. King, *Law and society in the Visigothic kingdom*, Cambridge studies in medieval life and thought, 3rd ser., vol. 5 (Cambridge, 1972), pp.122–58.
8. Among the numerous studies of the penitentials, Gabriel Le Bras, 'Pénitentiels', in *Dictionnaire de théologie catholique* (Paris, 1908–57), xii,1160–79, Cyrille Vogel, *Les 'Libri paenitentiales'*, Typologie des sources du moyen âge occidental, fasc. 27 (Turnhout, 1978), and Pierre J. Payer, *Sex and the penitentials* (Toronto, 1984) are particularly helpful. Henry Charles Lea, *A history of auricular confession and indulgences in the Latin church*, 3 vols (Philadelphia, 1896; repr. New York, 1968) also remains useful, despite its age.

The aim of private penance was curative: sin was envisioned as a moral sickness that required treatment to restore the sinner to spiritual health. Penitentials, then, represented a kind of spiritual pharmacopoeia that supplied confessors with a list of the sins they might encounter, together with a menu of expiatory acts appropriate for each type of sin. This allowed the confessor to prescribe a course of penance to match the spiritual needs of each sinner. Numerous writers composed handbooks of this sort during the seventh and eighth centuries. All of them incorporated canons of behaviour based upon the councils and other traditional canonical sources, but also drew upon the author's own experience and practice as a confessor.

The earliest well-developed, methodical penitential, written by Finnian (or Vinnian) of Clonard, dates from the first half of the sixth century.[9] Finnian distinguished sharply in the penances he prescribed between the more demanding punishments appropriate for the clergy and the milder ones that the sins of the laity merited. Thus, for example, a cleric who quarrelled with his neighbour and entertained thoughts of killing him was to fast for six months on bread and water and to abstain from wine and meat for an additional six months before he could be readmitted to communion. A layman guilty of the same offence had to do penance only for a week since, as Finnian explained, 'he is a man of this world and his guilt is lighter in this world and his reward less in the world to come' (canons 6–7). Finnian's work, like most later handbooks of penance, devoted substantial space to a wide variety of sexual misbehaviours. Almost two-fifths of Finnian's canons deal with sexual offences of one kind or another, a proportion that remained fairly typical of later penitentials.[10] Subsequent penitential handbooks, of which

9. The standard edition of Finnian's text appears in Ludwig Bieler, *The Irish penitentials*, Scriptores Latini Hiberniae, vol. 5 (Dublin, 1963), pp.74–95; an English translation from an earlier edition may be found in *Medieval handbooks of penance*, ed. and trans. John T. McNeill and Helena M. Gamer (New York, 1938; repr. 1965), pp.86–97.
10. Payer, *Sex and the penitentials*, pp.52–3 analyzes the proportion of sexual offences in a representative sample of penitentials.

many dozens survive, considerably enlarged the range of sins that Finnian treated and often prescribed punishments different from his. Some consisted of little more than extended tariffs of sins and suggested penalties, while others attempted to explain more amply the reasons for distinguishing between different offences and to set their prescriptions within a broader theological context.

Since priests throughout Western Christendom consulted these manuals and relied upon them for guidance in dealing with the sinners who confessed to them, the penitentials became in effect new sources of law, although few of their authors held high offices in the ecclesiastical hierarchy and were seldom vested with formal legislative power.

One of the most peculiar new sources of church law in the early Middle Ages was the collection of canons that we now call the Pseudo-Isidorian Decretals. This work comprised a vast compendium of genuine conciliar canons and papal letters, interwoven with falsified canons composed by forgers whose precise identity remains a mystery. The collection was ascribed to 'Isidore Mercator' and was apparently confected in the mid-ninth century by reformers in the archdiocese of Reims who sought to bolster the authority of bishops and the papacy by composing a battery of 'ancient' texts, supposedly from the 'golden age' of the early church, that would support their contention that the hierarchical structure of the church went back to its very foundations.

This pious fraud was immensely successful. Almost a hundred medieval manuscripts of the Pseudo-Isidorian collection still survive, which makes it the most frequently copied canonical collection of its age. Its comprehensive range, moreover, made it seem an especially valuable reference work, one that bishops and abbots wished to have at hand when legal questions arose and they needed to consult past authorities and precedents. Although a few contemporaries suspected the authenticity of the collection, most students of canon law and authors of later canonical collections used Pseudo-Isidore freely as a source and copied both genuine and spurious texts from the work for their own compilations. Thus the forgeries quickly entered the mainstream of canon law, where they remained, largely undetected, for centuries.[11]

Pseudo-Isidore's influence was pervasive. The forgers inserted a wholly new office into the church's hierarchy, that of primate, intermediate in authority between the metropolitan and the patriarch. The forgers' inventions also seemed to demonstrate that the bishops of Rome had dominated Christian life from the earliest times and that papal approval was essential for the validity of conciliar and synodal canons. Such exaltations of papal prerogatives furnished later reformers in the eleventh century with ammunition that they used effectively in their campaigns to centralize the church's administrative authority at Rome. The forgers likewise invented new procedural forms and evidential requirements that considerably complicated litigation in the medieval church.[12]

The emergence during the eighth and ninth centuries of a new European political hegemony under Frankish monarchs of the Carolingian family not only united many of the Germanic kingdoms politically for a brief period, but also fostered a new unity in canon law. Charlemagne (768–814), who appears to us, as he did to his contemporaries, the most successful ruler of the Carolingian dynasty, made the renewal of canon law a goal of his imperial policy and sought to enhance the effectiveness of the ecclesiastical courts. To this end, he asked Pope Adrian I (772–95) to furnish him with an up-to-date compendium of the canons that could serve as the fundamental statement of the church's current law. The pope's response was to dispatch to the emperor in 774 the *Hadriana*, a newly-revised version of the *Dionysiana*, an old compilation of canons composed by Dionysius Exiguus towards the end of the fifth century. The synod of Aachen (802) directed bishops throughout the Carolingian empire

---

11. A Calvinist pastor, David Blondel (1591–1655), first demonstrated in 1628 that the work of 'Isidore Mercator' was a forgery; A. Lambert, 'Blondel (David)' in *Dictionnaire de droit canonique*, 7 vols (Paris, 1935–65; cited hereafter as DDC), ii, pp.926–7; Schafer Williams, *Codices Pseudo-Isidoriani: A palaeographico-historical study*, MIC, Subsidia, vol. 3 (New York, 1971), pp.105–7.

12. Horst Fuhrmann, *Einfluss und Verbreitung der pseudoisidorischen Fälschungen von ihrem Auftrachtung bis in die neuere Zeit*, 3 vols, MGH, Schriften, vol. 24 (Stuttgart, 1972–74), esp. i, pp.39–53.

to use this revised collection, in conjunction with the collection of Spanish conciliar canons known as the *Hispana,* as the fundamental lawbooks in their courts.

Charlemagne and his successors also made ambitious efforts to reform ecclesiastical institutions and discipline. The capitularies, or regulatory directives, that Charlemagne and his successor, Louis the Pious (814–40), issued often dealt with ecclesiastical matters. One of the most important of these, the Capitulary of Herstal (779), for example, greatly improved the church's ability to fund its activities by calling upon imperial officials to enforce payment of the tithe, the 10 per cent tax on most types of income that remained the basis of church finance for more than a thousand years. The resulting growth of ecclesiastical resources made it possible to multiply the numbers of parishes and to bring regular religious services and instruction to many parts of the empire where they previously had been haphazard and occasional. Other capitularies dealt with monastic schools and libraries, with standardization of liturgical observances, with clerical discipline, and a host of other matters vital to the well-being of the Carolingian church. The capitularies further made it clear that Charlemagne viewed himself as the head of both the religious and civil establishment within his empire. Indeed he apparently saw no sharp dividing line between royal and ecclesiastical powers. Regulation of the church was in his estimation an integral part of his royal functions. Later canonists came to treat the Carolingian capitularies as legitimate sources of ecclesiastical law and routinely incorporated them in subsequent collections of the canons.

Charlemagne's efforts to reinvigorate canon law formed part of his larger effort to renew the church throughout his realm. His church reform policy, while it was very likely rooted in a genuine concern to improve the quality of religious life in his empire, also had political objectives. Charlemagne, like Constantine and his successors, used church institutions and personnel as instruments of political power. He selected his bishops – and the emperor emphatically saw them as his appointees – with a keen eye to their potential usefulness as officers of government, as well as religious leaders. And he held bishops and other prelates, once in power, strictly accountable for the faithful exercise of their offices. Charles employed other clergymen as secretaries in his own household and entrusted them with a significant share of responsibility for orderly administration and record-keeping. Still other clerics taught his children the skills they would need to govern, and to this end Charlemagne collected scholars from throughout Europe to staff his palace school.

The emperor sought to bring order into every aspect of church life. He was concerned about the liturgy and demanded that worship be conducted according to a uniform ritual throughout his domains. He cared about church music and took pains to see that choirs were properly instructed so that their performances would enhance, rather than detract from, the solemnity of liturgical ceremonies. He directed bishops and abbots to provide more adequately for the education of their monks and clerics. He encouraged missionaries to spread the Gospel and baptize pagans and supported their work actively, in part at least because he viewed their labours as an important element in the pacification of newly conquered territories. He likewise enforced the collection of taxes for church support, especially the tithe, which funded many of the church's activities.

Charlemagne's reforms raised the status of the church and greatly increased both its effectiveness and importance as an institution. At the same time, however, the emperor sought and achieved greater control over church life in all its aspects than any ruler of late antiquity had ever done.

This reinvigoration of ecclesiastical institutions and the renewal of canon law that formed part of it did not long outlast Charlemagne himself. After the great emperor's death in 814, the regime that he had built up soon began to falter and ultimately to fail. Although Charlemagne's sole surviving son, Louis the Pious, may well have been the most intelligent member of the Carolingian dynasty, he was not clever enough to save the fragile empire that his father's conquests had put together. Louis's reforms of the Frankish church and government, however commendable in their goals, provoked widespread resentment among the ruling aristocracy, while his second marriage, which added a further heir to vie for power with the two sons of his first marriage, complicated dynastic politics. Rivalries among Louis's heirs, combined with the greed, ambition, and fecklessness of his grandsons, resulted in a territorial breakup of the Carolingian realm, inevitably accompanied by a diminution in the political power of its rulers.

It was the great misfortune of the Carolingians that dynastic jealousies, political intrigues, and territorial fragmentation coincided with attacks by powerful foreign enemies. The later Carolingians found themselves beset simultaneously by Vikings from Scandinavia, Magyars from central Europe and the Russian plains, and Muslims from Spain and North Africa. The convergence of internal stresses and external pressures ultimately tore the Carolingian Empire into fragments.

As the central government began to crumble and foreign enemies appeared on the horizon, local officials, war lords, and strongmen commenced to take over many of the functions that Carolingian monarchs had once managed. Dukes, counts, and other war lords who lacked formal titles or public authority assumed responsibility for organizing the defence of their regions against the ravages of invaders. They also imposed taxes on local populations to defray the expenses of defence, sat as judges in local courts, supervised the building and maintenance of roads, bridges, and other public works, and sometimes even minted their own coinage to pay for it all. Since churches, monasteries, and convents of nuns were especially attractive targets for the Vikings and other outside attackers, local military leaders put a large part of their effort into defending these institutions. In return, the defenders soon asserted control over bishops, monasteries, and other church establishments. By the tenth century new structures of government, based on networks of relationship between these local authorities, had emerged throughout most of the former Carolingian territories. This new style of government we conventionally, if perhaps unfortunately, call feudalism.[13]

13. The usefulness of the term 'feudalism', and of the concept that underlies it, has been vigorously questioned. The terminology of 'feudalism' is so deeply entrenched in historical literature, however, that I have elected to employ it here, rather than to venture into an examination of its defects and limitations. For a lucid explanation

During the tenth and eleventh centuries, canonical rules for choosing members of the church's hierarchy often fell into abeyance. Bishops, abbots, and other church officials, down to and including parish priests, typically came to be named by local landowners and noblemen, who often demanded concessions of church property from the successful candidate in return for securing his appointment. Similarly, should a local strongman wish to provide his son with a dignified and comfortable living as a bishop or abbot, for example, the chances were extremely good that the boy would be taken care of, no matter how meagre his qualifications for the position. Numerous other provisions of canon law also fell by the wayside during this period. Knights and nobles almost everywhere claimed the right to appropriate part, and sometimes all, of the tithe and other church revenues from their manors for their own use in compensation for the protection that they offered against even more voracious competitors. Or, to cite another common situation, when a local landowner wished to divorce one wife and marry another, canonical authorities might be hard-pressed to resist the pressures he could exert to get his way. We conventionally describe this state of affairs as 'the proprietary church regime' (*Eigenkirchentum*), a term coined by German scholars, who have studied the phenomenon with particular interest.[14]

The changed situation of the church in the tenth and eleventh centuries required revised lawbooks. Among the numerous compilations of canon law that appeared during.

---

13. (*Continued*)
    of the problems that 'feudalism' presents, see Elizabeth A. R. Brown, 'The tyranny of a construct: Feudalism and historians of medieval Europe', *American historical review* 79 (1974), 1063–99.

14. The classic study remains Ulrich Stutz, 'The proprietary church as an element of mediaeval Germanic ecclesiastical law,' even though some of his conclusions have been superseded by more recent research. His essay appears in *Medieval Germany, 911–1250*, ed. and trans. Geoffrey Barraclough, 2 vols (Oxford, 1938), ii, pp.35–70. More recently Timothy Reuter has argued that the proprietary church system in the German-speaking lands was not nearly so unusual or so systematic as Stutz believed, but that similar regimes were common in other parts of Europe; ' "The imperial church system" of the Ottonian and Salian rulers: A reconsideration', *Journal of ecclesiastical history* 32 (1982), 347–74.

the tenth century perhaps the most widely influential was the collection in two books (*Libri duo de synodalibus causis et disciplinis ecclesiasticis*) composed about 906 by Abbot Regino of Prüm (ca. 845–915). A notable feature of Regino's collection was the prominence that Book II gave to the canon law concerning the duties of the laity, in addition to regulations for the clergy and church administration, which formed the subject matter of Book I.[15]

The outstanding canonical collection of the early eleventh century was the *Decretum* of Burchard, who was bishop of Worms between 1000 and 1025. Burchard's work circulated widely and remained a standard reference work in medieval libraries for many generations. Although large (it comprised 1,785 canons, organized in 20 books), it was not so vast as to be prohibitively expensive and time-consuming to copy. Burchard's *Decretum* might be described as a canonical and theological encyclopedia, since it attempted to cover the whole span of canon law, as well as many problems that later writers would classify as moral theology.

The opening book of Burchard's work dealt with the basic structure of the church, the powers of prelates and synods, their jurisdiction, and similar matters. Burchard's chapters on synods were particularly popular, since they constituted a practical handbook that bishops apparently consulted regularly as a guide to correct procedure during these recurrent assemblies of the clergy. Book II covered the lower clergy, while the third book contained regulations concerning individual churches and the services performed in them. Books IV and V dealt with the laws governing the sacraments, and Book VI treated the consequences of various forms of homicide: murder, manslaughter, patricide, fratricide, and the like. Burchard's seventh book concerned consanguinity and incest, while the eighth book dealt with monastic life of both men and women and the ninth book treated the legal problems of single women, both unmarried and widowed. Book X had

---

15. Paul Fournier and Gabriel Le Bras, *Histoire des collections canoniques en Occident depuis les fausses décrétales jusqu'au Décret de Gratien*, 2 vols (Paris, 1931–32; repr. Aalen, 1972), i, pp.244–68. The text of Regino's collection may be found in PL cxxxii, pp.185–370.

to do with magic and sorcery. Books XI and XII contained material on penal law and the punishments for various ecclesiastical crimes. The two following books of the *Decretum* focused on the law concerning fasts and feasts, as well as the moral shortcomings that resulted from overindulgence in food and drink. The fifteenth book of Burchard's collection treated civil rulers and the laity, the sixteenth dealt with procedures in church courts, the seventeenth with fornication and other sexual offences, and the eighteenth with matters that involved Christians who were ill or dying. Book XIX, sometimes called the *Corrector*, became a particularly popular reference work for confessors and for that reason was often copied separately from the rest of his *Decretum*. Scribes sometimes copied the twentieth and concluding book of the work separately as well, frequently under the title of the *Speculator*, since it dealt with theological topics such as providence, predestination, the coming of the Antichrist, the Last Judgement and the resurrection of the dead.

Although the logical structure of Burchard's work is not always easy to make out and the sequence of topics that it covered may seem bewildering, it had the considerable merit at least of grouping more-or-less closely related topics within the individual books of the collection. This made Burchard's collection somewhat easier to use than earlier non-systematic canonical collections had been and helps to account for its considerable popularity.

Burchard seems to have employed a number of assistants to help in compiling the *Decretum* and he and his collaborators drew upon an impressive range of sources, which they edited and updated as seemed necessary to make the work conform to practices current in the period between 1008 and 1012, when they were pursuing the project. Just as Burchard freely drew upon the work of his predecessors, so later canonists often mined his *Decretum* for canons that they borrowed for their own collections.[16]

While the *Decretum* of Burchard of Worms described how

16. Fournier and Le Bras, *Histoire des collections*, i, pp.364–421; J. Pétrau-Gay, 'Burchard de Worms', in DDC ii, pp.1141–57; the printed version of Burchard's *Decretum* in PL cxl, pp.537–1058 is not altogether reliable.

many eleventh-century bishops and prelates believed the church ought to work, the realities of church life in that period often differed substantially from what canon law said they ought to be. The subordination of ecclesiastical institutions and religious values to the whims and desires of soldiers, adventurers, and thugs – which in essence describes what the general run of early feudal knights and nobles really were – resulted in widespread pillaging of church property and its conversion to the private use of military families, accompanied by a drastic deterioration in the discipline of the clergy and of the spiritual services that they provided. Complaints about these matters began to surface by the beginning of the tenth century and over the following century-and-a-half they grew in frequency, in number, and in intensity. Writers complained about the ignorance, boorishness, lust, and greed of the priests whom local landowners appointed to parish churches. Even monks, they said, no longer fasted and prayed; instead they feasted and played their days away. Many monks, in truth, did enter the monastic life under compulsion, rather than out of idealistic aspirations for a life of asceticism and devotion. A substantial number of religious houses became little more than ecclesiastical country clubs, filled with the surplus offspring of noble families, who exiled their extra sons and daughters to monasteries where they would no longer be a drain on the family wealth. Nunneries, some said, were little more than brothels, although they were perhaps a trifle cleaner and more orderly than most such establishments.

This state of affairs was bound to provoke a reaction, and it soon did so. As early as the tenth century a few monastic houses successfully resisted attempts to bring them under the control of lay interests. The Burgundian monastery of Cluny (founded in 909) was prominent among the reformed religious communities and soon attracted others to the cause. Monasteries independent of lay control became centres from which more ambitious and far-reaching reform ideas began to flow. By the mid-eleventh century a church reform movement had begun to attract support among influential civil authorities, such as the German kings and emperors, Otto III (983–1002) and Henry III (1039–56), as well as the English king, Edgar the Peaceable (959–75), and others. In the mid-eleventh century reform-minded clerics began to be named as popes, with the active support of Henry III of Germany, and commenced to reassert papal leadership not only in the reform movement but also in the Western church as a whole.

A decisive event in the maturation of church reform was Henry III's appointment of Bruno of Toul (a reforming monk from Lorraine, who conveniently happened to be Henry's cousin) as Pope Leo IX (1048–54). The new pope brought with him to Rome a phalanx of fellow-reformers, including Frederick of Lorraine (later Pope Stephen IX), Humbert of Moyenmoutier (soon named as cardinal of Silva Candida), and Hildebrand (later Pope Gregory VII). These men and others in Leo IX's entourage helped to insulate the new pope from the demands and influence of the Roman aristocracy, who had controlled and used the papacy in much the same way that noblemen elsewhere dominated their local bishops and parish priests.

Leo IX and his advisers saw canon law as a key instrument for implementing the changes that they envisioned. They aimed to secure the independence of the church from control by laymen of any sort, whether they be kings, local strongmen, or simply wealthy donors. The clergy, as Leo and his circle saw things, were ordained to rule the church; interference by the laity, however well-intentioned, was intolerable. In order to secure the freedom from lay control that was their ultimate objective, the pope and his advisers believed that they must eliminate what they saw as the two chief vices of contemporary ecclesiastical life: simony and Nicolaitism.

Simony was so-called from Simon Magus, a New Testament villain, who tried to bribe St Peter to give him the power to confer the Holy Spirit through the laying on of hands (Acts 8:9–24). In the language of the reformers, simony covered a broad variety of sins: any transaction that involved the exchange of money or other worldly goods in return for ecclesiastical office or power was apt to be classed as simony, as was any other sort of arrangement that threatened to compromise the independence of the clergy from secular control.

Nicolaitism referred to an obscure sectarian group

mentioned in the New Testament (Apocalypse 2:6) and denounced by patristic writers as heretics who were given to sexual promiscuity. The eleventh-century reformers referred indiscriminately to married clergymen, to clerics who kept concubines or frequented prostitutes, and in general to all monks, priests, or other members of the clergy who were in any way sexually active as Nicolaites. St Peter Damian (1007–72) was by far the most outspoken and radical critic of Nicolaitism and Pope Gregory VII (1073–85) substantially adopted many of Damian's views as official papal policy. Damian and Gregory rationalized their rabid opposition to the ancient and widespread practice of clerical marriage by arguing that a clergyman who had a wife and children must inextricably be entangled in worldly values and could not properly attend to his family without neglecting his spiritual obligations.

The reformers' programme entailed a radical, indeed a revolutionary, change in the structure and operations of Western society. It would deprive kings and other powerful laymen of the income and power that many of them derived from control over ecclesiastical property and appointments, while at the same time it would require priests to forsake their wives, abandon their children, and embrace a life of sexual renunciation that few had probably contemplated when they were ordained.[17] It is scarcely surprising that such measures provoked stubborn and bitter resistance from those who stood to lose by it. Antagonism between the forces of reform and those whose lives the reformers sought to change was even further exacerbated by the uncompromising and self-righteous rhetoric that Gregory VII and other prominent reformers employed. The upshot was a long and acrimonious struggle, often called the Investiture Controversy, between church reformers and their opponents.[18]

Early in that conflict advocates of reform concluded that canon law must play a key role in their strategy. The

17. The radical nature of the church reform movement is particularly stressed by Harold Berman, *Law and revolution: The formation of the Western legal tradition* (Cambridge, MA, 1983), pp.99–113.
18. For the abundant literature on this topic see Uta-Renate Blumenthal, *The investiture controversy: Church and monarchy from the ninth to the twelfth century* (Philadelphia, 1982).

abolition of simony and Nicolaitism, they reasoned, must not only be grounded on legal prohibitions of the practices they abhorred, but must also be enforced by legal processes. They believed that the abuses they fought reflected structural weaknesses in the church's legal system, for they could not have taken root had adequate monitoring and enforcement mechanisms been in place.

Gregory VII and other reformers therefore concluded that they must achieve four tactical objectives in order to attain their ultimate goals. First, they needed to compile fresh collections of old law to demonstrate that their goals had a legitimate foundation in ecclesiastical tradition. Second, they needed to create new laws that would buttress their programme by repairing gaps in the existing legal corpus. Third, they must develop more adequate procedural mechanisms, as well as new and more effective courts to correct violations of church law. And fourth, the church required new and better means than it currently had in order to detect violators and to bring them to the courts for prosecution.

On the first score, the second half of the eleventh century saw the appearance of numerous compilations of canon law designed to further the objectives of church reformers. Several of these – such as the *Collectio canonum* completed about 1083 by Bishop Anselm of Lucca (d. 1086),[19] or the collection that Cardinal Deusdedit (ca. 1030–1100) assembled about 1087[20] – were the work of identifiable members of the reform party at the papal curia. One of the most successful of them all, however, *The collection in seventy-four titles* (completed by 1067), was compiled by an unknown author. Whoever he may have been, he clearly selected the 315 canons of his collection with a view to demonstrating the legal foundations of the reform programme.[21]

---

19. Anselm of Lucca, *Collectio canonum*, ed. Friedrich Thaner (Vienna, 1906–15; repr. Aalen, 1965). Thaner's edition (the only one ever published) was never finished and includes only the first eleven books of Anselm's work.

20. *Die Kanonessammlung des Kardinals Deusdedit*, ed. Victor Wolf von Glanvell (Paderborn, 1905).

21. *The collection in seventy-four titles: A canon law manual of the Gregorian reform*, trans. John Gilchrist (Toronto, 1980).

A still more ambitious and influential supporter of legal reforms was a French bishop and canonical expert, Ivo of Chartres (ca. 1040–1115). Ivo collected a vast repertory of canons in a collection entitled the *Decretum*, which comprised 3,760 canons divided into seventeen books.[22] This work was too bulky and complex, however, to achieve wide circulation and faulty organization made it inconvenient as a reference work. Ivo accordingly produced a second, more compact, canonical collection, comprising slightly more than a thousand canons, arranged in eight books. This collection, the *Panormia*, achieved far greater popular success than its bulkier companion; it was widely disseminated throughout Western Christendom and later canonists drew upon it freely for subsequent collections.[23] A third canonical manual, *The collection in three parts* (*Tripartita*) has also been ascribed to Ivo, although the basis for that ascription is rather shaky.[24]

An even more important contribution than his canonical collections to the development of systematic canon law was the prologue that appears in numerous manuscripts of Ivo's *Panormia*.[25] In the prologue he sketched out a much more sophisticated canonical methodology than appears in the work of any of his predecessors. Ivo's prologue set forth rules for the interpretation of canonical texts that became central to the work of later canonists, and especially to the work of Gratian.[26]

22. Ivo of Chartres, *Decretum*, in PL clxi, 59–1036. The published texts of Ivo's canonical collections must be used with care, for they teem with errors; Peter Landau, 'Das Dekret des Ivo von Chartres: Die handschriftliche Überlieferung im Vergleich zu dem Editionen des 16. und 17. Jahrhunderts', *Zeitschrift der Savigny-Stiftung für Rechtsgeschichte*, kanonistische Abteilung 70 (1984), 1–44.
23. Ivo of Chartres, *Panormia*, in PL clxi, pp.1045–344.
24. Martin Brett, 'Urban II and the collections attributed to Ivo of Chartres', in *Proceedings of the eighth international congress of medieval canon law*, ed. Stanley Chodorow, MIC, Subsidia, vol. 9, pp.27–46.
25. Bruce Brasington, 'The prologue of Ivo of Chartres: A fresh consideration of the manuscripts', in *Proceedings of the eighth international congress of medieval canon law*, ed. Stanley Chodorow, MIC, Subsidia, vol. 9 (Vatican City, 1992), pp.3–22.
26. Bruce Brasington, 'The *Nachleben* of Ivo of Chartres: The influence of his prologue on several Panormia-derivative collections', forthcoming in the *Proceedings of the ninth international congress of medieval canon law.*

Canonists found Ivo's prologue immensely valuable as a guide for resolving the discrepancies that they often encountered between contradictory ecclesiastical laws.[27] Faced with such conflicts Ivo advised canonists to examine the context in which the canons had been adopted. Such an examination might reveal that the apparently conflicting canons had addressed different problems or separate aspects of a single problem. In that case the canonist might be able to resolve apparent discrepancies by showing that the canons did not in fact conflict at all. Ivo also cautioned canonists to test the authenticity of their sources in order to eliminate forged or interpolated texts that might conflict with authentic canonical rules. In addition Ivo declared that when canonists interpreted the law, they must take account of the hierarchy of jurisdictions within the church. The basic principle here was that canons that originated with higher authorities took precedence over canons adopted by lesser authorities. Thus if the canons of a general council conflicted with the canons of a provincial council or a diocesan synod, the general council's enactments overrode those of the lesser body. Further, Ivo warned canonists that they must be alert to the distinctions between variable laws and invariable laws and between general and particular canons. Variable laws might be subject to dispensation by an appropriate authority, while invariable laws were not. The application of particular canons was limited to specific regions or situations or classes of persons, whereas general laws applied across the board to all Christians.

New canons to legitimize reform objectives were forthcoming as soon as reformers secured control of the papacy. Leo IX summoned a council of the French clergy in 1049, for example, and induced the assembly to adopt a series of canons that enunciated new and higher standards of discipline for the clergy and laity alike. At the Easter synod of the Roman clergy, also in 1049, the pope secured adoption of a canon that required all clerics from the rank

27. The only readily available copy of Ivo's prologue can be found in PL clxi, pp.47–60. This text, unfortunately, fails to measure up to modern critical standards and is not very reliable as a representation of what Ivo originally wrote.

of subdeacon upward to remain celibate. One of Leo's successors, Pope Nicholas II (1059–61), took an important step to assure that the papacy would remain independent from the control of the great Roman noble families who had long dominated papal politics. Nicholas's election decree of 1059 entrusted the exclusive power to choose the pope to a body of papal advisers, the College of Cardinals, who remain in control of papal elections to this day.[28] His successor, Alexander II (1061–73), not only reissued earlier canons against clerical concubinage and simony, but also forbade laymen to invest bishops with the ring and staff (or crozier) that symbolized episcopal power.

The most aggressive legislator among the eleventh-century reforming popes was Gregory VII (1073–85).[29] Gregory attacked the roots of political appointments to church offices in a series of canons that required that bishops, abbots, and other high-ranking officials henceforth be elected by appropriate groups of clerics, rather than put into office by feudal potentates. Gregory boldly asserted that the ecclesiastical power, and in particular the papacy, was superior in authority to all secular powers, including kings and emperors. Indeed, he went further to claim that the pope had the right, even the duty, to deprive kings and other temporal authorities of power if they disobeyed papal commands or infringed the independence of the church. Gregory VII's open challenge to the legitimacy of lay authorities did not go uncontested. A series of violent and dramatic confrontations between him and the German emperor Henry IV (1056–1106) ultimately forced Gregory to abandon Rome and seek refuge at Salerno under the protection of the Norman kings of South Italy.

28. I. S. Robinson, *The papacy, 1073–1198: Continuity and innovation*, Cambridge medieval textbooks (Cambridge, 1990), pp.33–120; Stephan Kuttner, '*Cardinalis*: The history of a canonical concept', *Traditio* 3 (1949), 129–214; reprinted with original pagination in Kuttner's *History of ideas and doctrines of canon law*, 2nd edn (London, 1992).
29. But Gregory's legislation, although voluminous and often original, paradoxically was seldom cited as an authority by later canonists; John Gilchrist, 'The reception of Pope Gregory VII into the canon law (1073–1141)', *Zeitschrift der Savigny-Stiftung für Rechtsgeschichte*, kanonistische Abteilung 59, (1973), 35–82.

Gregory VII's more diplomatically astute successors, notably Pope Urban II (1088–99), succeeded in retrieving control of Rome and restoring papal power over central Italy, while at the same time remaining loyal to the reform principles that Gregory had championed. In a series of reforming councils and synods, Pope Urban reaffirmed his precursors' condemnations of simony, clerical marriage and sexual irregularities, and all the other issues on the reforming agenda. Numerous canons from Urban's synods found their way into the principal canonical collections of the following generation and Urban II became in fact one of the chief legislative authorities for the reformed papacy.[30]

The third element of the reform strategy, more effective courts and enforcement mechanisms, required basic institutional innovations. This proved to be a slow, often frustrating, process. Early experiments in this area led to dead ends, and a reasonably successful system of ecclesiastical courts only began to emerge in the second half of the thirteenth century.

Before that, church reformers during the eleventh and twelfth centuries relied largely on synods, both at the diocesan level of the bishop and at the papal level, to enforce the canonical rules. Synods were in essence multi-purpose assemblies of all the clergymen of a region. Synods were, at least in principle, supposed to meet frequently in each diocese to hear complaints and settle disputes that had arisen since the previous meeting. The assembled clergy worked something like a jury, with the bishop as presiding judge and his chief lieutenants as experts who advised him and the rest of the group on legal issues and procedure.

While the synod thus functioned in part as a court, it also played other roles, notably as a legislative assembly that could set standards of conduct and adopt new laws and regulations binding on all the faithful, laymen as well as clerics, within its region. In addition the synod served as a forum for debates on theological issues and current local problems, as a staff meeting for administrative

---

30. Alfons Becker, *Papst Urban II. (1088–1099)*, 2 vols, MGH, Schriften, vol. 19 (Stuttgart, 1964–88).

announcements, and as a sounding-board for proposed initiatives and projects. Both because it met irregularly (and sometimes infrequently as well) and because many of its members were not especially well-informed about the niceties of legal analysis or the intricacies of procedure, the synod proved not to be particularly efficient as a tribunal. Ecclesiastical authorities continued to search for more desirable alternatives.

In addition to synods, reforming popes in the eleventh century also used papal legates with increasing frequency to supervise the implementation of canon law and papal policy. Papal legates functioned as travelling judges, dispatched from Rome (or wherever the curia might happen to be during those hectic decades) to deal with controversies and disputes that local authorities were either unable or unwilling to settle. Legates, like synods, were supposed to fill several different functions simultaneously. They were investigators, deputized to discover what was going on at the local level; they were legislators, authorized to promulgate rules for the region to which they were dispatched; they were diplomatic representatives, sent to convey the pope's plans and policies to kings and bishops and to report back to the pope the reactions they encountered. In addition to everything else, legates functioned as prosecutors, empowered to bring action against those who violated church law, and at the same time as judges, commissioned to hear and decide cases in the pope's name and with the force of papal authority. Given this bundle of roles, legates were not only busy, but often found it difficult to cope effectively with their incompatible functions.

At the level of the diocese and the parish, the eleventh-century church employed other mechanisms to detect and prosecute infractions of canon law. Bishops were supposed to conduct visitations; that is, they were expected to inspect each parish and monastery in their diocese at frequent intervals and to correct any irregularities they might discover. Since episcopal visitations in practice took place only occasionally, however, bishops typically depended upon resident authorities (known variously as rural deans, archdeacons, or archpriests) to keep track of routine problems and to enforce the disciplinary canons among the clergy and laity in their vicinity.

Enforcement of the rules at the local level was complicated by the exemptions that many monasteries and even some parishes enjoyed from the supervision of local authorities. Grants of exemption made the exempt parish or monastery answerable exclusively to some distant superior, usually the pope, rather than to local authorities. Since the pope was rarely in any position to know much about problems or abuses that might arise far from Rome, say in a monastery in the Yorkshire Dales, he could scarcely ever exercise much effective supervision over the exempt institution, which for practical purposes enjoyed immunity from any outside supervision whatever. It is scarcely surprising that situations of this sort often led to lax discipline, abuses of authority, and not infrequently to scandals.

The lack of efficient and reliable detection, prosecution, and adjudication mechanisms was a major weakness of the Western church at the end of the eleventh century and remained a hindrance to its effective functioning for generations thereafter. This, combined with the absence of any reasoned and thorough compendium of canon law that would give church authorities adequate guidance to pursue and punish offenders, seriously limited the church's capacity to enforce the norms that the canons prescribed.

As of 1100 the Western church needed some authoritative guide, some agreed-upon body of law that would permit judges and administrators to find their way through the tangled underbrush of the law with reasonable certainty and at tolerable speed. Towards the middle of the twelfth century such a guide at last appeared in the *Decretum* of Gratian.

Chapter 3

GRATIAN AND THE SCHOOLS OF LAW IN THE CLASSICAL PERIOD (1140–1375)

Bologna by the middle of the twelfth century had been Europe's premier centre of legal studies for more than a generation. During the closing decade of the eleventh century a self-taught jurist named Irnerius was drawing crowds of students there from all over Italy. Early in the new century Irnerius's reputation as an original and inspiring teacher with a unique knowledge of Roman civil law had spread to Germany and beyond. Consequently non-Italian students soon began to trickle across the Alps in the hope of acquiring a grasp of legal principles that would qualify them as men of practical learning and might lead to profitable careers in the service of powerful rulers, either in church or state.[1]

1. Within the large (and often controversial) literature on Irnerius and the beginning of law teaching at Bologna, Kenneth Pennington, 'Medieval law', in *Medieval studies: An introduction*, ed. James M. Powell (Syracuse, NY, 1992), pp.333–52, provides a recent and balanced overview. The standard history of medieval universities presents a conventional picture of the central role that Irnerius played in the revival of Roman law; Hastings Rashdall, *The universities of Europe in the Middle Ages*, rev. edn by F. M. Powicke and A. B. Emden, 3 vols (Oxford, 1936), i, pp.113–20 , as does Paul Vinogradoff, *Roman law in medieval Europe* (Oxford, 1929; repr. Cambridge, 1968), and Giulio Silano, 'Irnerius' in *Dictionary of the Middle Ages*, 13 vols (New York, 1982–89; referred to hereafter as DMA), vi, pp.554–5 also provides a brief but helpful account. For greater detail see especially Ennio Cortese, *Il rinascimento giuridico medievale* (Rome, 1992), as well as Enrico Besta, *L'opera di Irnerio: Contributo alla storia del diritto italiano*, 2 vols (Turin, 1896). Charles M. Radding, however, has recently argued that these conventional accounts are altogether mistaken. Radding advances in their place a radically dissenting view of the whole process of legal revival in *The*

The teaching of law during Irnerius's generation and the generation of his disciples (the Four Doctors,[2] who carried on his tradition) was a private enterprise, without public subsidy, institutional framework, or governmental control. An individual could set up in business as a law teacher simply by buying or renting a house with a hall large enough for lectures, furnishing it with a desk and chair for the teacher, and perhaps adding a few benches for students. He announced the times and topics of the lectures he proposed to give, then waited for students to show up – and pay their fees. If he possessed a reputation for learning, had a circle of friends well situated to publicize his talents, and possessed the necessary amount of luck he might succeed in attracting enough students to make a living. He might also pad out his living by renting rooms in his house to students, and might in addition dole out the allowances their families sent to them, or even advance them a loan now and again during hard times. The success-ful law teacher was also apt to attract clients who would pay generously for his legal advice. Appointments as a judge or an ad hoc judge-delegate might also come his way, thus enhancing his reputation as well as lining his pockets.

Law teachers and students gained a further measure of security and prestige in 1155, when the German king and Holy Roman Emperor, Frederick Barbarossa (ca. 1122–90)

---

1. (*Continued*)
   origins of medieval jurisprudence: Pavia and Bologna, 850–1150 (New Haven, 1988). It is fair to say that legal historians have overwhelmingly rejected Radding's thesis; see, for example, the reviews by André Gouron in *Tijdschrift voor Rechtsgeschiedenis* 57 (1989), 178–81; Richard M. Fraher, in *The American historical review* 94 (1989), 732–33; Johannes Fried in *Deutsches Archiv für Erforschung des Mittelalters* 45 (1989), 287–8; and Stanley Chodorow in *Speculum* 65 (1990), 743–5. All the extant documents concerning Irnerius are conveniently collected in Enrico Spagnesi, *Wernerius Bononiensis iudex: La figura storica d'Irnerio* (Florence, 1970).
2. They were Bulgarus Bolgarini, Martin Gosia, Ugo da Porte Ravennata, and James. On their careers see Paul Vinogradoff, *Roman law in medieval Europe* (Oxford, 1929; repr. Cambridge, 1968), pp.61–2; J. A. Clarence Smith, *Medieval law teachers and writers, civilian and canonist* (Ottawa, 1975), pp.12–13; O. F. Robinson, T. D. Fergus, and W. M. Gordon, *An introduction to European legal history* (Abingdon, 1985), pp.94–6.

published a decree, known as the *Authentica 'Habita'*, that placed them under imperial protection and authorized judges to penalize with fourfold damages anyone who in future dared to molest them. The emperor further bestowed exclusive jurisdiction over students upon their teachers and the bishop of the city in which they studied. This in principle exempted students from the jurisdiction of local or municipal authorities and made them answerable for their misdeeds solely to academic and ecclesiastical authorities.[3]

It is highly unlikely that this decree was an entirely spontaneous expression of the emperor's concern for law teachers and their students – imperial privileges seldom materialized save in response to urgent requests, usually by some interested party. The fact that Barbarossa over the next several years sought legal advice from the Four Doctors of Bologna concerning his rights over the northern Italian communes suggests that perhaps the inspiration for the *Habita* may have come from them.

Towards the end of the twelfth century, moreover, foreign law students at Bologna (that is, those who were not Bolognese citizens) organized a student guild, an *universitas scholarum*, to protect their interests against landlords, shopkeepers, tavernkeepers, stationers, booksellers, and teachers who attempted to exploit the student market for goods and services. This event, whose date unfortunately cannot be precisely fixed, marked the beginning of the University of Bologna. In self-defence Bolognese law teachers (and ultimately teachers of the liberal arts, medicine, and theology as well) formed their own guilds, or *universitates doctorum*, to safeguard their interests against those of their students. By the 1220s Bolognese municipal authorities were discussing the possibility of putting some of the most eminent law teachers on the city payroll in order to make sure that the city would continue to attract students from abroad and thus assure its lasting prosperity. Such an arrangement in fact only materialized about 1280, by which time numerous towns and other public authorities

3. Winfried Stelzer, 'Zum Scholarenprivileg Friedrich Barbarossas (Authentica "Habita")', *Deutsches Archiv für Erforschung des Mittelalters* 34 (1978), 123–65.

elsewhere in Italy, Spain, and southern France had begun to do the same.[4]

Gratian's book appeared just as organized and officially sanctioned law teaching was becoming well-established at Bologna, probably sometime close to 1140. About Gratian himself we know little. His book makes it evident that he taught canon law in a school of some kind. Both circumstantial evidence and tradition tie him to Bologna; and there is good reason to think that he was a monk.[5] Virtually nothing else can be said with certainty about him, save that he wrote, and perhaps compiled in part from the work of others, a canon law textbook that he entitled *A harmony of conflicting canons (Concordia discordantium canonum)*. The title aptly described Gratian's purpose: to reconcile differing canonical traditions and prescriptions into an intellectually consistent and unified system. Since this title, although accurate, was rather cumbersome, canonists and others soon began to call it simply *Gratian's Decree (Decretum Gratiani)*, the name that most writers still use for it.

Beginners usually find the *Decretum* mystifying at first. Not only is the overall structure of the book inconsistent and confusing, but beyond that the meaning and thrust of the arguments themselves often seem difficult to follow the first time through.[6] Gratian's book was not a collection of

4. Alan B. Cobban, 'Elective salaried lectureships in the universities of southern Europe in the pre-Reformation era', *Bulletin of the John Rylands Library of Manchester* 67 (1984/85), 662–87 at 663.

5. John T. Noonan, Jr, 'Gratian slept here: The changing identity of the father of the systematic study of canon law', *Traditio* 35 (1979), 145–72; but see also C. Mesini, 'Postille sulla biografia del "Magister Gratianus", padre del diritto canonico', *Apollinaris* 54 (1981), 509–37. As for the likelihood that Gratian was a monk (which Noonan doubts), the *Summa Parisiensis*, a detailed commentary on Gratian's work, written about 20 years after the *Decretum* first appeared, flatly states that 'Gratian was a monk', but gives no further details; *The Summa Parisiensis on the Decretum Gratiani* to C. 2 q. 7 d.p.c. 52 and C. 16 q. 1 c. 61, ed. Terence P. McLaughlin (Toronto, 1952), pp.115, 181.

6. A brief glance at the recent English translation of the first 20 Distinctions of Gratian's *Decretum* will quickly make the problem clear; see *The treatise on laws (Decretum DD. 1–20)*, trans. Augustine Thompson and James Gordley, Studies in medieval and early modern canon law, vol. 2 (Washington, D.C., 1993). On the structure of the *Decretum* see Appendix I, pp.190–20.

legislative enactments, such as one might expect to find, for example, in a statute book. Nor was it a logically structured compendium of general norms, of the sort that make up a code. Rather, Gratian deployed his sources so as to bring out the contradictions between them and then sought to reconcile those differences through a process of dialectical reasoning. For this reason he marshalled the conflicting authorities that he found into units and sub-units. Each group of canons within a unit announced one view of a topic, which the next group contradicted. Gratian typically sought to resolve the contradictions by drawing distinctions between the conflicting authorities that would enable him either to reject one set and adopt the other, or else to apply each set of authorities to a different situation or context.

The dialectical argumentation of the *Decretum* is what made Gratian's work far more attractive to teachers of canon law than any available alternative. It is precisely because of the book's complex and sometimes subtle argumentation that canon law teachers within a decade or two of its appearance overwhelmingly adopted it as the fundamental textbook of their subject. It marked such a crucial break with earlier canon law collections that it has become customary to count its appearance as the beginning of the so-called 'classical' period of canon law (1140–1375), the period when canon law attained its definitive shape and most enduring characteristics.[7] The *Decretum* provided a splendid vehicle for classroom exposition of the intricacies of the law, since it required students and teachers to explore the ways in which rules could be understood in differing situations, and demonstrated concretely how abstract legal principles could be applied to resolve the messy disputes that continually arise between real people in the real world. Gratian's book seemed so useful and important, indeed, that a twelfth-century scholar, whose identity remains uncertain, found it

7. The standard scholarly treatment of this period is Gabriel Le Bras, Charles Lefebvre, and Jacqueline Rambaud, *L'âge classique, 1140–1378: Sources et théorie du droit* (Paris, 1965), which is vol. 7 of the series *Histoire du droit et des institutions de l'église en Occident* (Paris, 1955–).

worthwhile to translate the *Decretum* into Old French, presumably for the use of laymen whose Latin was inadequate to the task of reading the book in its original form.[8]

We know that Gratian's *Decretum* quickly became the standard textbook in the canon law schools because many early manuscripts of the work record in their margins questions and explanations that teachers raised in their lectures about various problems, together with cross-references to other relevant parts of Gratian's text. These individual comments and queries we conventionally call 'glosses', while a collection of numerous glosses by an individual teacher often bore the title of 'gloss apparatus' or '*lectura*'. A systematic commentary on a legal text, shorn of the sort of detailed examinations of individual words and phrases that characterize an 'apparatus', will frequently be called a '*summa*'.[9]

The earliest surviving collection of glosses on Gratian's text is ascribed to a Bolognese teacher named Paucapalea, who composed his glosses on Gratian before 1148.[10] Another early Bolognese law teacher who commented in detail on Gratian's text was Master Rolandus.[11] Master Rolandus wrote shortly after Paucapalea and modern scholars used to assume that he was the same Rolandus who later became Pope Alexander III (1159–81), although this identification now seems mistaken.[12]

8. *Gratiani Decretum: La traduction en ancien français du Décret de Gratien*, ed. Leena Löfstedt, Commentationes humanarum litterarum [of the Finnish society of sciences and letters], vols 95, 99 (Helsinki, 1992–; 2 vols to date).

9. For further details about the various genres of canonistic writing see Antonio García y García, 'The faculties of law', in *A History of the University in Europe*, vol. 1: *Universities in the Middle Ages*, ed. Hilde de Ridder Symoens (Cambridge, 1992), pp.394–7.

10. See John T. Noonan, Jr, 'Paucapalea' in DMA ix, pp.466–7, as well as the published version of Paucapalea's work in *Die Summa des Paucapalea über das Decretum Gratiani*, ed. Johann Friedrich von Schulte (Giessen, 1890).

11. *Die Summa magistri Rolandi nachmals Papstes Alexander III*, ed. Friedrich Thaner (Innsbruck, 1874).

12. John T. Noonan, Jr, 'Who was Rolandus?' in *Law, church, and society: Essays in honor of Stephan Kuttner*, ed. Kenneth Pennington and Robert Somerville (Philadelphia, 1977), pp.21–48; Rudolf Weigand, 'Magister Rolandus und Papst Alexander III', *Archiv für katholisches Kirchenrecht* 149 (1980), 3–144.

The commentaries of numerous other Bolognese teachers survive from the second half of the twelfth century, and their authors are often referred to collectively as 'decretists'.

Among the most important twelfth-century Bolognese decretists were Rufinus (d. before 1192),[13] and Huguccio (d. 1210),[14] whose ideas and insights have continued to influence some basic legal and political ideas right down to the present.[15] Rufinus and Huguccio furthermore exemplified a career pattern that became extremely common among later canonists, for while both began their careers as law teachers, they also engaged occasionally in practice as legal experts or consultants (*iurisperiti*) both to high-ranking church officials and also to civil authorities of various kinds. Both men received appointments to the church's hierarchy towards the close of their careers, Huguccio as bishop of Ferrara in 1190, Rufinus first as bishop of Assisi and later as archbishop of Sorrento.

Although the schools of teachers such as these had not yet become part of a formal institutional structure, the Bolognese decretists were nevertheless interconnected, for they almost certainly knew one another personally and both adopted and criticized one another's ideas. It seems appropriate, therefore, to refer to them collectively as the Bolognese school of canon law.

---

13. Rufinus, *Summa Decretorum*, ed. Heinrich Singer (Paderborn, 1902; repr. Aalen, 1963). See also Stephen C. Ferruolo, 'Rufinus' in DMA x, pp.545–6, and Robert L. Benson, 'Rufin' in *Dictionnaire de droit canonique*, ed. R. Naz, 7 vols (Paris, 1935–65; hereafter cited as DDC), vii, pp.779–84.

14. Kenneth Pennington, 'Huguccio' in DMA vi, pp.327–8; and Alfons M. Stickler, 'Uguccio de Pise' in DDC vii, pp.1355–62. More recently Wolfgang Müller, 'Huguccio of Pisa: Canonist, bishop, and grammarian?', *Viator* xxii (1991), 121–52, has questioned some conventional assumptions about Huguccio's identity.

15. For example, Brian Tierney, *Foundations of the conciliar theory* (Cambridge, 1955; repr. 1968) and his *Religion, law, and the growth of constitutional thought* (Cambridge, 1982); Gaines Post, *Studies in medieval legal thought: Public law and the state, 1100–1322* (Princeton, 1964); Ernst H. Kantorowicz, *The king's two bodies: A study in mediaeval political theology* (Princeton, 1957; repr. 1970); Kenneth Pennington 'Law, legislative authority and theories of government, 1150–1300' in *Cambridge history of medieval political thought, c.350–c.1450*, ed. J. H. Burns (Cambridge, 1988), pp.424–53.

Soon after the Bolognese school's appearance, other masters, beginning in the 1160s and 1170s, were creating a similar school of canon law at Paris.[16] Early Parisian teachers of canon law included Stephen of Tournai (1128–1203)[17] and the unknown author who wrote the *Summa Parisiensis* shortly before 1170.[18] Other schools of decretists in the late twelfth century included a Rhineland school, identified with Bertram of Metz (d. 1212),[19] Gérard Pucelle (d. 1184),[20] and the anonymous author of the *Summa 'Elegantius'* (completed about 1169),[21] as well as an Anglo-Norman school that flourished especially at Oxford by the 1190s.[22]

Teaching in the medieval law schools was almost exclusively done by dialectical text analysis, which methodically followed the structure and organization of the textbook and sought to explain the meaning and application of each sentence and paragraph of the text, commencing at the beginning and proceeding

16. Stephan Kuttner, 'Les débuts de l'école canoniste française,' *Studia et documenta historiae et iuris* 4 (1938), 193–204, repr. with original pagination in his *Gratian and the schools of law* (London, 1983).
17. G. Lepointe, 'Etienne de Tournai', in DDC v, pp.487–92; Herbert Kalb, *Studien zur Summa Stephans von Tournai: Ein Beitrag zur kanonistischen Wissenschaftsgeschichte des späten 12. Jahrhunderts* (Innsbruck, 1983); only part of Stephen's *Summa* has been published: *Die Summa des Stephanus Torniacensis über das Decretum Gratiani*, ed. Johann Friedrich von Schulte (Giessen, 1891; repr. Aalen, 1965).
18. *The Summa Parisiensis on the Decretum Gratiani*, ed. Terence P. McLaughlin (Toronto, 1952).
19. Stephan Kuttner, 'Bertram of Metz', *Traditio* 13 (1957), 501–5.
20. Charles Lefebvre, 'Gérard Pucelle', in DDC v, p.955; Stephan Kuttner and Eleanor Rathbone, 'Anglo-Norman canonists of the twelfth century: An introductory study', *Traditio* 7 (1949/51), 279–358, at 296–303, repr. with original pagination in Kuttner's *Gratian and the schools of law*.
21. *Summa 'Elegantius in iure diuino' seu Coloniensis*, ed. Gérard Fransen and Stephan Kuttner, 4 vols, in the series *Monumenta iuris canonici* (cited hereafter as MIC), Corpus glossatorum, vol. 1 (New York, Vatican City, 1969–90).
22. Kuttner and Rathbone, 'Anglo-Norman Canonists', pp.304–39; Leonard E. Boyle, 'The beginnings of legal studies at Oxford', *Viator* 14 (1983), 107–31 and 'Canon law before 1380', in *The history of the University of Oxford*, ed. T. H. Aston, vol. 1: *The early Oxford schools*, ed. J. I. Catto (Oxford, 1984), pp.531–64.

systematically to the end. Odofredus, a thirteenth-century teacher of civil law, described for his students the standard method of teaching a legal text:

> First, I shall give you the summaries of each title before I come to the text. Second, I shall put forth well and distinctly and in the best terms I can the purport of each law. Third, I shall read the text in order to correct it. Fourth, I shall briefly restate the meaning. Fifth, I shall solve conflicts, adding general matters (which are commonly called *brocardica*) and subtle and useful distinctions and questions with the solution, so far as Divine Providence shall assist me. And if any law is deserving of a review by reason of its fame or difficulty, I shall reserve it for an afternoon review session.[23]

Teachers of canon law adopted a nearly identical lecturing style.[24] Students generally attended the review sessions (*repetitiones*) that Odofredus mentioned in the afternoons, after spending the morning listening to lectures by the senior members of the school's faculty.

Medieval law schools also required their students to perform considerable feats of concentration and memory. Students memorized as a matter of course enormous numbers of laws and had to be able to recall them readily and in proper order, since the lectures they heard bristled with references and citations. Martino de Fano, a thirteenth-century legist, demanded that his students make it a daily practice to commit references to memory; he added: 'And finally, as you lie in bed or walk about the street, go over what you have learned and say, "Today I have learned so many laws, and these are the opening words of each".'[25] The need for abundant memorization

23. Odofredus, in Friedrich Carl von Savigny, *Geschichte des römischen Rechts im Mittelalter*, 7 vols (Heidelberg, 1834–51; repr. Aalen, 1986), iii, pp.541–42, 553; translation adapted from Lynn Thorndyke in *University records and life in the Middle Ages* (New York, 1944, repr. 1975), p.67.

24. Hostiensis, *Summa aurea*, 5 tit. De magistris §6 (Lyon, 1537 ed., fol. 235ra–rb); Antonio García y García, 'The faculties of law', pp.398–400.

25. Quoted from Martino's *De regimine et modo studendi* by F. M. Powicke, 'Some problems in the history of the mediaeval universities', *Transactions of the Royal Historical Society*, 4th ser., 17 (1934), 1–18 at 14.

and ready recall was reinforced by practices such as the one prescribed in the canon law school (or Faculty of Decrees) at the University of Paris; here, lectures were delivered without notes and, during the hour before daybreak, without light either.[26]

As the study of canon law using Gratian's textbook began to attract ever-increasing numbers of students, the making of new law also continued and indeed accelerated considerably. This spurt of new law-making was stimulated, at least in part, by the success of Gratian's work, for the teachers who expounded his *Decretum* discovered in the process numerous problems for which existing canon law either furnished unsatisfactory solutions or none at all. Most of the new law was issued as papal letters of a kind known as 'decretals'. Hence the new law is often called 'decretal law' and those who commented on it are accordingly styled 'decretalists'.[27]

Decretals generally announced papal decisions on individual cases and frequently spelled out in some detail the rationale that underlay the decision; thus many of them resemble, at least roughly, modern appellate court decisions. Decretal letters in the usual course of events were simply dispatched to the parties involved. Copies of some decretals were recorded in the papal correspondence files, or registers, that the curia maintained, but others were not. Hence practising canonists and teachers of canon law found it useful, indeed essential, to make copies of any decretals that came their way, since this allowed them to keep abreast of the current views of the church's highest court of appeals.

Some early decretal collections were nothing more than haphazard copies, without any obvious logical order, of the papal letters that an individual teacher, practitioner, or official chanced across. During and after the pontificate of Pope Alexander III, however, more systematic collections

---

26. *Chartularium universitatis Parisiensis*, ed. Heinrich Denifle and Emile Chatelain, 4 vols (Paris, 1889–97; repr. Brussels, 1964), iii, 425–39 (no 1528–31).
27. Stanley Chodorow, 'Decretals', in DMA iv, pp.122–4; Gérard Fransen, *Les décrétales et les collections de décrétales*, in the series *Typologie des sources du moyen âge occidental*, fasc. 2 (Turnhout, 1972).

began to appear.[28] One especially important collection was the *Breviarium extravagantium* that Bernard of Pavia (d. 1213) compiled between 1188 and 1192.[29] Bernard organized the decretals he had gathered – nearly a thousand of them – into five books. Each book dealt with a single theme; Bernard further subdivided each book into titles that focused on subtopics within the book's principal theme. He arranged the individual decretals within each title in chronological order, so that readers could determine which were the most recent decisions on that subject. Bernard's decretal collection was no doubt the product of his own experience as a canon law teacher at Bologna and other teachers there and elsewhere quickly adopted it as a supplement to Gratian's text and incorporated it into their syllabi.[30]

Bernard of Pavia's *Breviarium* was the first of five such systematic decretal collections that the next generation of law teachers adopted as part of the curriculum, both in the nascent canon law faculties of the universities and also in the private classes that individual teachers offered in monasteries, cathedral chapters, and religious houses of studies, as well as in towns and cities throughout Western Europe.[31] As decretals grew more numerous, however, record-keeping and security measures failed to keep pace. By the early thirteenth century the papal curia had become seriously alarmed by an increasing traffic in counterfeit decretals, some of them fabricated in the interests of parties to disputes, others put together by unscrupulous notaries and copyists who sold them for profit to law students and teachers.[32] The popes accordingly became anxious to control the process of publishing authentic decretals for use in courts and classrooms. After two of his

---

28. Charles Duggan, *Twelfth-century decretal collections and their importance in English history*, University of London historical studies, vol. 12 (London, 1963).
29. Gabriel Le Bras, 'Bernard de Pavie', in DDC ii, 781–89.
30. On the structure of Bernard's *Breviarium* see below, Appendix I, pp.192–3.
31. For details on the others see Appendix I below.
32. Stephen of Tournai, letter to the pope, in *Chartularium universitatis Parisiensis*, i, 47–48 (no 48); translated by Thorndyke, *University records*, pp.23–4.

predecessors had issued official collections of their own decretals, Pope Gregory IX (1227–41) commissioned an eminent Catalan canonist, Raymond of Penyafort (d. 1275) to prepare a new official decretal collection that would include all of the relevant papal and conciliar law since Gratian up to his own time. The resulting text, entitled the *Gregorian decretals (Decretales Gregorii IX)*, but more informally known as the *Liber extra*, was a massive compilation of almost 2,000 decretals, arranged according to the plan that Bernard of Pavia had employed in his *Breviarium*. The pope published the work officially in September 1234, and in his letter of transmission to the Universities of Bologna and Paris directed that it be taught in the law faculties as the official law of the Roman church. The *Liber extra* remained officially in force among Roman Catholics until 1918.[33]

The writing and publication of decretals did not come to a halt in 1234, however, and within a few years the publication of both official and unofficial collections of them commenced once again. Pope Innocent IV (1243–54) published no less than three collections of *New laws* (*Novellae*) in 1245, 1246, and 1253, while Gregory X (1271–76) promulgated a further collection called, logically enough, the *Newest laws* (*Novissimae*) in 1276. Pope Boniface VIII (1294–1303) incorporated most of the decretals officially published by his predecessors, together with other constitutions of his own, in the *Sext* or *Sixth book of decretals* (*Liber sextus*) in 1298. Despite its title, the *Sext* consisted of five books structured on the conventional pattern of other decretal collections. Early in the fourteenth century another, and much smaller, official collection of new canons, the *Clementine constitutions* (*Constitutiones Clementinae*) was published by order of Pope John XXII (1316–34) in 1317, while in 1325 William of Montlezun (*de Monte Lauduno*), a professor of canon law at Toulouse, brought forth a small private collection of John XXII's decretals entitled the *Extravagantes of John XXII*, which found a place in the curricula of later medieval

---

33. Stephan Kuttner, 'Raymond of Peñafort as editor: The "decretales" and "constitutiones" of Gregory IX', *Bulletin of medieval canon law* (hereafter BMCL) 12 (1982), 65–80.

schools of canon law.[34] This collection represented the final academic harvest of new law from papal decretals, which had been the main source of canonical innovation since Gratian's time. By 1325 decretal letters had ceased to be the principal vehicles for legal innovation in the Western church. Instead the decisions of the papal courts, especially the Roman Rota, assumed an increasingly prominent role, not only for clarifying existing law, but also for creating new canonistic rules through judicial decisions.[35] Reports of the Rota's decisions survive in hundreds of manuscripts, most of them still unpublished. Collections of select rotal decisions circulated among legal professionals during the late Middle Ages and several of these were among the earliest legal texts to be published after the invention of printing. The decisions of the Rota constituted a canonistic case law, whose importance increased steadily from the fourteenth century onwards.[36]

By the end of the fifteenth century, after the invention of printing in Europe, publishers began to issue sets of the classical canonical texts – Gratian's *Decretum*, the *Liber extra*, the *Sext*, the *Clementine constitutions*, and the *Extravagantes of John XXII*, sometimes supplemented by additional material – as textbooks under the collective title the *Body of canon law* (*Corpus iuris canonici*), which they intended to parallel their publication of Justinian's codification of Roman law, entitled the *Body of civil law* (*Corpus iuris civilis*).

As decretal law proliferated during the late-thirteenth and fourteenth centuries, the major collections were incorporated into the curricula of the canon law schools almost immediately upon their publication. This, in turn,

34. The term *extravagantes* was commonly used to describe official papal utterances that had not yet been incorporated in an official collection of canons. In 1500 a Parisian canonist, Jean Chappuis, published another such collection, the *Common Extravagantes* (*Extravagantes communes*), which secured wide circulation.
35. See below, ch. 6, pp.125–6.
36. R. C. Van Caenegem, *An historical introduction to private law*, trans. D. E. L. Johnston (Cambridge, 1992), pp.95–6. On collections of rotal decisions see also Gero Dolezalek and Knut Wolfgang Nörr, 'Die Rechtsprechungssammlungen der mittelalterlichen Rota', in *Handbuch der Quellen und Literatur der neueren europäischen Privatrechtsgeschichte*, ed. Helmut Coing, vol. 1, Mittelalter (Munich, 1973), pp.849–56.

led quickly to the production of numerous commentaries on the decretals, beginning with glosses and gloss apparatuses. Bernard of Parma (d. 1266) completed an apparatus that became the *Standard gloss* (*Glossa ordinaria*) on the *Gregorian Decretals* as early as 1241, but continued to revise the work until just before his death. Bernard drew much of his material from the glosses and other commentaries of others, such as Lawrence of Spain[37] and his pupil, Tancred,[38] who had lectured and written glosses on the earlier, pre-Gregorian, decretal collections.[39]

The abundant literature on the decretal law was almost invariably a by-product of the teaching process and represented lectures and observations on the decretal texts made by eminent law teachers of the period. Many of the more celebrated writers combined teaching with private practice, administrative careers, or judicial appointments – and sometimes with all of these. Thus Geoffrey of Trani (d. 1245), author of an early and much-copied *Summa* on the *Liber extra*, followed his teaching years, first at Naples, then at Bologna, with a judicial appointment at the papal curia, and finally with appointment as a cardinal.[40] One of Geoffrey's patrons was Sinibaldo dei Fieschi, who, after teaching for a time at Bologna and holding a succession of increasingly important curial positions, ultimately became Pope Innocent IV. Even during his eventful pontificate, Sinibaldo continued his work as a legal scholar and completed his *Apparatus* on the *Liber extra* shortly before his death.[41] One of Sinibaldo's contemporaries during his

37. Kenneth Pennington, 'Laurentius Hispanus' in DMA vii, 385–86; Alfons M. Stickler, 'Laurent d'Espagne' in DDC vi, pp.361–4.
38. Stanley Chodorow, 'Tancred' in DMA xi, p.584; L. Chevailler, 'Tancrède', in DDC vii, pp.1146–65.
39. Paul Ourliac, 'Bernard de Parme ou de Botone', in DDC ii, pp.781–2; Stephan Kuttner and Beryl Smalley, 'The "Glossa ordinaria" to the Gregorian Decretals', *English historical review* 60 (1945), 97–105, repr. with original pagination in Kuttner's *Studies in the history of medieval canon law* (Aldershot, 1960), together with Kuttner's 'Notes on the Glossa ordinaria of Bernard of Parma', BMCL 11 (Berkeley, 1981), 86–93.
40. Stephan Kuttner, 'Der Kardinalat des Gottfried von Trani', *Studia et documenta historiae et iuris* 6 (1940), 124–31.
41. Elisabeth Vodola, 'Innocent IV, pope' in DMA vi, pp.465–7; J. A. Cantini and Charles Lefebvre, 'Sinibalde dei Fieschi', in DDC vii, pp.1029–62.

student years at Bologna was Henry of Susa (ca. 1200–71), who taught canon law for a brief period at Paris, but spent much of his mature life as an adviser to kings and popes. Like Sinibaldo, Henry of Susa continued to revise and expand his legal writings long after he had stopped lecturing. He completed a short *Summa* on the titles of the *Liber Extra* (which later came to be called the *Golden Summa*, or *Summa aurea*) while he was archbishop of Embrun and his lengthy *Lectura* on the *Liber extra* after he had become cardinal-bishop of Ostia in 1262. As a consequence of this last and highest of his ecclesiastical offices, Henry of Susa is usually referred to as Hostiensis.[42] William Durand (ca. 1230–96), a younger contemporary of Hostiensis and Innocent IV, likewise combined scholarship and an academic career with judicial and administrative appointments. After completing his doctorate at Bologna, Durand taught there for a while and later took a professorship at Modena. Subsequently he was appointed to a judgeship in the curia, then returned to Bologna as its papal governor, and late in life became bishop of Mende in the French Midi. Durand's contemporaries rightly regarded him as a distinguished scholar, especially for his *Speculum iudiciale*, which he completed while serving as a judge and which he subsequently revised while he was a bishop. Durand's *Speculum* became the leading procedural textbook of the later Middle Ages.[43]

One of the last of the great figures of what we now regard as the classical age of canon law (1140–1375) was Giovanni d'Andrea, commonly known by the Latinized form of his name as Johannes Andreae (ca. 1270–1348). Giovanni d'Andrea, unlike the others, was a married layman and taught throughout most of his life, mainly at Bologna, where he took his doctorate between 1296 and 1300. To be sure, Giovanni combined his teaching with service as a legal adviser to the municipality of Bologna and to several popes, notably John XXII, who appointed him a papal legate – a most unusual position for a layman to hold. Giovanni compiled the *Standard gloss* to the *Sext* and

42. Elisabeth Vodola, 'Hostiensis' in DMA vi, pp.298–9; Charles Lefebvre, 'Hostiensis' in DDC v, pp.1211–27.
43. Ronald John Zawilla, 'Durand, William' in DMA iv, pp.314–15; L. Falletti, 'Guillaume Durand' in DDC v, pp.1014–75.

to the *Clementine constitutions*, wrote a lengthy *Lectura* (which he entitled *Novella*, in honour of one of his daughters who bore that name) and composed numerous additional comments on the *Speculum iudiciale* of William Durand.[44] One of Giovanni d'Andrea's granddaughters married another major fourteenth-century canonist, Giovanni da Legnanao (ca. 1320–83), a member of a noble family from Milan, who studied law at Bologna and later played prominent roles in politics and public affairs. Giovanni da Legnano, like his wife's grandfather, was a voluminous and influential writer. His most widely influential work, *A treatise on war, reprisals and the duel*, laid the foundations upon which later writers, such as Francisco Suarez (1548–1617), a Spanish Jesuit, and Hugo Grotius (1583–1645), a Dutch Calvinist, built the modern theory and practice of international law.[45]

One particularly significant development during the generations following Gratian was the fast-growing interdependence between canon law and the revived Roman civil law. Gratian apparently included few, if any, references to Roman law in the original version of the *Decretum*, but early in its history anonymous interpolators added almost 150 further canons to his book, including substantial numbers of Roman law texts.[46] Canonists in the late twelfth century habitually borrowed terms, ideas, concepts, and institutions from the civilians, while civilian writers frequently compared canonical institutions and practices with those that they found in Roman legal texts.[47] By the early thirteenth century the symbiotic relationship between the two learned laws (so called in contrast to customary law and municipal statutory law, which were not

44. Sven Stelling-Michaud, 'Jean d'André' in DDC vi, pp.89–92; Hans Peter Glöckner, 'Johannes Andreae' in DMA vii, p.118.
45. *Tractatus de bello, de represaliis et de duello*, ed. and trans. Thomas E. Holland (Oxford, 1917); Sven Stelling-Michaud, 'Jean de Legnano' in DDC vi, pp.111–12.
46. Le Bras, Lefebvre, and Rambaud, *L'âge classique*, pp.100–14.
47. E. C. C. Coppens, 'L'interpétation analogique des termes de droit romain en droit canonique médiéval', in *Actes du colloque 'Terminologie de la vie intellectuelle au moyen âge* (Turnhout, 1988), pp.54–64; Charles Lefebvre, 'La glose d'Accurse, le Décret et les décrétales', in *Atti del convegno internazionali di studi accursiani*, 3 vols (Milan, 1968), i, pp.249–84.

typically subjects of formal study in university law faculties) had grown so close and pervasive that scholars sometimes speak of a 'reception' of Roman law by the canonists. 'Reception' in this context means that canonists accepted the law of Justinian's *Corpus* as a supplementary source of canon law. Thus when canonical sources failed to supply answers to a question or solutions to a problem, canonists sometimes drew the information and legal rules that they needed from Roman law sources.[48] In a practical sense, as well, the two laws were interdependent. Law students who realistically hoped to make a living as practising lawyers needed to study both laws in order to acquire the skills necessary to assure themselves a livelihood. Short handbooks of civil law for canonists and of canon law for civilians consequently found an eager readership and circulated widely.[49]

From the second half of the thirteenth century onward, moreover, we find increasingly frequent references to the 'general law' or *ius commune*, meaning those principles of substantive law and procedure that were in common use throughout Christendom.[50] In effect the general law usually

48. Canonists prior to the late thirteenth century usually refrained from using the term 'law' (*lex*) to describe the material of their discipline. 'Law' comes into general use to describe the canons only after the Council of Trent in the mid-sixteenth century. Stephan Kuttner, 'Some considerations on the role of secular law and institutions in the history of canon law', in *Scritti di sociologia e politica in onore di Luigi Sturzo* (Bologna, 1953), ii, pp.351–62, and 'Reflections on gospel and law in the history of the church', in *Liber amicorum Monseigneur Onclin* (Gembloux, 1976), pp.199–209. Both of these studies are reprinted with original pagination in Kuttner's *Studies in the history of medieval canon law*. See also Gérard Fransen, 'De analogia legis apud canonistas', *Periodica de re morali, canonica, liturgica* 66 (1977), 535–47.

49. Ingrid Baumgärtner, ' "Was muß ein Legist vom Kirchenrecht wissen?" Rofredus Beneventanus und seine *Libelli de iure canonico*', in *Proceedings of the seventh international congress of medieval canon law*, ed. Peter Linehan, MIC, Subsidia, vol. 8 (Vatican City, 1988), pp.223–45; Arturo Bernal Palacios, 'La *Concordia utriusque iuris* de Paspicoverus', in *Proceedings of the sixth international congress of medieval canon law*, ed. Stephan Kuttner and Kenneth Pennington, MIC, Subsidia, vol. 7 (Vatican City, 1985), pp.139–51.

50. Despite the similarity in the terms, the *ius commune* must not be confused with English common law, which was (and for that matter still is) the body of customary rules worked out in English practice from the mid-twelfth century onward.

meant romano-canonical legal concepts and practices that municipal and royal courts could invoke to settle problems for which appropriate local custom or statute was lacking.[51] Further, the *ius commune* included not only the texts of romano-canonical law, but also acceptance of the standard glosses and opinions of the commentators as authoritative sources of legitimate law.[52] The *ius commune* relied heavily upon canonical civil procedure as a model, which it adapted for its own purposes with relatively minor changes. The *ius commune* in many regions also incorporated principles of 'canonical equity' as well, which allowed judges to adjust the rules to fit the circumstances of a particular situation where justice seemed to require departure from strict law. Thus the *ius commune* in effect transformed romano-canonical law into sets, or 'blocks' of legal practices and principles that were conceived as underlying local custom and statute.[53] Judges could and did exercise discretion to invoke the 'blocks' of principles or practices that they deemed useful in order to resolve a dispute and make peace within a community.[54]

The developments discussed thus far in this chapter show that canon law by the mid-thirteenth century had become a distinctive academic discipline, increasingly technical and increasingly distanced intellectually from theology and civil law, yet still conceptually related to both. It is scarcely surprising in these circumstances to find that

51. Robinson, Fergus, and Gordon, *Introduction to European legal history*, pp.179–207; Francesco Calasso, *Introduzione al diritto comune* (Milan, 1951).
52. Alan Watson, *Failures of the legal imagination* (Philadelphia, 1988), pp.135–6; Woldemar Engelmann, *Die Wiedergeburt der Rechtskultur in Italien durch die wissenschaftliche Lehre: Eine Darlegung der Entfaltung des gemeinen italienischen Rechts und seiner Justizkultur im Mittelalter* (Leipzig, 1938), pp.189–92.
53. Alan Watson, *The making of the civil law* (Cambridge, MA, 1981), pp.14–22.
54. The standard account of the development of *ius commune* is now Manlio Bellomo, *Storia del diritto comune* (Rome, 1989). For the role that *ius commune* played in late medieval Germany see also James Q. Whitman, *The legacy of Roman law in the German romantic era: Historical vision and legal change* (Princeton, 1990), pp.7–9. On romano-canonical law in Italy, France, and Scotland see also Alan Watson, *Sources of law, legal change, and ambiguity* (Philadelphia, 1984), pp.51–75.

by the second quarter of the thirteenth century canonists began to affirm their distinctive identity. They did so in part by creating specific academic titles to differentiate men qualified in canon law from those trained in other disciplines. Even before 1200 titles such as 'master of decrees' (*magister decretorum*) appear from time to time in the records, but such a title did not at that time necessarily imply any specific course of study or signify that the person to whom it applied held a university degree.[55] Within two decades, however, designations of this sort were beginning to carry more precise academic implications. A 'master of decrees' by the 1220s was likely to mean a person who had pursued a prescribed course of studies in canon law at a university and at the end of it had passed an examination given by his teachers, who certified that he was competent both to teach and to practise as a canonist. By the 1250s degree structure and nomenclature had grown more complex. The title 'doctor of decrees' (*doctor decretorum*) had by then come into common use to designate a fully-trained canonist, one who had not only completed a course of studies that stretched over five years or more, but had also passed both a preliminary private examination and a public one and had also lectured in canon law at the university that conferred his title. Those who had completed the first year or two of canonical studies were coming by this time to be described as 'bachelors of decrees', while those who had progressed far enough to take and pass the private examination often bore the title 'licentiate in decrees'.[56]

This burgeoning of degrees, titles, and formal requirements for certified graduates indicates beyond serious doubt that canonists around the beginning of the thirteenth century were coming to think of themselves, and to be seen by others, as a distinctive occupational group. By about 1250 university-trained canonists had become a 'profession' in something reasonably close to the sense that the word has come to have in modern speech and

---

55. Savigny, *Geschichte*, i, pp.469–72.
56. Peter Weimar, 'Zur Doktorwürde der Bologneser Legisten', in *Aspekte europäischer Rechtsgeschichte* (Frankfurt a/M, 1982), pp.421–2.

writing.[57] Medieval canonists may, indeed, have been the earliest occupational group to develop a professional identity in the strict sense of the term.[58]

That is not to deny, of course, that before 1250, or for that matter even before 1200, considerable numbers of individuals made a living, either wholly or in large part, from the teaching or practice of canon law. On the contrary, there is ample evidence that there were numerous such people – and a good many writers from about 1150 onward were upset about it. But an 'occupation' is not the same as a 'profession'. A 'profession' denotes a special type

57. The concepts of 'profession' and 'professionalism' have been the subject of much discussion and dispute among sociologists in the twentieth century. John Kultgen, *Ethics and professionalism* (Philadelphia, 1988) seeks to simplify these disagreements by reducing the competing views of professionalism to two: the functionalist model and the conflict model. Functionalists, in Kultgen's analysis, are those who believe that institutions, such as professions, help societies to meet their needs and thus contribute to social stability by reducing conflict and competition within a community. Advocates of the conflict model argue that professions and other institutions originate in a need to resolve the conflicts that arise within communities as a result of competition for scarce resources. Professional groups, in this view, represent a compromise between competing interests, whereby members of the profession partially meet some special needs of the rest of the community. In return for this professionals receive monopolistic privileges that allow members of the profession to amass rewards that are often wholly disproportionate to their social contribution. Thus professions are inherently the tools of oppressive minorities and when the oppressed majority becomes sufficiently incensed at this situation, social discord and instability will inevitably result. The conflict model assumes that societies are therefore inherently unstable and that any form of social organization will ultimately be overturned and its place taken by another, equally unstable, social structure. Andrew Abbot, *The system of professions: An essay on the division of expert labor* (Chicago, 1988), on the other hand, argues that such theoretical quibbling about the origins of professions misses the essential point, namely that competition and jurisdictional disputes between occupational groups determine the way in which professions emerge and develop. For theoretical discussions that deal specifically with the legal profession see Richard L. Abel and Philip S. C. Lewis, eds, *Lawyers in society*, vol. 3, *Comparative theories* (Berkeley and Los Angeles, 1989).

58. See also James A. Brundage, 'The rise of the professional jurist', forthcoming in the *kanonistische Abteilung* of the *Zeitschrift der Savigny-Stiftung für Rechtsteschichte*.

of occupation, one that requires higher and more rigorous learning and skills than do ordinary jobs, an occupation to which admission is stringently controlled (in part through educational requirements), and whose members are held to stricter standards of behaviour than those demanded of ordinary workers. In theory at least, members of a 'profession' must enforce their own standards of conduct because non-professionals lack competence to do so. 'Professionals' usually pride themselves on the notion that the work they do constitutes a public service and that they perform their functions not simply to make money, but also to benefit society as a whole.

Canon law became a profession in all of these senses between about 1200 and about 1250. Before 1200 there is no evidence of a formal ceremony by which canonical advocates and proctors were admitted to practice, while by 1250 this was commencing to become common.[59] The admissions ceremony involved the swearing of an oath of office and the entry of the new practitioner's name on a register of practitioners. The admissions oath, in turn, spelled out in general terms some basic professional obligations that the newly admitted practitioner undertook to observe. Fledgling practitioners swore that they would represent and advise their clients with the utmost diligence and zeal. They further swore that they would not knowingly accept unjust or ill-founded causes, that they would neither fabricate evidence themselves nor introduce evidence fabricated by others, that they would not conceal relevant evidence from their opponents or the court, and that if during the course of proceedings they became aware that their client's case was frivolous or maliciously brought in order to harass their opponent, they would immediately abandon the client, withdraw from the case, and inform the judge of their reasons for doing so.[60]

Although control of entry into the profession was

---

59. The earliest canonical admissions oaths date from 1231; Council of Rouen, c. 45 and Council of Château Gontier, c. 36, in *Sacrorum conciliorum nova et amplissima collectio*, ed. Giovanni Domenico Mansi, rev. edn, 53 vols (Paris, 1900–27), xxiii, pp.218–19, 240–1.

60. James A. Brundage, 'The calumny oath and ethical ideals of canonical advocates', forthcoming in *Proceedings of the ninth international congress of medieval canon law*, ed. Peter Landau.

formally in the hands of the judges in the courts to which practitioners were admitted, in practical terms the profession itself largely determined who would be admitted and who would not. The universities played a pivotal role in the process, since university teachers certified that prospective practitioners possessed the required training and skills. In addition, in many jurisdictions, especially in Italy, local guilds or associations of university-trained lawyers might impose their own examinations and other requirements upon those who sought to qualify as advocates or proctors in the courts.

Enforcement of standards of professional conduct lay formally in the hands of the judges, who had the power to hear complaints and impose sanctions upon those who failed to measure up. While it was not unknown for a judge to initiate disciplinary proceedings, the initiative much more commonly lay with aggrieved clients. Punishment of canon lawyers found guilty of improper conduct ranged from fines to temporary suspension from practice to permanent exclusion and disbarment for the most egregious offenders.

Canonists made a living from their profession either by charging fees for services or else by securing ecclesiastical appointments that brought them an income. Law teachers and other legal writers elaborated complex rules concerning the etiquette that canonists were supposed to observe when establishing and collecting fees. Thus, for example, it was considered bad form for a client to pay a fee directly to his advocate; instead, the client paid the proctor (a practitioner of lesser dignity, with fewer academic qualifications than an advocate), who in turn paid the advocate. Even then the proctor customarily hid the money in a bag or basket when presenting it to the advocate, so as to avoid any vulgar counting out of coins.[61]

Legal writers who addressed themselves to practitioners strongly urged their readers to reach an agreement with their clients concerning the amount and payment schedule

---

61. Rufinus, *Summa decretorum* C. 3 q. 3 d.p.c. 3 §5 v. *praebitis sportulis*, ed. Singer, p.264. On fees generally see also James A. Brundage, 'The profits of the law: Legal fees of university-trained advocates', *American journal of legal history* 32 (1988), 1–15.

of fees at the very outset. A few authorities held that it was improper for an advocate to demand payment in advance, but Gratia of Arezzo, author of a thirteenth-century manual for practising canonists, advised that fees be made payable at the conclusion of closing argument, but before the court's decision was handed down. At this point, he suggested, litigants were apt to be optimistic about the outcome and were thus likely to pay cheerfully and in full; whereas if one waited until the outcome was known, clients who lost their cases might be disinclined to pay at all.[62] Academic writers sometimes argued by analogy with the doctor-patient relationship that it was improper even to discuss legal fees, much less pay them, until the case was concluded. Although Accursius (d. 1263) included this opinion in his *Standard gloss* to Justinian's Code, it seems unlikely that his view was much heeded in practice.[63]

In point of fact, powerful clients and many ecclesiastical institutions, whether powerful or not, habitually kept one or more advocates and proctors on standing retainer, usually paid to them as an annual pension, to make sure that they would have expert legal assistance available when needed. This was a sensible precaution: the practising bar in many ecclesiastical courts was relatively small – a half-dozen or even fewer trained advocates or proctors were available in many jurisdictions – and an influential litigant with money to spare could place all of them on retainers, which would make it impossible for them to act on behalf of his adversary.[64] Given the fairly elaborate rules that canonists devised concerning conflicts of interest, this

62. Gratia of Arezzo (Aretinus), *Summa de iudiciario ordine* 2.9, in *Pillius, Tancredus, Gratia libri de iudiciorum ordine*, ed. F. C. Bergmann (Göttingen, 1842; repr. Aalen, 1965), pp.378–9.

63. Accursius, *Glos. ord.* to Cod. 2.6.6 v. *contractum ineat*. The civilian *Glossa ordinaria* will be cited throughout from the edition in 5 vols published at Lyon in 1584, while Roman law texts are cited from the critical edition of the *Corpus iuris civilis* by Paul Krueger, Theodor Mommsen, Rudolf Schoell, and Wilhelm Kroll, 3 vols (Berlin, 1872–95; often reprinted).

64. This may still happen occasionally. In 1993 a private individual who was suing a multinational corporation in the State of Delaware complained that he was unable to find a single lawyer in the State who was free to represent him; *New York Times*, 19 May 1993, C1, C 14.

could well leave his opponent without skilled legal assistance. The canons, to be sure, provided a remedy for this situation, as they also did for the litigant who could not afford to pay the usual legal fees, through a process called 'distribution of counsel'. The process was apt to be cumbersome and time-consuming, however, and even the simple process of petitioning for distribution might well have been beyond the capacity of many litigants.

Venerable tradition prescribed that the amount of legal fees ought to reflect the nature of the case, the skill of the advocate, the circumstances of the client, and the custom of the court in which an action was argued.[65] Advocates and proctors were admonished to keep their fees reasonable and modest. For those who had difficulty in following that advice, some courts tried to set ceilings on legal fees and promised sanctions against those who violated their scales of maximum fees. In practical reality, however, the determining factor usually tended to be the resources of the client: rich clients paid more, often a great deal more, than poor ones for essentially the same services.

The maturing of canon law and the growth of the canonical legal profession during the classical age had important intellectual and social implications for Western Christendom during the high and later Middle Ages. Men trained in romano-canonical law included some of the keenest minds and most ambitious spirits in Europe, for by the end of the fourteenth century anyone who hoped to achieve high office in either ecclesiastical or civil society needed either powerful connections or a legal education, and preferably both.[66] Since legal training cultivated both verbal and reasoning skills, as well as recall of a vast battery of rules and procedures, lawyers as a group tended to be articulate and learned, their talents tempered by the

65. The rule goes back to classical Roman law: Dig. 50.13.1.10 (Ulpian), from which the canonists adopted it; Johannes Teutonicus, *Glos. ord.* to C. 11 q. 3 c. 71 v. *iustum*. The canonistic *Glossa ordinaria* will be cited throughout from the 4 volume edition published at Venice in 1605. Texts of the *Corpus iuris canonici* are cited from the standard edition by Emil Richter, revised by Emil Friedberg, 2 vols (Leipzig, 1879; repr. Graz, 1959).
66. Myron P. Gilmore, 'The lawyers and the church in the Italian Renaissance', *Studi Senesi* 75 (1963), 7–29 at 12–13.

requirements of a complex and demanding discipline. Successful teachers and practitioners of the law, moreover, often accumulated sufficient wealth to be able to afford the luxuries not only of collecting books, but also of reading and reflecting on them,[67] while many achieved sufficient social status and influence to assure that their views were listened to with respect. It is scarcely surprising, then, to discover that many of the leading fourteenth and fifteenth-century humanists had trained as lawyers.[68]

Indeed, lawyers by the thirteenth century had become prominent figures in nearly every department of medieval society. They were active almost everywhere in civic affairs and frequently dominated town governments in Italy and elsewhere.[69] Pietro Andrea (1480–1528) claimed that jurists occupied a position of special authority in society, and many of his contemporaries obviously agreed, for men learned in the laws exercised influence out of all proportion to their numbers.[70]

As early as the close of the twelfth century we find Pope Innocent III already describing jurists as a privileged class (*ordo*) in the church,[71] while the *Standard gloss* to Gratian's *Decretum* asserted that advocates were entitled to be treated as knights and other authorities claimed that law professors

67. Roger Doucet, *Les bibliothèques parisiennes au XVIe siècle* (Paris, 1956), pp.20–9; Donald R. Kelley, *Foundations of modern historical scholarship: Language, law, and history in the French Renaissance* (New York, 1970), p.244; Lauro Martines, *Lawyers and statecraft in Renaissance Florence* (Princeton, 1968), p.84.

68. William J. Bouwsma, 'Lawyers and early modern culture', *American historical review* 78 (1973), 303–27.

69. Francesco Calasso, *I glossatori e la teoria della sovranità: Studio di diritto commune pubblico*, 2d edn. (Milan, 1951), pp.85–90; Mario Sbriccoli, *L'interpretazione dello statuto: Contributo allo studio della funzione dei giuristi nell'età communale*, Università di Macerata, Pubblicazioni della Facoltà di giurisprudenza, ser. 2, vol. 1, p 67.

70. Petrus Andrea, *Tractatus de cognitione iuris et interpretatione verborum*, in *Tractatus universi iuris*, 22 vols in 28 (Venice, 1584–86), i, fol. 1va; Carlo M. Cipolla, *Before the industrial revolution: European society and economy, 1000–1700* (New York, 1976), pp.82–3.

71. X 5.7.12 (1199); Gabriel Le Bras, 'Velut splendor firmamenti: Le docteur dans le droit de l'église médiévale', in *Mélanges offerts à Etienne Gilson* (Toronto and Paris, 1959), pp.373–88 at 380.

with 20 years of teaching experience ranked as counts.[72] These bold claims of status in fact did bear some relationship to social reality, for jurists were often treated as de facto noblemen, and significant numbers of them actually belonged to knightly or noble families.[73] Whatever their social origin, moreover, successful advocates and other lawyers tended to accumulate wealth and a combination of wealth, learning, and access to power earned them high rank on the social scale.[74] Successful lawyers, in addition, often founded something very like legal dynasties, which generation after generation produced prominent, well-connected jurists, and these families often intermarried with one another to create close-knit webs that bound together members of the legal patriciate.[75] Although entrenched legal families often took steps to give their descendants easier access than outsiders enjoyed to a legal career, nevertheless the law remained throughout the Middle Ages one of the most promising avenues of advancement for able and ambitious men.[76]

72. Johannes Teutonicus, *Glos. ord.* to C. 23 q. 1 c. 5 v. *militiae*; also Bernard of Parma, *Glos. ord.* to X 3.34.9 v. *maturitate tamen consilio* and Giovanni d'Andrea, *Glos. ord.* to VI 3.12.4 v. *castrense*; Ernst H. Kantorowicz, 'Kingship under the impact of scientific jurisprudence' in *Twelfth-century Europe and the foundations of modern society*, ed. Marshall Clagget, Gaines Post, and Robert Reynolds (Madison, 1961), pp.89–111 at 91–92.
73. Daniel Waley, *The Italian city republics* (New York, 1969), pp.28–9; J. K. Hyde, *Padua in the age of Dante* (New York, 1966), p.146.
74. See, for example, G. W. Coopland's 'Introduction' to his edition of Philippe de Mézières's *Songe du vieil pelerin*, 2 vols (Cambridge, 1969), i, pp.39; Bernard Guenée, *Tribunaux et gens de justice dans la bailliage de Senlis à la fin du moyen âge (vers. 1380–vers 1550)* (Strasbourg, 1963), pp.200–2; André Gouron, 'Le role social des juristes dans les villes méridionales au moyen âge', *Annales de la Faculté des lettres et sciences humaines de Nice*, 9/10 (1969), 55–67, reprinted with original pagination in his *La science du droit dans le Midi* (London, 1984), pp.55–60.
75. Among canonists, Giovanni d'Andrea was notably successful as the founder of a dynastic tradition; see the accounts mentioned above at n. 44. See also René Fédou, *Les hommes de loi lyonnais à la fin du moyen âge: Etude sur les origines de la classe de robe*, Annales de la Université de Lyon, 3rd ser., vol. 37 (Paris, 1964), pp.153–78; Ernst Bertin, *Les mariages dans l'ancienne société française* (Paris, 1879; repr. Geneva, 1975), p.416.
76. Robert L. Reynolds, *Europe emerges* (Madison, 1961), pp.188, 267–8.

Chapter 4

CANON LAW AND PRIVATE LIFE

The jurisdictional boundaries of canon law – like medieval political boundaries – were often fuzzy and many jurisdictional frontiers remained uncertainly defined throughout the Middle Ages. Medieval church courts claimed, and often exercised, authority over numerous aspects of life that people in modern secularized societies tend to regard as the business of civil government, rather than of church authorities. In the nineteenth and twentieth centuries, moreover, people who live in what we call 'the developed nations' have generally come to accept the notion that some areas of human thought and behaviour should be treated as purely private matters, free from supervision or control by public authorities of any kind, civil or ecclesiastical. Thus, religious and political beliefs, as well as most kinds of sexual conduct, in this view, are private concerns that the community should not try to regulate. These affairs are the exclusive business of the individuals involved in them, and should be free from public interference so long as the parties do not invade the autonomy of those who do not share their views or who choose not to participate in their activities. Personal conduct becomes a matter for public intervention only if it creates problems that affect the rest of society.

Medieval views on these matters differed profoundly from those current in the modern world. Medieval churchmen claimed authority over virtually every aspect of human beliefs and actions. They believed that they had not merely the right but the duty to repress any religious or moral ideas that departed from orthodox norms. Deviant beliefs, they thought, not only endangered the salvation of those who entertained them, but threatened to infect the rest of the community as well. Hence church authorities claimed the right to prosecute and, if necessary, to remove from society those who harboured heretical ideas. Church leaders claimed, furthermore, that they must protect society and its individual members from immoral behaviour as well as unorthodox thought, and so they claimed a broad jurisdiction over all varieties of sinful actions, commercial and non-commercial, sexual and non-sexual, civil and criminal, among the clergy and laity alike.

Thus church authorities claimed, and academic canonists taught, for example, that canonical courts possessed full and exclusive jurisdiction over all crimes and offences committed by clerics of whatever description. This meant that anyone in holy orders, together with many others who enjoyed the benefits of clerical status (such as students, monks, hermits, regular canons, nuns, and the like) was answerable only to church courts, no matter what the issue might be – ecclesiastical judges accordingly claimed jurisdiction over rape, murder, arson, treason, robbery, or fraud, for example, when committed, or alleged to have been committed, by clerics. The controversy over criminous clerks that erupted in twelfth-century England and culminated in the murder of Thomas Becket (1170), illustrates dramatically how hotly that particular jurisdictional claim might be contested, as well as how important it seemed to the parties.

Among the laity, religious authorities likewise asserted the right to regulate most common varieties of human conduct from the cradle to the grave. Church courts exercised jurisdiction, for example, over marriage and the termination of marriage, the legitimacy of children, all types of sexual conduct, commercial and financial behaviour, the legitimate times and conditions of labour, poor relief, wills and testaments, and burial of the dead.

Canonists were able to secure their claims to jurisdiction over marriage without the kind of murderous confrontation that marred their efforts to judge criminous clerics. Canonical authorities, moreover, were prepared to compromise with civil authorities on some issues that involved marriage jurisdiction. Churchmen usually conceded the right of lay courts to adjudicate marital property issues that arose in connection with dower, dowry, and succession to decedents' estates.

Civil courts, notably the English common law courts, were disinclined to yield passively to the jurisdictional imperialism of the canonists. Civil authorities in England and elsewhere claimed the right to define the boundaries of ecclesiastical jurisdiction, a claim that ecclesiastical authorities vigorously resisted.[1] Settlements on issues of the precise jurisdictional frontiers between canonical courts and the civil courts varied somewhat from one region to another and from one period to the next. But regardless of the outcome of competition between civil and ecclesiastical courts in a particular region and over a particular segment of the law, the range of canonical jurisdiction remained broad enough to encompass matters that sooner or later were bound to affect almost everyone.

The issues that brought the largest numbers of people into personal contact with canonical courts at the local level had to do with marriage, family, and sexual behaviour. The exclusive competence of church courts to deal with these matters was well established by the tenth century and was only rarely challenged thereafter.[2] Bishops' consistory courts typically seem to have spent a large part of their time dealing with cases that involved one or more of these issues. Although the lower-ranking courts of archdeacons were not supposed to rule on the more serious issues of marriage law, they frequently did so in practice, so that the precise jurisdictional frontiers were often the subject of contention between bishops and their archdeacons – and these disputes were of course fought out in the courts of even higher-ranking prelates, often reaching the papal courts before they secured final resolution.

A substantial part of the matrimonial cases that ecclesiastical courts heard concerned questions about the formation of marriage. The basic issue that canonical

1. Richard H. Helmholz, 'Conflicts between religious and secular law: Common themes in the English experience', *Cardozo law review* 12 (1991), 707–28.
2. Pierre Daudet, *Les origines carolingiennes de la compétence exclusive de l'église en France et en Germanie en matière de juridiction matrimoniale* (Paris, 1933).

judges often had to decide, in other words, was: Are these two people married to each other, or are they not?

We might expect that such a question, at least in most situations, ought to be relatively simple to answer. In fact it frequently proved far from simple or straightforward to discover the proper solution. The matter fell within the jurisdiction of the bishop's court – on that nearly everyone agreed. The relevant law seemed straightforward and simple – deceptively so, in fact. Canon law by the late twelfth century deemed that two people were married when they exchanged mutual consent to marry one another, provided that they were free to marry (of lawful age, not currently married to anyone else or bound by a vow of chastity, not too closely related to each other, and so on), their consent was voluntary, and it was given in the present tense. Alternatively a couple might exchange consent in the future tense, in which case they became husband and wife the next time they had sexual intercourse with each other. No registration, no licence, no prior announcement, no witnesses, no wedding ceremony – none of these was necessary for a valid marriage. Canon law, to be sure, did require that couples announce their intention to marry before they exchanged consent, that the wedding take place publicly, and that a priest be present to witness their vows and bestow a nuptial blessing on them – but these conditions, although important, were not essential for a valid marriage. It was, of course, in the best interests of most couples to comply with these important but non-essential requirements. Should they fail to do so, however, their marriage was nonetheless valid and they were thenceforth bound to one another for life.[3]

Thorny problems arose, however, when an informal or clandestine marriage – that is, one that took place in private, without priest, witnesses, or formal ceremony – was called into question. One party, for example, might have a change of heart and run off with a wealthier or more attractive partner, whereupon the deserted spouse brought

3. James A. Brundage, *Law, sex, and Christian society in medieval Europe* (Chicago, 1987), pp.348–64; Charles Donahue, Jr, 'The canon law on the formation of marriage and social practice in the later Middle Ages', *Journal of family history* 8 (1983), 144–58.

legal action to demand that the errant partner return. The first party might then deny that they had ever exchanged marital consent, while the other insisted that they had. Proof in such a situation presented judges with formidable problems.[4]

Sometimes, too, one or both partners (or their families) might decide that their union was a mistake, even after they had been living together for years and had numerous children. Pressure from one of the families, or sometimes from the community, often made it impractical for such a couple simply to separate. Instead they needed to convince a canonical judge that they had never exchanged marital consent or that they had not been free to marry, or that some previously unrecognized canonical impediment had undermined the validity of their union, so that they could now go their separate ways – and perhaps marry new partners. In this situation the problems of evidence could be even more formidable.

Or again, in another fairly common situation, a couple might marry clandestinely, produce children, live out their lives in reasonable harmony and contentment, and leave their property to any child or children who survived them. So far, so good; but if the children's inheritance was challenged – say, by one of those wicked uncles so common in folklore – on the grounds that the parents had never been validly married, proof of the marriage might be exceedingly difficult to produce.

In addition to litigants who came to court with the aim of securing a legal termination of their unions, many others petitioned ecclesiastical judges to pronounce a formal judgment to affirm the validity of their marriages and to force a wandering spouse to return to the matrimonial home. Canonical courts also had to deal with the consequences of the marriages that they annulled, such as alimony, child support, custody, and the like. Church courts, however, did not attempt by and large to resolve disputes over the division of marital property, for these

---

4. Charles Donahue, Jr, 'Proof by witnesses in the church courts of medieval England: An imperfect reception of the learned law', in *On the laws and customs of England: Essays in honor of Samuel E. Thorne*, ed. Morris S. Arnold et al. (Chapel Hill, NC, 1981), pp.127–58.

matters lay within the competence of civil courts. Ecclesiastical judges did deal occasionally with questions of marital conduct, notably complaints about physical abuse and sexual maladjustment, either of which might constitute grounds for separation, or even annulment.

The policies that families adopted concerning the marriages of their children were also subject to judicial review, especially when family interests resulted in pressure to marry persons related within the forbidden degrees of kinship.[5] To complicate matters further, persons related by legal ties were also forbidden to intermarry, so that in-laws, for example, could not marry one another, nor could the godparents who stood as sponsors at baptism marry one another or any close relatives of their godchild.[6]

Beyond their civil jurisdiction over marriage formation, canonical courts also exercised criminal jurisdiction over all types of extramarital sexual conduct. Thus fornication, adultery, bigamy, rape, incest, prostitution, and sodomy were all subject to ecclesiastical penalties and church courts, especially in archdeacons' courts, while some diocesan consistory courts also tried to enforce regulations about sexual morals. Such cases brought numerous persons unwillingly into contact with the disciplinary mechanisms of canon law.

Canon law also had significant impact on certain features of medieval commerce and finance. While theologians wrestled with moral problems concerning the equitable distribution of wealth and access to resources, canonists were obliged to devise mechanisms to implement the economic policies that church authorities adopted.[7] One

---

5. Canonical rules on consanguinity and affinity were quite complex and also changed over time. Canonists up to 1215 held that the law forbade marriage within seven degrees of kinship, which for many people must have restricted the choice of marital partners quite severely. The Fourth Lateran Council modified this rule, however, and reduced the forbidden degrees from seven to four: 4 Lat. (1215) c. 50, in *Constitutiones concilii quarti Lateranensis una cum commentariis glossatorum,* ed. Antonio García y García, MIC, Corpus glossatorum, vol. 2 (Vatican City, 1981), pp.90–1.

6. Joseph H. Lynch, *Godparents and kinship in early medieval Europe* (Princeton, 1986).

7. John T. Gilchrist, *The church and economic activity in the Middle Ages* (London, 1969).

basic tenet of medieval economic morality concerned the concept of the just price. The prices of commodities, according to this view, can be equitably determined only in the market place – a just price thus means the price that the buyer was willing to pay and the seller was willing to accept.[8]

Simple rules of this sort invariably mask a tangle of complexities that become apparent as soon as one peers beneath the surface, and so it was with the just price doctrine. What if producers of some vital commodity, such as salt, for example, artificially manipulated the market by withholding supplies in order to drive up prices? This is called forestalling; canonists deemed it illegal and church courts were prepared to penalize those who engaged in the practice. Similarly, an individual or a small group might try to corner the local market in foodstuffs, such as wheat, and refuse to sell any of their hoard until buyers were prepared to pay steeply for it. This was engrossing and was also a canonical offence. Likewise canon law punished regraters, who bought commodities in bulk at a market town and then resold them in the countryside at many times the purchase price. In short, manipulation of market prices ran contrary to theological concepts of fair play and canonical courts supplied the means to force opportunists to abide by this belief.[9]

It also needs to be said, however, that canon law sometimes applied just price theory inconsistently when services rather than commodities were at issue. Thus when journeymen attempted to drive up wages by withholding labour from the guild masters who employed them, canonists were prepared to treat this as illegal interference with market economics. When guild masters resorted to collective action to drive wages lower, however, the issue of market manipulation seemed to become much fuzzier and canonical sanctions were seldom invoked. Under some

8. John W. Baldwin, *Medieval theories of the just price*, Transactions of the American Philosophical Society, new ser., vol. 49, no 4 (Philadelphia, 1959).
9. John W. Baldwin, 'The medieval merchant before the bar of canon law', *Papers of the Michigan Academy of Science, Arts, and Letters* 44 (1959), 287–99.

circumstances, moreover, canonists were prepared to tolerate intervention in the marketplace in order to set limits on the return for services. Thus, for example, government was held entitled to cap the fees and honoraria that lawyers might claim by imposing schedules of maximum fees for legal services. The rationale here taught that intervention was justified because of the power disparity involved between lawyer and client. But although canonists recognized that a similar power disparity might exist in the relationship between a physician and a critically ill patient, they were not inclined to impose limits on medical fees, but rather contented themselves with exhorting physicians to restrain their greed and predicting dire consequences post mortem for medical profiteers.[10]

Finance was another realm of economic life that concerned the canonists. Here their attention fastened chiefly upon the charging of interest for loans. Church authorities had claimed the right to regulate this matter as early as the first Council of Nicaea in 325, which forbade clergymen to charge interest on loans.[11] Later authorities gradually broadened the prohibition by extending it to Christian laymen and to all classes of loans. Any return in addition to the principal of a loan constituted usury and usury was a canonical crime for which church courts could impose substantial penalties. Usurers who took or demanded interest upon a loan must return their unlawful gains to the borrower and might suffer further penalties, both spiritual and temporal, as a consequence of their unlawful actions.[12] They were also subject to excommunication and canonical *infamia*, which rendered them ineligible to hold positions of public trust, to bring accusations in court, to testify at a trial, or to make a valid will. The penalties for usury could even survive the usurer's

---

10. James A. Brundage, 'The profits of the law: Legal fees of university-trained advocates', *American journal of legal history* 32 (1988), 1–15.
11. 1 Nicaea c. 17, in COD, p.13.
12. Gilchrist, *The church and economic activity*, pp.62–76, 104–15; Fedor Schneider, 'Das kirchliche Zinsverbot und die kuriale Praxis im 13. Jahrhundert', in *Festgabe, enthaltend vornehmlich vorreformations-geschichtliche Forschungen, Heinrich Finke ... gewidmet* (Münster i/W., 1904), pp.127–67.

death and be passed on to his heirs, until restitution was completed. Beyond all this, the usurer's fate in the afterlife was also thought to be exceedingly grim, and Dante, among others, described in exquisite detail the tortures reserved for the souls of usurers in the seventh circle of hell.[13]

Punishment in this world, however, seems to have been more uneven than it reportedly was in the next. Small-time usurers, pawnbrokers, and petty moneylenders were indeed haled before the ecclesiastical courts with considerable frequency and forced to disgorge their unlawful gains. Even this was subject to considerable variation, however, since the courts tended to ignore complaints when the rate of interest charged was relatively modest.[14] Moreover, although players on a grander scale – wealthy investors, prosperous merchants, and well-to-do entrepreneurs – regularly sought and received returns far in excess of the capital they advanced to others, they often evaded prosecution for usury and escaped with their gains intact by disguising interest payments in various ways. A lender might, for example, discount loans in advance, so that the written record obliged the borrower to repay a larger sum than he in fact received. Creditors could also disguise interest as a penalty charged for late payment, as a security deposit against the risk of loss, as a share in profits from an enterprise funded by the loan, or even as a free-will gift by the grateful debtor to his creditor. Although canon lawyers and church authorities often worked diligently to enforce the usury laws, imaginative bookkeepers and inventive notaries regularly enabled their employers to defeat prosecutions.

The anti-usury regulations of the medieval church represented an early effort to formulate an economic theory that rested on the perception that economic policy involves moral issues. The reigning theory perceived correctly that the price of credit is a key factor in any economic system. Acting on this premise, however, church authorities further assumed (wrongly as it turned out) that

13. Dante, *Inferno* 11.94–111.
14. Richard H. Helmholz, 'Usury and the medieval English church courts', *Speculum* 61 (1986), 364–80, repr. in his *Canon law and the law of England* (London, 1987), pp.323–39.

the abolition of interest charges on loans would make consumer credit readily available to those who required it – peasants, for example, who needed an advance of seed to plant their crops for the following year, or small traders who needed additional capital in order to purchase stock for resale. Although ecclesiastical courts and lawyers strove diligently to try to make their economic theories work, people stubbornly refused to act in ways that theory predicted they should. Reality ultimately triumphed: by the end of the Middle Ages church authorities had begun to modify the canonical prohibition of all interest charges and to permit lenders to collect modest amounts of interest legally, while still condemning excessive interest as the social evil of usury.

Church courts further claimed jurisdiction over other areas of commercial law. Dishonest gain (*turpe lucrum*), or as we might call it, excess profit, was also an ecclesiastical crime. The aim of the law here was primarily to discourage commodity speculation. A buyer who purchased goods where they were abundant, transported them to another locality where they were scarce, and there sold them at a higher price than he paid was entitled to profit from his labour and commercial skills. Likewise the buyer who purchased more of some commodity than he required for his own use and immediately sold the surplus for a profit was acting within the law. But a transaction in which a buyer purchased goods at a low price when they were abundant, held them for a time until the supply had dwindled, and then sold them off at a much higher price when they were in short supply could be penalized for receiving dishonest gains. The law clearly sought to protect consumers by either preventing or penalizing unscrupulous manipulation of the market economy. Since so much depended upon the intentions of the parties, however, this part of the law was never easy to enforce.[15]

It is worth noting, too, that medieval canonists, especially from the thirteenth century onward, became increasingly

15. Gilchrist, *The church and economic activity*, pp.53–62. John F. McGovern, 'The rise of new economic attitudes – economic humanism, economic nationalism – during the later Middle Ages and the Renaissance', *Traditio* 26 (1970), 217–53.

vocal champions of the social values of private property and the accumulation of wealth. Although it is still popularly believed, and often taught, that modern capitalistic veneration of private property and individual rights dates only from the seventeenth and eighteenth centuries, scholarly studies in recent years have demonstrated that many notions about property rights put forward by writers of the Age of Enlightenment, such as Thomas Hobbes (1588–1679), John Locke (1632–1704), Sir William Blackstone (1723–80), and Adam Smith (1723–90), for example, had been anticipated centuries earlier by medieval jurists, both civilian and canonist.

Canonists, like other jurists of the *ius commune* tradition, were vocal champions of sturdy individualism and of an economy based on private ownership which must, they thought, entitle a rightful owner to enjoy as much property as he could accumulate and to dispose of it in any way that he pleased, provided that its disposition threatened no harm to others. Thus the industrious, well-connected and lucky entrepreneur, for example, had every right to amass as enormous a fortune as he could, and likewise to give every penny of it away if and when that suited his fancy. He would be within his rights to turn his estate, say, into a home for superannuated sheepdogs, so long as they posed no danger to surrounding landowners and livestock. The law would not permit him to set his house alight, however, if in so doing he would endanger the life, limbs, or property of others. In property matters medieval jurists were staunchly on the side of individual proprietors and, by the same token, were deeply suspicious of joint-proprietorship arrangements, since they feared that tenants-in-common would be more apt than a single owner to neglect property, to allow it to fall into disuse or decay, and to stifle its effective exploitation because of conflicts and jealousies among the co-owners. Both canonists and civilians, in addition, zealously defended the rights of property owners against efforts by public authorities to expropriate their wealth through taxation or by any other means. Expropriation by a ruler, they agreed, was tyranny and subjects had every right to resist it. An owner might, of course, consent to be taxed, if the tax was levied for an appropriate purpose, but free consent of the subject was as essential to taxation as it was to matrimony: coerced consent rendered the transaction void and illegal.[16]

The economic individualism of medieval canonists and civilians reflected their more general views on individual human rights. Modern historians have again usually ascribed these notions to the inventive genius of seventeenth and eighteenth-century writers, but in fact the central tenets of rights theories first began to surface not long after 1200, during the extraordinarily fertile early period of the classical canon law.[17]

Medieval lawyers, together with some humanists and scholastic theologians, also wrote of work and thrift as values in their own right and, more important, as means of accumulating wealth that benefited both the individual owner and the Christian commonwealth at large. Lawyers perceived, perhaps earlier than other writers, that the strength of a kingdom and its ruler depended largely upon material wealth. The legist Azo, writing during the first decade of the thirteenth century, for example, urged rulers to encourage economic prosperity for the general good of their realms.[18] Giles of Rome (ca. 1263–1316) argued that law and virtue can only prevail when supported by adequate material resources,[19] while Giovanni Dominici (d. 1419) praised the virtues of thrift.[20]

Although canonists believed that work was virtuous, canon law postulated a hierarchy of labour, in which some types of work occupied more favoured positions than

---

16. John F. McGovern, 'Private property and individual rights in the commentaries of the jurists, A.D. 1200–1550', in *In iure veritas: Studies in canon law in memory of Schafer Williams*, ed. Steven B. Bowman and Blanche E. Cody (Cincinnati, 1991), pp.131–58.
17. Brian Tierney makes this case persuasively in 'Villey, Ockham and the origin of individual rights', in *The weightier matters of the law: Essays on law and religion, a tribute to Harold J. Berman*, ed. John Witte, Jr, and Frank S. Alexander (Atlanta, 1988), pp.1–31.
18. Azo, *Summa Codicis* to Cod. 4.62.1 (Pavia, 1566; repr. Turin, 1966), p.168; Gaines Post, *Studies in medieval legal thought* (Princeton, 1964), pp.450–2.
19. Aegidius Romanus, *De ecclesiastica potestate* 3.11, ed. Richard Scholz (Berlin, 1929; repr. Aalen, 1961), pp. 200–6; also trans. R. W. Dyson (Woodbridge, Suffolk, 1986), pp.197–203.
20. Giovanni Dominici, *On the education of children*, trans. Arthur B. Coté (Washington, D.C., 1927), pp.27, 60, 66.

others. The law forbade clerics to engage in occupations that church authorities deemed immoral or conducive to immorality and in still others that seemed marginal. This in turn implied a series of judgments about the dignity and social value attached to various kinds of labour, judgments that, with few exceptions, have tended to remain fixtures in later Western societies. This hierarchy postulated a primary distinction between those superior occupations that involved intellectual or spiritual work, such as reading, writing, meditation, scholarship, and the exercise of mental skills, on the one hand; and a lower, less dignified category of occupations that involved manual labour and/or personal service, such as innkeeping, tavernkeeping, farming, and the like, as well as trade and craft occupations, such as butchering, shoemaking, black-smithing, carpentry, tailoring, the textile trades, and other work of that sort, no matter how skilled it might be. The first group comprised the 'clerical' occupations, that is those that were compatible with the status of a cleric. The second group, sometimes called 'servile' occupations, were not deemed appropriate employment for members of the clergy. Among the 'servile' occupations canonical writers made a further distinction between respectable work, such as making shoes, weaving cloth, and the like, and morally suspect occupations, such as acting, dancing, music-making, tavernkeeping, conjuring, and fortune-telling, for example, which seemed at best frivolous and at worst were liable to lead to immorality, particularly to sexual immorality. Commercial and financial occupations, notably money changing, were often placed in the morally dangerous category as well, since they seemed liable to lead to the practice of usury. Hence employment in these fields, too, was ruled incompatible with clerical status.[21] Even quite respectable occupations such as estate management or employment in royal service entailed so many temptations to engage in morally dubious practices – such as misuse of

---

21. 1 Nicaea 17, in COD, p.13, trans. Gilchrist, *The church and economic activity*, p.155; 2 Lateran 13, in COD, p.176, trans. Gilchrist, p.165; 3 Lat. 25 = X 5.19.3, in COD, p.199, trans. Gilchrist, p.173; 1 Lyon, const. 2.1, in COD, pp.169–70, trans. Gilchrist, pp.189–92; Vienne 8 = Clem. 3.1.1, in COD, pp.340–1, trans. Gilchrist, pp.197–8.

church property by clerical merchants who stored their merchandise in churches – to say nothing of sharp dealing, fraud, or outright corruption, that clerics were forbidden to participate in them and laymen who were involved in them became ineligible for ordination to the higher ranks of the clergy.[22]

Canon law further imposed limits upon the periods when people could legally engage in work, especially 'servile' work. The law mandated abstinence from work on Sundays and holy days throughout the year. Prohibition of labour on these occasions was grounded, at least in theory, on the premise that the holiday would enable everyone to attend Mass and participate in other devotional exercises and would thus provide spiritual as well as corporal refreshment for the entire community.[23] By the twelfth century saints' days and other festivals in the Roman liturgical calendar added about 40 days annually of enforced leisure to the 52 Sundays when work was forbidden.[24] Further, workers were obliged to refrain from labour on the feast days of local saints celebrated in their own region, and these averaged about 30 additional days each year when work was illegal. In total, then, canonical regulations subtracted something in excess of 120 days, the equivalent of four months every year, from the time available for productive labour.

These regulations entailed serious economic and social consequences both for employers and employees. Workers paid by the day or hour saw their potential income reduced by ecclesiastical holidays, while employers who engaged workers by the week, month, or quarter, for example, frequently paid full wages for considerably less than a full period's labour.

Still, frequent holidays no doubt contributed in some measure to social well-being, since they afforded workers periodic and frequent respite from monotonous, repetitive

22. Chalcedon 3, in COD, pp.64–5, trans. Gilchrist, p.155; Gratian, *Decretum* D. 51 c. 1–3, D. 53 c. 1; 4 Lateran 19 = X 3.44.2, ed. García 66–67, trans. Gilchrist, pp.176–7.
23. Christopher R. Cheney, 'Rules for the observance of feast-days in medieval England', *Bulletin of the Institute for Historical Research* 34 (1961), 117–47.
24. Gratian, D. 3 de cons. c. 1.

tasks that no doubt dulled both mind and body. Holiday celebrations, moreover, often featured dances, feasts, dramas, pageants, and revelry that presumably went some way toward enlivening the dreary round of agricultural life in the villages and the monotonous routines of artisans, craftsmen, and merchants in towns and cities. Such bursts of merriment punctuated the unexciting chores of daily life and helped to ease the strains of what was doubtless for many a drab and torpid existence.

At the same time, however, churchmen inveighed against indecorous and worldly enjoyments that distracted the faithful from their religious obligations on festival days and not infrequently enticed the weak-minded into serious sin – especially drunkenness, gambling, and sexual debauchery. Moralists found customary festivities, dances, drinking, and frivolity wholly inappropriate as means of commemorating the heroic virtues of saintly virgins, martyrs, and church fathers. The critics no doubt had a point, perhaps even a more ironic one than they may have suspected, for at least some customary celebrations represented pagan practices that early generations of missionaries and churchmen had re-channelled into Christian festivities. The bonfires lit in honour of St John the Baptist's feast on Midsummer Eve, for example, were in fact survivals of pre-Christian pagan sacrifices to Druidic gods. Maypole dances, similarly, originated in celebrations of the pagan fertility spirits formerly deemed responsible for the renewal of life that spring and summer usher in. Even Christmas festivities in all likelihood originated in celebrations of the winter solstice and the old gods who had once been credited with ensuring the turn of the seasons.

Poor relief was another area where canon law controlled a vital element of medieval social structure. The church had from early on accepted special responsibility for alleviating poverty and providing support for the disadvantaged.[25] Gratian and his early commentators put the matter clearly: the bishop bore primary responsibility for assisting the poor in his diocese and defending them against oppressors, while the rest of the clergy shared in

25. See above p. 71.

that duty.[26] Funding for poor relief in medieval society came in the first instance from tithes, the 10 per cent tax on most forms of income that the church levied, at least in principle, on everyone.[27] A fourth part of the revenue of each parish was supposed to be earmarked for assistance to the poor, according to some canonical texts, although other authorities prescribed that as much as a third should be allocated to this function.[28] In theory this should have yielded quite substantial funding for poor relief, but the administration of tithes in practice was fraught with problems and conflicts. In many regions lay proprietors – often the lords of manors – converted tithe revenues to their own uses. Elsewhere the rectors of parishes treated tithes as part of their personal income and shared them only grudgingly with the other nominal beneficiaries.

Tithes, together with other ecclesiastical taxes and revenues, were naturally matters of great interest to canon law and canon lawyers.[29] In addition to tithes, churchmen collected a great variety of additional revenues, such as the mortuary tax that the parish priest demanded from families when the head of the household died, the annual *census* that many monasteries paid to the papacy in return for exemption from the jurisdiction of local bishops, the tribute that popes demanded from monarchs (such as the Peter's pence in England), the special taxes levied periodically to finance crusades, the subsidies that bishops

26. Brian Tierney, *Medieval poor law: A sketch of canonical theory and its application in England* (Berkeley and Los Angeles, 1956), pp.68–71; James A. Brundage, 'Legal aid for the poor and the professionalization of law in the Middle Ages', *Journal of legal history* 9 (1988), 169–79. On voluntary poverty as a religious ideal see Lester K. Little, *Religious poverty and the profit economy in medieval Europe* (Ithaca, NY, 1978).
27. Catherine E. Boyd, *Tithes and parishes in medieval Italy: The historical roots of a modern problem* (Ithaca, NY, 1952); Giles Constable, *Monastic tithes from their origins to the twelfth century*, Cambridge studies in medieval life and thought, new ser., vol. 10 (Cambridge, 1964); Piotr Górecki, *Parishes, tithes and society in earlier medieval Poland, ca. 1100–1250*, Transactions of the American Philosophical Society, vol. 83, pt 2 (Philadelphia, 1993).
28. Gratian, *Decretum* C. 12 q. 2 c. 23, 26–31; Tierney, *Medieval poor law*, pp.72–5.
29. Vivian H. H. Green, 'Taxation, Church', in *DMA* xi, pp.605–11 provides a useful overview of the subject.

collected when they visited the parishes of their dioceses – the list is very long indeed.

These revenues, together with the profits from its landholdings and other assets, made the medieval church, taken as a whole, an extremely wealthy institution. Ecclesiastical wealth was unevenly distributed, however, so that while some fortunate dioceses and parishes regularly enjoyed revenues substantially in excess of their needs, others hovered perennially on the brink of financial disaster. These variations represented in part more-or-less random fluctuations in the generosity of donors, the fertility of lands, the managerial effectiveness of landlords and rectors, the consequences of storms, floods, and other natural disasters, and the unpredictable fortunes of individual villages and regions within an institution whose divisions and subdivisions blanketed every corner of Western Europe.

It is deeply misleading to think of the medieval church as if it formed a single, uniform, monolithic institution. The economic circumstances of medieval churches and the clergy who served them varied enormously. Some parishes were splendidly endowed: their coffers overflowed with surplus wealth, while their rectors and attendant clergy lived in conspicuous luxury. Neighbouring parishes, by contrast, might be grindingly poor, scarcely able to keep the church roof intact, and to provide the incumbent clergyman with a hovel for a parsonage and a near-starvation diet to go with it. Similarly dioceses, monasteries, nunneries, and other ecclesiastical institutions varied immensely in their resources. Even popes and cardinals were sometimes hard put to it to find cash to meet current expenses and had to borrow – sometimes at truly usurious interest rates – in order to make ends meet.

Since the medieval church as a whole was by no means poor, but at the same time the distribution of wealth among its constituent units was so markedly uneven, economic diversity posed serious problems of policy. Canon law consequently had to cope with enormous institutional disparities, while at the same time maintaining the principle that uniform rights and obligations prevailed throughout the institution.

The canons maintained that in principle church

property was inalienable: property that belonged to an ecclesiastical institution could never be disposed of.[30] Even the most rigorous canonists, however, had to admit exceptions to this principle. A monastery, for example, might need to trade one property for another in order to consolidate its land holdings and work them more efficiently. A bishop might find it appropriate in hard times to sacrifice a jewel-studded reliquary in order to buy food for the starving, while an abbot might need to dispose of a surplus pasture in order to repair a monastic church struck by lightning. The principle of inalienability of church property was a central tenet of the eleventh-century church reformers and provided the rationale for the claims of churchmen to exemption from royal taxation, an issue that brought monarchs and popes into several bitter confrontations – notably in the struggle between Pope Boniface VIII (1294–1303) and the French king Philip the Fair (1285–1314).

The church, its clergy, and its legal system were also critical in the development during the high Middle Ages of those mechanisms for transmission of property between generations that we usually style last wills and testaments. Testamentary disposition had been common, at least among the wealthy, in late Roman antiquity, but the practice, although it never quite disappeared, certainly diminished markedly in importance during the early Middle Ages.[31] The Germanic peoples who settled in Western Europe preferred to transmit property by intestate succession rather than by testamentary disposition. Roman observers in antiquity, notably Tacitus (ca. 56–ca. 115), had found it remarkable that the testament had no place in Germanic legal systems and that property usually passed from one generation to the next according to fixed rules.[32] This Germanic preference for inheritance according to rule, rather than permitting the decedent to choose how

---

30. This was the significance of *mortmain* (the dead hand): the church clutched its property with the iron grip of a corpse in rigor mortis; see also William Chester Jordan, 'Mortmain' in DMA viii, pp.488–9.
31. David Daube, 'The prevalence of intestacy at Rome', *Tulane law review* 39 (1965), 253–62.
32. Tacitus, *Germania* 20.4, ed. Henry Furneaux and J. G. C. Anderson, Oxford Classical Texts (Oxford, 1900; repr. 1962).

property would be distributed among survivors, presumably reflected the intimate relationship that Germanic society saw between the possession of family property and personal identity. Thus custom dictated that property holders in any given generation must allow their survivors to share the family goods according to community norms, rather than expressing a personal preference about the matter through a will.

These Germanic inheritance practices persisted through the early Middle Ages, but both canon law and changes in social structure gradually nudged Europeans toward flexible and voluntary, rather than fixed and automatic, methods of dividing the property of deceased family members. From the eleventh century onward population growth and increasing mobility, together with the reappearance of towns, commercial development, and the consequent loosening of ties between family identity and real property holdings meant that flexible inheritance practices slowly began to replace the older pattern of automatic property distribution.

Church authorities emerged early on as enthusiastic supporters of voluntary inheritance mechanisms. Their enthusiasm was no doubt partly due to institutional self-interest, for clerics routinely urged the elderly and the ill to secure their prospects of a blessed survival hereafter by making generous provision for pious causes toward the end of this life. Widespread acceptance of the practice of testamentary disposition undoubtedly worked to the advantage of the medieval church.[33]

Revived awareness of Roman law from the beginning of the twelfth century further stimulated reintroduction of ancient testamentary practices (and, more especially, their adaptation to fit contemporary conditions), especially in regions such as Italy, the south of France, and northern Spain, where the influence of the civil law tradition remained especially strong. But even in areas such as

---

33. Although not, I suspect, quite as routinely as Jack Goody maintains in *The development of the family and marriage in Europe* (Cambridge, 1983). See the criticisms of Goody's position in Lloyd Bonfield, 'Canon law and family law in medieval Western Christendom', *Continuity and change* 6 (1991), 361–74.

England and Germany, where continuity between the Roman past and the medieval present was either tenuous or entirely lacking, the last will and testament slowly made inroads against traditional distribution practices.

In England, more than in most regions of medieval Europe, canonical courts became the regular forum for the probate of wills and testaments and the disposition of claims arising under them.[34] The dominance of canon law over probate jurisdiction was already well-established by the end of the twelfth century and Glanvill refers to it as if it were a routine matter that secular courts did not contest.[35] During the late medieval period, however, the common law courts succeeded in wresting debt claims against a decedent's estate away from the canonical courts and into their own jurisdiction.[36]

Civil law and secular courts on the Continent were less ready than their English counterparts to yield control over testamentary matters to the church. Instead, testamentary questions were usually treated as matters of mixed jurisdiction. Church courts secured control in cases where the formalities of making a testament were at issue and also over legacies and bequests for pious causes, as well as the testaments of clerics; while the civil courts dealt with most other disputes that arose from testamentary disposition of property.[37]

34. Michael M. Sheehan, *The will in medieval England: From the conversion of the Anglo-Saxons to the end of the thirteenth century*, Studies and texts, vol. 6 (Toronto, 1963).
35. *Tractatus de legibus et consuetudinibus regni Anglie qui Glanvilla vocatur*, 7.8, ed. and trans. G. D. G. Hall (Edinburgh, 1965), p.81; Sir Frederick Pollock and Frederic William Maitland, *The history of English law before the time of Edward I*, 2nd edn, 2 vols (Cambridge, 1968), ii, pp.331–3.
36. Richard H. Helmholz, 'Debt claims and probate jurisdiction in historical perspective', *American journal of legal history* 23 (1979), 68–82; repr. in his *Canon law and the law of England*, pp.307–21.
37. For example, Philippe de Beaumanoir, *Coutumes de Beauvaisis*, 11.317, 333, and 12.427–28, ed. A. Salmon, 2 vols (Paris, 1899–1900; repr. 1970), i, pp.156, 162, 206–7; also trans. F. R. P. Akehurst (Philadelphia, 1992), pp.120, 124, 153; *Registre des causes civiles de l'officialité épiscopale de Paris, 1384–1387*, ed. Joseph Petit, Collection de documents inédits sur l'histoire de France (Paris, 1919), p.xxviii and passim; Carlo Calisse, *A history of Italian law*, trans. Layton B. Register, Continental Legal History Series (London, 1928), pp.638–41.

Canon law concerning inheritance also reflected other ecclesiastical interests. Eleventh-century church reformers, for example, bent on penalizing sexual misbehaviour among clergy and laity alike, insisted that the canons curtail the practice of allowing illegitimate offspring to share in the property of their deceased parents. Romano-canonical law not only strongly encouraged people of substantial means to distribute their estates by testament whenever possible, but also worked to modify other inheritance practices. Legal devices – such as *inter vivos* gifts in lieu of legacies, the renunciation of property by younger children and especially by married daughters (who received dowries in place of inheritances) – strengthened the powers of the heads of propertied families. Regrettably, but inescapably, they also provided fuel for litigation and bitter dissension between family members who saw themselves disadvantaged as a result.

Even a decedent's burial-place might become the subject of hotly contested litigation before ecclesiastical courts. Laymen attached great importance to the disposition of their bodies after death and often sought to be buried in or near a monastery or other religious community where they hoped that the prayers and intercession of the community's members might secure favourable treatment in the afterlife and help to turn aside some of God's wrath merited by their sins. The rectors of parishes understandably resisted attempts to bury the deceased elsewhere than in his or her home parish, since cemetery fees and offerings for burial services contributed significant income to many parishes. Disputed burials frequently produced bitter quarrels between competing ecclesiastical institutions and these contests, of course, often came to church courts for resolution.[38]

In addition to their civil jurisdiction, ecclesiastical courts also exercised jurisdiction over a wide variety of criminal matters. As mentioned earlier, church courts asserted

---

38. The title *De sepulturis* in the *Liber Extra* (X 3.28) contains the basic regulations on this subject. Marcus Bull, *Knightly piety and the lay response to the first Crusade: The Limousin and Gascony, c. 970–1130* (Oxford, 1993), pp.146–53 provides numerous examples of these contests in southwestern France.

exclusive control over clerical discipline and, in particular, over all criminal complaints against members of the clergy.[39] They also prosecuted usury, as a criminal offense and successful prosecutions on this count could bring quite sizeable sums of money into ecclesiastical coffers, both as fines and confiscations, as well as in the form of court costs. Church courts sometimes dealt with marriage problems as criminal matters,[40] and exercised, as we have seen, a broad jurisdiction over sex crimes. Perhaps not surprisingly, fornication, adultery, and other common sex offenses usually accounted for the largest part of the criminal business that came before local ecclesiastical tribunals.[41]

Defamation was a major source of both private and criminal prosecutions in church courts. Many sorts of hurtful words, if uttered maliciously, might give rise to an action. A taunt that another was a thief could do so, as could a wide range of other invectives that imputed criminal behaviour – 'whore', 'harlot', 'murderer', 'perjurer', 'pimp', 'rapist', and the like furnished grounds for legal action in canonical courts. Mere unpleasantnesses, however, which stated or implied some personal defect, disreputable habit, or socially dubious parentage – such as 'whore's son', 'bastard', 'leper', 'serf', 'liar', 'knave', and so-on – were not adequate to sustain a defamation action. Interestingly enough, however, utterance of these and other such personal epithets by the sixteenth century had become grounds for a civil action for slander in the English royal courts.

Truth was no defence to a canonical defamation action, provided that the alleged defamatory words had been spoken outside of court. Accusations made formally before

---

39. See above, p.7.
40. French canonical courts seem to have treated marriage cases as criminal matters much more often than English courts did; Donahue, 'The canon law on the formation of marriage', pp.144–58.
41. Charles Donahue, Jr, 'Roman canon law in the medieval English church: Stubbs v. Maitland re-examined after 75 years in the light of some records from the church courts', *Michigan law review* 72 (1974), 647–716 at 56–61; Brundage, *Law, sex, and Christian society*, p.481, n. 317.

a judge and sustained by evidence, however, could not be prosecuted as defamation.[42]

Matters involving heresy, blasphemy, and sacrilege fell naturally under canonical jurisdiction, although ecclesiastical judges usually called upon secular officials to carry out the punishment of convicted heretics when that entailed corporal penalties, such as branding, mutilation, or execution, in which the law forbade clerics to participate.[43] Prior to the early thirteenth century investigation of suspected heretics had been a matter for local bishops to deal with when they encountered reports of deviant religious beliefs and practices. As claims of papal authority became increasingly ambitious in the early thirteenth century, however, the popes began to involve themselves with increasing fervour in this branch of ecclesiastical criminal law and created the inquisition in order to centre its administration in the Roman curia.

The inquisition comprised a group of loosely-related ecclesiastical courts that specialized in cases where doctrinal deviance was at issue. The best-known of these specialized courts was the Roman inquisition, whose history began in 1231, when Pope Gregory IX commissioned a priest named Conrad of Marburg to investigate reports of heresy in Germany. Two years later the pope entrusted a similar commission to Robert le Bougre, a Dominican friar, whom he dispatched on a heresy-hunting expedition in the north of France. Within a short time the process of appointing individual examiners to investigate reports of heresy commenced to take shape as an institution when the pope sent dozens of mendicant friars (overwhelmingly Dominicans and Franciscans) to sniff out heretics in the south of France, where the Cathar heresy had attracted widespread support. By the end of the 1230s other mendicant inquisitors were busily at work searching for heretics in Lombardy and central Italy, where the

---

42. Richard H. Helmholz, *Select cases on defamation to 1600*, Selden Society publications, vol. 101 (London, 1985) provides a full and thorough treatment of the subject; for a brief introduction see also his 'Canonical defamation in medieval England', *American journal of legal history* 15 (1971), 255–68.
43. X 3.50.5; 4 Lat. (1215) c. 18 in *Constitutiones concilii quarti Lateranensis*, ed. García, p.18 (= X 3.50.9).

Waldensian heresy had put down roots. In the decades that followed, inquisitorial courts appeared in Sicily and southern Italy and the institution ultimately spread as far afield as Armenia, Morocco, and Norway. A few regions, notably England, failed to attract the attention of the inquisition, presumably because they played no major role in thirteenth-century outbreaks of religious dissent.

The specialized inquisitorial courts adopted a newly-developed type of criminal procedure, the inquisitorial procedure, to facilitate their work. Standard canonical procedures were strongly orientated toward safeguarding defendants from unwarranted or malicious prosecutions. Hence the established *ordo iuris* by the late twelfth century required an accuser to bring a charge, so that unless someone was prepared to step forward and make a public accusation, no prosecution could commence. Accusation was hazardous for the accuser, because if he failed to prove his allegations he became liable to punishment himself. Proof of an accusation, moreover, required the accuser to bring forward testimony from two credible persons who were prepared to testify under oath that they had personally witnessed the events or the behaviour complained of. This evidential requirement made it extremely difficult to assemble adequate legal proof to support a charge of heresy. Few individuals were likely to swear out a public accusation of heresy against a friend, relative, or neighbour, while the chances remained rather slim of finding two credible adults who were themselves untainted by heresy and who had enough direct, personal, eyewitness knowledge of the heretical activities of the accused to convince a judge that the charge was justified.[44]

As early as the late eleventh century, church reformers had become acutely aware that the accusatory procedure just described made it nearly impossible to prosecute 'occult crimes' successfully. The 'occult crimes' that most immediately bothered the reformers were sex offences, especially clerical concubinage, fornication, and adultery, as well as simony. Concern over the inadequacy of the procedural system to cope with essentially private matters

44. See below, pp.144–7.

such as sexual behaviour and simony increased noticeably during the twelfth century. Gratian's *Decretum* reflects the difficulties that the problems posed. The fact that Gratian moved directly from his treatment of simony to deal with criminal procedure may reflect the connection that he saw between these two topics.[45] But while Gratian seemed clearly aware of the difficulty, he was also aware that the canonical sources he worked with had been framed with a view to protecting the rights of defendants against groundless accusations. 'A person who is accused is not immediately called convicted, but only when he has been judged guilty', declared a ninth-century papal text that Gratian incorporated into the *Decretum*.[46] The canonical tradition thus operated on a presumption of innocence until guilt was proved and criminal procedure was designed to safeguard that presumption.[47] The concern with defendants' rights, it should be said, appears to have been motivated in great part by a desire to protect priests from the vindictiveness of disaffected parishioners and the other malcontents who seemed endemic even in Christian communities. Still, the doctrine operated to shield concubinous priests, lecherous laity, and secret manipulators from the consequences of criminal activities.

Efforts to mend this obviously unsatisfactory situation began to take shape around 1200 in the form of a new type of criminal process designed to deal more adequately with the 'occult crimes' that escaped successful prosecution under the accusatory system. The new criminal process was an inquisitorial procedure, so-called because it was conceived of as an investigatory process initiated by public authorities, such as judges, who operated through inquiry (*per inquisitionem*) into wrongdoing that was a matter of

45. In Part II of the *Decretum*, C. 1 is devoted primarily to the crime of simony, while C. 2 deals with the problem of proof in a criminal process.
46. Gratian, C. 15 q. 8 c. 5: 'non statim qui accusatur reus est, sed qui conuincitur criminosus'.
47. Richard M. Fraher, ' "Ut nullus describatur reus prius quam convincatur": Presumption of innocence in medieval canon law?', in *Proceedings of the sixth international congress of medieval canon law*, eds Stephan Kuttner and Kenneth Pennington, MIC, Subsidia, vol. 7 (Vatican City, 1985), pp.493–506.

common knowledge or grave suspicion (*notorium, manifesta,* and *fama* were the terms generally used to describe such affairs).[48] No accuser was necessary under inquisitorial procedure. In addition the rules of evidence were relaxed so as to make conviction easier to obtain than it was under the old procedure. Inquisitorial procedure did not require 'full proof', but instead demanded only an accumulation of 'partial-proofs', such as inferences or presumptions (*indicia*) that pointed to the defendant's guilt, provided that some more-or-less direct evidence was available to confirm them. Thus, for example, if a priest kept an attractive young woman in his house, if parishioners generally suspected that she was his mistress, and if, say, the sacristan was prepared to testify that he had once glimpsed the priest and his lady friend lying naked in the same bed, this accumulation of partial proofs would be sufficient to prove concubinage, despite the fact that no one (much less two independent and credible witnesses) could actually testify to having witnessed the couple in the act of coitus.

It is not difficult to see how inquisitorial procedure soon emerged as the preferred method of dealing with suspected heretics. Even so, evidential problems continued to thwart heresy prosecutions and to deal with this problem church authorities also sanctioned the use of questioning under torture when testimony was otherwise likely to be unavailable. Canonists and jurists approved the use of torture only in extreme cases where a strong presumption of guilt already existed. Legal authorities were inclined to be conservative on this issue, for they were aware that testimony induced by torture was apt to be unreliable (a *res fragilis* they sometimes called it) and that pain and fright were likely to wring false confessions from terrified defendants.[49] They tried to justify its use in exceptional circumstances, however, on grounds that public welfare (*publica utilitas*) demanded that crimes should not go

48. See below, pp.147–50.
49. Albertus Gandinus, *Tractatus de maleficiis*, rubr. *A quo vel a quibus possit fama incipere et ex quo tempore*, §5, in Hermann Kantorowicz, *Albertus Gandinus und das Strafrecht der Scholastik*, 2 vols (Berlin, 1907–27; repr. 1981) 2:64–9; John Langbein, *Torture and the law of proof: Europe and England in the ancien régime* (Chicago, 1977), pp.3–17, 45–9.

unpunished, and argued that even though torture sometimes forced people to confess to crimes they had not committed, its use would nevertheless deter others from committing real crimes.[50]

Two things should be evident from what has been said here about the private law of the medieval church. First, the influence of canon law permeated the entire medieval social order. It would have been difficult, indeed almost impossible, for an individual, regardless of social status or occupation, to remain untouched from one year's end to the next by canonical regulations. Canon law was by no means a matter that concerned solely the clergy or the devout. In a society where everyone (save for members of scattered Jewish communities, occasional Muslims in Spain and southern Italy, and some pagans in northern and central Europe) was at least nominally Christian, canon law repeatedly touched the lives of practically every person from cradle to grave. Its fasting regulations controlled what people ate and when they ate it. Its tax system demanded contributions from every peasant and workman, while its usury laws made life difficult (although not necessarily unrewarding) for money changers, merchants, bankers, and financiers. Its feasts, festivals, and holidays shaped patterns of work and play. Both Christian worship and beliefs provided the context within which individuals prayed and thought. From baptism to burial canon law was a major presence in everyday life from top to bottom of the social scale.

Second, medieval canon law and civil law developed a close symbiotic relationship with one another. Canonists had to study a good bit of elementary Roman civil law as

50. Richard M. Fraher, 'The theoretical justification for the new criminal law of the high Middle Ages: "Rei publicae interest, ne crimina remaneant impunita"', *University of Illinois law review* (1984), 577–95 and 'Preventing crime in the high Middle Ages: The medieval lawyers' search for deterrence', in *Popes, teachers, and canon law in the Middle Ages*, eds James R. Sweeney and Stanley Chodorow (Ithaca, NY, 1989), pp.212–33. But cf. Kenneth Pennington, *The prince and the law, 1200–1600: Sovereignty and rights in the Western legal tradition* (Berkeley and Los Angeles, 1993), pp.42–4, 157–60. Pennington is sceptical that the use of judicial torture was as routine as it is conventionally said to have been.

part of their training, while jurists who studied Roman law in the schools also had to acquire more than a slight facility with canon law in order to make a reasonable living. Church law and the laws of civil society complemented each other, but also competed with each other on many matters. Lawyers and judges within each legal system borrowed procedural practices unashamedly from the other and even adopted the other's ideas and doctrines when those seemed useful or appropriate. Although civil law and canon law remained formally distinct legal systems, each operated within the same geographical region and served much the same population as the other. Since the two laws not infrequently offered alternative methods for dealing with the same problem or situation, they provided prospective consumers with a choice of courts and judges in which to settle their disputes. Civilians and canonists jealously tried to guard their own turf from encroachment by their competitors, while at the same time they sought to attract business away from their rivals. We have seen examples of this competition in dealing with marriage problems, for example, where civil courts generally handled problems of marital property while canonical courts dealt with questions about the formation and termination of the marital relationship. Likewise when it became time to pass property from one generation to the next, canon law favoured flexible disposition by testament, while civil law tended to prefer succession according to fixed rules. Prospective decedents in practice frequently disposed of part of their estates by the one method and part by the other. Similarly canon law and civil law each developed its own taxation system in order to defray the expenses that the rulers of church and state incurred. Again, canon law intruded into the bailiwick of secular rulers by regulating certain aspects of labour, finance, and commerce, while civil courts claimed jurisdiction over the remainder of the workaday world.

This pattern of symbiotic competition, as we shall see, carried over into matters of government and politics as well.

Chapter 5

CANON LAW AND PUBLIC LIFE

Medieval canon lawyers, even more than civil lawyers, needed to create tools to analyse and solve the legal problems inherent in corporate organization and structure. Bodies corporate were among the most important clients that canonists dealt with. Ecclesiastical corporations ranged from the college of cardinals, religious orders, and cathedral chapters at the upper end of the hierarchy to individual monasteries, nunneries, confraternities, and parishes, toward its lower end.

Despite variations in size, power, and resources, these organizations shared common structural characteristics and faced similar kinds of problems. Each comprised a collective group of persons whose common identity persisted across generations, even though the individuals who made up the group changed with the passage of time and the inescapable mortality of its members. Thus the corporation did not die: it was immortal, even if its members were not. Each group had a leader or chief officer and, although their titles and the range of their authority varied considerably, the head of each group invariably claimed executive powers over the other members, usually served as the group's official spokesman to the outside world, played a critical role in defining and implementing group policies, and exercised (or at least claimed the right to exercise) some degree of control over whatever property the group possessed in common.

But what was, or ought to be, the proper relationship between the chief officer and the other members of such a corporate body? Did the head, by virtue of his office, enjoy an all-encompassing right to exercise absolute power over the members? If not, what were the limits of the head's powers? Could the head single-handedly alienate property given to the whole group? What if the head of the group proved to be greedy, irresponsible, incompetent, immoral, or otherwise unfit for office? What if he became a heretic? Could he be removed? If so, how, under what circumstances, and by whom could this be achieved? Could the members impose legitimate constraints upon their leader's policies and actions? If so, how could they do this? Who was to judge if the head exceeded his authority? Who could enforce such a judgment and how?

Each of these questions required answers and supplying those answers was the task of canon law and canon lawyers. Problems of power and authority within corporate bodies cropped up everywhere within the church establishment and did so more often, certainly, than in most con- temporary royal governments. Corporate entities within lay society were relatively scarce, while the structure of the medieval church depended upon corporate groups at every level.

Discovering a satisfying analytical scheme that would yield workable solutions to the problems of continuity and change within corporate structures was not simple. An inherent paradox of corporate bodies lies in the fact that they continually change and yet (in principle at least) always remain the same. Early medieval attempts to deal with this paradox proved inadequate or unsatisfactory.

We do not know who first perceived that the legal concept of 'person' might hold a key to the solution of this paradox. Lawyers use the word 'person' in a rather different sense from the broad meaning of 'human being' that most of us assign to it in everyday speech and writing. In legal discourse 'person' stands for a more restricted and more abstract idea. At law a 'person' means an entity capable of possessing and using legal rights and subject to legal liabilities. Many human beings, to be sure, are legal 'persons', but other human beings may lack legal personality, in the sense that they cannot sue or be sued, they may not be empowered to own or sell property, they cannot make contracts and, in general, their actions fail to have legal effect. In Roman law, for example, slaves were not 'persons', nor under most circumstances were women –

two groups who, taken together, undoubtedly comprised the great majority of the population under Roman rule. In modern law, likewise, minors usually enjoy only a limited legal personality, as do a few other groups of people, such as the insane and prisoners.

The notion that legal 'persons' need not always mean human beings is certainly a very old one, but it long remained a relatively minor and obscure feature of legal thought. During the latter part of the twelfth century, however, canonists began to see that applying the idea of legal personality to groups such as monasteries, nunneries, dioceses, and other ecclesiastical institutions might furnish a useful analytical tool to explain some of the apparent anomalies that had puzzled their predecessors. By 1200 canonists had begun to distinguish between natural 'persons' in the traditional legal sense and juristic 'persons' (*persona quoad iuris intellectum*), or bodies corporate, who possessed the same attributes of legal personality as natural 'persons'.[1]

It was an easy and natural further step to think of juristic persons as having a head and members, just as natural persons did. Huguccio (d. 1210) and the author of the anonymous *Glossa Palatina* (written between 1210 and 1215),[2] among others, approached the problem of the relationship between the head and members of a corporate body on the basis of Gratian's teachings about the relationship between the pope and the remainder of the Christian church. Was the pope bound, they asked, by the decisions of a general council or could he single-handedly overrule them? What, for that matter, about the relationship between the pope and the College of Cardinals? The cardinals elected the pope; but did that imply that if they found him unsatisfactory, or if somehow he fell into heresy, they could depose him? It was well-established custom by the late twelfth century that the pope routinely sought the advice of the cardinals who served in the curia on difficult or delicate issues. But if the

1. See above, pp.19–20.
2. Cardinal Alfons Stickler has made a strong case that Laurentius Hispanus was probably the author of the *Glossa Palatina*; see 'Il decretista Laurentius Hispanus', *Studia Gratiana* 9 (1966), 463–549.

pope should choose not to consult the cardinals on some matter, did that render his disposition of the matter invalid because of a procedural defect?[3]

Although decretists and early decretalists discussed these and related questions, they failed to arrive at a coherent theory of corporate structure and power relationships within a corporate body. Two distinguished thirteenth-century canonists, Pope Innocent IV (1243–54) and Cardinal Hostiensis (d. 1271), undertook more elaborate analyses of canonical corporation law. They disagreed in their conclusions, however, since each began with a fundamentally different conception of how corporate entities ought to conduct their business.

Innocent IV grounded his treatment of ecclesiastical corporations on the premise that power within these institutions ought to be concentrated in the hands of the principal officer. The head of the group, to be sure, might delegate partial responsibility and limited authority over some matters to subordinate officers, who were answerable to him for the proper discharge of their duties. Innocent's view of corporations, accordingly, may be described as authoritarian. The head of the corporation is ultimately the sole legitimate source of power and the members are dependent upon him. The exercise of power by the head is not subject to review or limitation by the other members of the group. Innocent envisioned the corporate head as an authoritarian ruler, responsible only to higher authority and ultimately to God.[4]

Hostiensis rejected this view. Instead, he taught that head and members shared corporate authority and responsibility. The head of the body, Hostiensis conceded, was entitled to make the final determination on matters that solely affected the rights and property that belonged to his office. Even on those issues, however, he must consult the other members of the group before taking final action. The members, according to Hostiensis's view, retained

3. See particularly Brian Tierney, *Foundations of the conciliar theory* (Cambridge, 1955), pp.23–84, and Kenneth Pennington, *Pope and bishops: The papal monarchy in the twelfth and thirteenth centuries* (Philadelphia, 1984), pp.71–72.
4. Innocent IV, *Apparatus* to X 1.2.8 v. *sedis* §2 (Frankfurt a/M, 1570; repr. 1968), fol. 4ra-rb.

authority over matters that affected them alone. On these the members could make final disposition, although the head of course retained the right to participate in discussions of these affairs and even to vote on them, since he remained, after all, a member of the corporate body. On matters that involved the joint interests of head and members, according to Hostiensis, the two shared authority and responsibility, so that neither could act without the consent of the other.[5]

Although Hostiensis and Innocent IV differed in their basic concepts of corporate structure, each felt obliged to adjust his position on particular issues to conform to the canons. Thus, for example, canon law forbade either a bishop or his cathedral chapter to dispose unilaterally of church property. Bishop and chapter shared joint responsibility for that decision and both must participate in such transactions. Disposing of benefices that were in the gift of the church similarly required joint action by bishop and chapter.

But what did joint action or joint responsibility mean in practical terms? Was it enough for a bishop simply to notify his chapter that, for example, he intended to sell off a rental property or trade one farm for another? Or did the chapter have a voice in these transactions? Did the chapter's responsibility extend beyond merely discussing a matter and advising the bishop of the chapter's views about it? Or did the chapter have to agree to the bishop's proposal (as well as inform him about the chapter's feelings) before church property could be alienated?

Situations such as these led teachers of canon law to distinguish between three major classes of corporate business. One class of business, they said, pertained exclusively or mainly to the prelate or other head of the corporate body. A second pertained primarily to the members of the body, while a third class consisted of matters in which head and members had joint interest. In dealing with matters that fell into the first of these classes, the corporate head must ask the advice of the members, but did not require their consent. The members of the

---

5. Hostiensis, *Lectura* to X 1.2.8 §§7–8, 5 pts in 2 vols (Venice, 1581; repr. Turin, 1965), pt 1, fol. 9va.

corporation could take action on matters in the second class, even without the consent of the head, although the head was entitled to be heard and to vote on these issues because he was a member of the corporation. Matters that fell into the third class, where joint interests were involved, required that both head and members agree before lawful action could be taken.[6]

This analysis of corporate decision-making required those who taught canon law in the schools to define the meaning of terms such as 'advise' and 'consent'. Thirteenth-century academic lawyers who taught canon law in universities such as Bologna, Paris, and Oxford, accordingly took up this task. Although some early writers used the terms 'advise' and 'consent' as if they were synonyms, Hostiensis and others by mid-century distinguished them sharply from one another. When the head of a corporate group, such as a chapter, a monastery, or perhaps the college of cardinals, was required only to take counsel with the members, but was not bound to abide by the advice he received from them, then 'advise' was the appropriate verb to describe the situation. But if the 'consent' of the members was required, the head must not only consult with the members, but also win their approval. The result was to impose limits upon the authority and discretion of the head of a corporation and to allow the members a voice in the determination both of corporate policy and actions.

As early as the time of Innocent III some writers had seen the theological teaching that the church formed the mystical body of Christ as grounds for classifying the entire Latin church as a corporate entity, with the pope as its head and the college of cardinals as members. Later canonists, such as John of Paris (d. 1306) and Cardinal Zabarella (d. 1417) in the fourteenth and fifteenth centuries, pushed this analysis much further. Just as the powers of the heads of other ecclesiastical corporations were limited by the powers of the members, they argued, so likewise papal power was not absolute. Instead, the cardinals and especially the general councils of the church

6. Bernard of Parma, *Glos. ord.* to X 1.3.21 v. *debeant.*

103

enjoyed the right to limit the exercise of papal discretion and to establish boundaries within which popes must operate.[7] The pope, like other Christians, they asserted, was bound to observe the laws of the church. Should he defy the limits that the law established, he acted illegitimately and, in extreme circumstances, might even be deposed. These issues concerning the limits of papal authority and the relationship between popes, cardinals, and councils lay at the heart of the conciliarist controversies in the later Middle Ages.

Canonistic corporation theories also influenced debates concerning the limits of the power of kings and other rulers within civil society. Just as canonists conceived of the church as the mystical body of Christ, so civil lawyers likewise adopted the notion that the commonwealth (*respublica*) formed another mystical body, the body politic, in which the ruler was the head and his subjects were the members of a corporate entity. In theory, at least, the mystical body of the church and the mystical body of the common-wealth were not separate. Instead, one (the commonwealth) was described as contained within the other (the church), which rather seriously muddied the organic metaphor.[8]

Out of these discussions, and in particular out of the elaboration of canonical corporation theory, emerged some novel political ideas that have subsequently become basic to modern Western notions about constitutional government.[9] Fundamental ideas of this sort are now so much a part of our everyday thinking that they appear self-evident and it requires some effort to imagine a world in which these concepts seemed so novel and dangerously radical that they threatened to undermine the foundations of the social order.

Among these novelties in the political and legal

7. Tierney, *Foundations*, pp.157–237.
8. On these issues see the magisterial treatment by Ernst Kantorowicz, *The king's two bodies: A study in mediaeval political theology* (Princeton, 1957).
9. Brian Tierney, 'Medieval canon law and western constitutionalism', *Catholic historical review* 52 (1966), 1–17, reprinted in his *Church law and constitutional thought in the middle ages* (London, 1979), with original pagination; Kenneth Pennington, 'Law, legislative authority and theories of government, 1150–1300', in the *Cambridge history of medieval political thought, c. 350–c. 1450*, ed. J. H. Burns (Cambridge, 1988), pp.436–53.

discourse of the high Middle Ages was the rule of law, which has since become a fundamental axiom in modern ideas about legitimate government. The rule of law in its broadest sense means that rulers, like their subjects, must obey the laws and that no one, however mighty or powerful, is above the law. The rule of law thus imposed limits upon the power of rulers, who, understandably enough, preferred to ignore laws that restricted their powers and hampered their conduct of either personal or public policy. Rulers had, after all, ignored inconvenient laws from time immemorial, and although discontented subjects had many times protested at excesses of royal power, they usually did so in vain.

Some thirteenth-century canonists and theologians began to argue, however, that ignoring or contravening established law jeopardized both the legal and moral bases of a monarch's right to exercise power. Rulers who acted in defiance of the law were tyrants, according to this view, and thereby forfeited even their legitimate claims to power if they transgressed the bounds that law established. Subjects had a moral right to resist tyrannical rulers, theologians maintained, and resistance to a tyrant was not merely justifiable, but even praiseworthy and virtuous. Since actions taken by a ruler contrary to law were illegitimate, moreover, it seemed to follow that they must be legally void and that those who lost property as a result of them were entitled to compensation. But who was empowered to judge a scofflaw ruler? And if the charges against him were proved, what authority could depose and make good the claims of his victims?[10] These were terribly difficult questions in theory and even more difficult to implement in practice. Human societies have yet to arrive at entirely satisfactory solutions to them.[11]

10. On these issues see especially Kenneth Pennington, *The prince and the law, 1200–1600: Sovereignty and rights in western legal tradition* (Berkeley, 1993), as well as Jean Dunbabin, 'Government' in Cambridge history of medieval political thought, esp. pp.493–8.
11. The Nuremberg trials at the close of World War II represented the most dramatic and explicit effort thus far to deal with these matters. At the same time the war crimes trials raised nearly as many questions as they solved and although similar prosecutions have been proposed since then, none have thus far taken place.

Canonistic discussions about problems of representation and consent within ecclesiastical institutions likewise furnished solutions for technical problems in corporation law that civil society ultimately found worth adapting. One important tool for dealing with the perennial problem of decision-making processes in corporate bodies, for example, was a Roman legal rule originally fashioned to govern the conduct of business when a minor or other person legally unable to manage property had two or more guardians. The rule seems almost absurdly simple: 'What touches all should be approved by all', or in other words, all parties with a legal interest in any matter must consent before a legitimate transaction concerning it can be completed.[12] Applied to a small group of two or three elderly patricians acting as guardians for a minor heir, this *quod omnes tangit* rule proved simple and straightforward. When applied to corporate bodies, and especially to large corporate groups, with hundreds or even thousands of members, however, the *quod omnes tangit* maxim seemed difficult, indeed nearly impossible, to implement. It would be ludicrously impractical to secure the consent of each member of a group of thousands – all the Christians within a diocese, for example, to say nothing of all the members of the Latin church – to every transaction that a bishop or pope proposed to take. It was not at all impractical, however, to require a prelate to secure the consent of a small advisory council, such as a cathedral chapter or the College of Cardinals, before embarking upon an enterprise that affected the interests of the larger group – the diocese or the Latin church – of which they were a part.

Even so, the *quod omnes tangit* rule seemed to require unanimous consent for every proposed transaction, with the result that each individual member of the group possessed a potential veto power that could overrule the wishes of all the other members.[13] This could obviously

12. Gaines Post, 'A romano-canonical maxim, "Quod omnes tangit" in Bracton', *Traditio* 4 (1946), 197–251, reprinted in Post's *Studies in medieval legal thought: public law and the state, 1100–1322* (Princeton, 1964), pp.163–238.
13. Ulpian had remarked upon this difficulty when he discussed problems of municipal property: Dig. 41.2.22.

create serious problems, and lawyers soon devised at least partial solutions to them. One obvious approach was to require that only the numerical majority of the body need consent to a proposal, rather than that everyone must consent unanimously to every item of business. Legal precedents for such a majority principle were not difficult to find. Justinian's *Digest*, for example, included a passage that taught that the decision of a majority of a group of arbitrators should prevail over the minority opinion.[14]

But what entitled some small group, such as cathedral canons or the Roman cardinals, to speak on behalf of the entire population of a diocese or the whole church? To account for this required a theory of representation, whereby one person could act on behalf of another with the same legal effect as if the principal had taken the action in person. Again Roman law supplied a mechanism that medieval canonists adapted for purposes very different from those that the classical jurists had originally envisioned. The mechanism this time was the mandate, a specialized kind of contract used in Roman law to create a proctor (*procurator*) – the Latin term that gave rise to the English word proxy. Romans in late antiquity mandated proctors to transact all sorts of business that would have been impossible or inconvenient for the principal to execute in person. Depending upon the terms of his mandate, the proctor might be empowered to buy or sell goods, pay or receive money, conclude contracts, or act upon the principal's behalf in litigation – any or all of these with the same force or effect as if the principal had done them himself.

The lawyers of the medieval church used the mechanism of mandated powers of representation to explain how and why a cathedral chapter could act on behalf of all the members of a diocese or the college of cardinals on behalf of all baptized Christians. The chapter of canons, canonists said, represented their constituents just as a proctor represented his principal. So long as his mandate authorized what the proctor did, his actions were

14. Ulpian in Dig. 4.8.17.6–7. See also Jeanine Quillet, 'Community, counsel and representation' in the *Cambridge history of medieval political thought*, pp.557–8.

equivalent at law to actions taken by the person he represented. This theory proposed that cathedral canons possessed an implied mandate to represent all the faithful within their diocese, while the cardinals had an implied mandate to represent all the members of the catholic church. Thus when these bodies gave their advice and consent to proposals from bishop or pope, that consent legally ratified the superior's action just as much as if every member of the diocese or the whole church had been consulted and had agreed to it.

This theory of representation vested consultative bodies, such as chapters and cardinals, with a great deal of power. At the same time it supplied a theoretical basis for established consultative practices, while it also placed a check upon the unbridled power of bishops and popes to do as they pleased. This approach to the problem of the division of power within a corporate body raised further difficulties, however; among them was the problem of establishing what constituted the mandate whereby the faithful could be said to entrust cathedral canons or the college with representative powers. Here academic lawyers maintained that the *quod omnes tangit* doctrine in Roman co-tutorship law entitled them to assert that, by analogy with quasi-contracts, a mandate could sometimes be inferred and that its terms need not necessarily be spelled out explicitly in a written agreement.[15] They could also fall back upon the *lex regia*, the belief that the power of Roman emperors to create legitimate laws was grounded in the assignment of that power by the people as a whole to their rulers.[16]

These various devices, then, enabled thirteenth and fourteenth-century canonists to devise an orderly law of ecclesiastical corporations, grounded on theories of representation and consent that they fabricated out of elements that they found at hand in Roman law. Other lively minds soon perceived that the intellectual foundations the canonists had constructed for church corporations could readily be adapted to fit institutions of

15. Post, *Studies in medieval legal thought*, pp.91–162.
16. Ulpian in Dig. 1.4.1.

civil government as well. The problem of defining the limits (if any) of a monarch's power was not, in principle, vastly different from that of describing the boundaries to the powers of popes and bishops. Civil rulers had long been accustomed, at the very least as a matter of prudence, to seek the advice of counsellors before embarking on major ventures and the similarities between the relationship of the king to his royal council, the pope to the college of cardinals, or a bishop to his cathedral chapter were quite striking. Thus ecclesiastical corporation law, the rules that governed the relationship between head and members and defined the limits within which each could legitimately act, furnished models that civil lawyers and political propagandists alike found useful.

These speculations, in turn, raised another fundamental question: Was a king, or other ruler, above the law or subject to the law? On the one hand, kingship seemed to imply some sort of law-giving power and a famous passage in Justinian's *Digest* even declared that 'What pleases the prince has the force of law' (*Quod placuit principi legis habet vigorem*).[17] By the thirteenth century, however, many learned lawyers and law teachers had come to reject the inference that might be drawn from that statement, namely that whatever a ruler may do is lawful. Instead writers of legal treatises had begun to explore the limits of princely power.

Natural law, legal writers agreed, established some boundaries that rulers must not transgress and so also did divine law as revealed in sacred scripture (or at least those parts of it that Christians deemed operative). Beyond these vague limits, however, opinions differed sharply as to whether rulers could be bound in any meaningful sense to obey the positive laws of the church and even of their own kingdoms. Enforcement of the law against the ruler posed a particularly vexing problem for legal and political writers who needed to explain how a ruler could be made to obey a rule that displeased him. Presumably he would eventually have to account to God for his actions, but that might not

17. This is, in fact, part of the same passage (Dig. 1.4.1) that describes royal power as originating from the Roman people.

necessarily check his unlawful actions here and now.[18] How could kings and other secular rulers be held accountable in this life for violations of the law? Fear of an avenging God seemed to many writers an inadequate safeguard against the actions of an arbitrary and wicked prince.

Canon lawyers generally agreed that the pope had the power to excommunicate and even to depose a king who repeatedly violated canon law and cited situations in which popes had taken these actions. Civil authorities, however, were understandably reluctant to acknowledge that the popes possessed any right to intervene in the affairs of secular governments and sought instead to devise alternative sanctions to restrain despotic rulers.

Canonical legal theories about the nature of representation and consent provided useful analogies for writers concerned with the problems of civil government. Civil lawyers, like canonists, began to speculate during the thirteenth century about the sources of royal power and some concluded that subjects, speaking through representatives, might lawfully impose limits upon the exercise of kingly prerogatives. Out of the questions and the answers that corporation theory suggested emerged the basic elements of what we may call 'parliamentary constitutionalism'.[19] These included the notion of the rule of law, which holds that rulers like their subjects must obey the law, combined with theories of representation and consent that entitled relatively small groups of a ruler's subjects to speak for the rest and to impose some limits upon the ruler's freedom from control. The conceptual framework that made possible the development of legislative assemblies, such as the English Parliament, the Spanish Cortes, and the French Estates-General, among others, emerged gradually out of speculative arguments among academic lawyers in the thirteenth and fourteenth

18. The Scriptures strongly implied that this would be the ultimate sanction; Romans 12:19; Apocalypse 18:19. Legal writers sometimes referred to these and similar passages as safeguards against royal caprice; e.g., Bracton, *De legibus et consuetudinibus Angliae*, fol. 1b–2, ed. George E. Woodbine, rev. and trans. Samuel E. Thorne, 4 vols (Cambridge, MA, 1968–77), ii, p.21.
19. Tierney, 'Medieval canon law and western constitutionalism', see above, n. 9.

centuries about these and related matters of legal principle.

Professors of canon law during the same period debated similar ecclesiological issues concerning the limits of papal power. What if the pope himself violated canon law, for example by falling into heresy? Who, this side of heaven, had the power to judge the pope? The college of cardinals? A general council? If one or both of these found him guilty, could the pope be deposed? But if so, who had the power to carry out the deposition? The gradual emergence during the thirteenth and fourteenth centuries of parliamentary institutions that would ultimately limit the power of civil rulers was thus paralleled by the emergence among the canonists of conciliar theories that held the pope answerable for his actions to the general councils of the church.[20]

Parallels between canonistic and civilian thinking on these matters were not coincidental. The emergence of similar ideas about these issues among civil lawyers and canonists reflected, at least in part, the long-standing intellectual interdependence of civil and canon law. That interdependence reached far back into the early history of the Christian church and the notion that 'The church lives by Roman law' (*ecclesia vivit lege Romana*) was a familiar aphorism.[21] The Roman law revival that flourished during the twelfth century reinforced the canonists' inclination to mine Roman law for ideas and practices that they could apply to canonical problems. In consequence, as we have seen, some formal training in Roman law was essential for every canonist, while for practical reasons men trained in civil law usually needed to learn some canon law.[22]

The intellectual cross-fertilization between students and teachers of the two learned laws led, perhaps inevitably, to borrowings in practice. Paradoxically during the thirteenth century, when law teachers within the universities commonly separated themselves into two distinct faculties

20. Tierney, *Foundations of conciliar theory*, traces these developments in detail.
21. Carl-Gerold Fürst, 'Ecclesia vivit lege Romana?', *Zeitschrift der Savigny Stiftung für Rechtsgeschichte*, Kanonistische Abteilung 61 (1975), 17–36.
22. Above, pp.59–60.

of civil and canon law, the interdependence between them became increasingly marked. At the same time, intellectual interaction and practical borrowing between the learned laws and the local customary laws that flourished in great profusion throughout Europe also grew in frequency and importance. When judges and pleaders in customary law courts or (especially in Italy) municipal courts could discover no method in their local law for resolving a dispute, they often turned to romano-canonical practices as a substitute for custom or statute. The implicit theory that justified such borrowings from the learned laws maintained that Roman law comprised in some sense a universal law of venerable antiquity, and that the principles of 'canonical equity' were likewise applicable everywhere in Christian society. The two learned laws, in this view of things, comprised 'everyone's general law' (*lex omnium generalis*) that judges could legitimately fall back upon to supply lacunae in the particular laws of any region in Christendom. The belief that romano-canonical law constituted a universally applicable *ius commune* proved particularly helpful in dealing with conflict-of-law problems that arose when the courts had to adjudicate disputes between parties from different cities or regions. It enabled the judge in such a situation to resolve the problem by calling upon an impartial rule, rather than choosing between the laws that the parties relied upon. The *ius commune* thus emerged in the late Middle Ages and the early modern period as a 'peacemaker's law', which allowed courts to settle issues definitely and finally, while at the same time maintaining a degree of flexibility to choose the solution that seemed most appropriate and least likely to promote further discord.[23]

The intellectual interdependence between civilians and canonists also shaped the ways that the legal elite responded to changes in society and institutions during the

23. See generally Manlio Bellomo, *Storia del diritto comune* (Rome, 1989), as well as p.17 above pp.60–1. James Q. Whitman, *The legacy of Roman law in the German romantic era: Historical vision and legal change* (Princeton, 1990), pp.7–9 also provides a helpful overview of the role of the *ius commune* in late medieval and early modern Germany.

twelfth and thirteenth centuries. Growth of population, the increasing economic importance of commerce and manufacturing relative to agriculture, the emergence of large towns and cities, and the consequent increase in the resources of townspeople as compared with those available to rural landowners, all raised fresh problems of governance, as well as of facilitating and controlling finance, commerce, manufacture, and public order. These problems spurred both clerics and laymen to seek new legal mechanisms and procedures for dealing with them.

One complex, delicate, and hence controverted set of problems in late medieval public law centred around issues of public finance. When, under what circumstances, and for what purposes was a ruler justified in requiring his subjects to turn over part of their property to him as taxes? Conflicting answers to these questions animated discussions of public law during the later Middle Ages – and, for that matter, even now arouse sharp differences and debates that inevitably involve legal issues, as well as moral and political ones.

The church itself was an early experimenter in direct taxation of the general population, beginning with the tithes that, in principle, every Christian was obliged to pay. Church authorities could point to scriptural authority to justify the imposition of the tithe.[24] Commencing in 1166 and again in 1185 and 1188 the popes began to insist that all Christians, including the clergy, must also surrender a further fraction of their property to assist the defence of the Holy Land against Muslim incursions.[25] The papacy could not realistically implement such schemes, of course, without cooperation from secular rulers and in fact twelfth-century crusade subsidies received enthusiastic support from the kings of England and France. Monarchs soon discovered that money thus raised could be useful for many purposes and that, although they might have to take the cross in order to secure access to the funds, this need not mean that they must necessarily depart for the Holy

24. For example, Lev. 27:30–33; Num. 18:26–30; Deut. 14:22–27.
25. Fred A. Cazel, 'Financing the crusades', in *History of the crusades*, ed. Kenneth M. Setton et al., 6 vols (Madison, Wisconsin, 1969–89), vii, pp.116–49.

Land at once. Kings sometimes managed to postpone their departures for decades and a few died before they got around to leaving for Jerusalem. King Henry III of England (1216–72), for example, took the cross no less than three times during a reign of well over half a century, but died in 1272 without ever setting out for the Holy Land.[26] Meanwhile, however, crusading taxes yielded handsome piles of lovely money that the monarch could use to meet all sorts of contingencies, some of them only remotely related (if related at all) to crusading.

It was scarcely surprising that monarchs who found revenues from crusading taxes so helpful in meeting their cash flow problems should wish to impose taxes themselves directly on the property-holders in their realms, both clerical and lay, without waiting for the pope to take the initiative and without contracting an obligation, however loosely enforced, to go on crusade. Popes resisted such moves, of course, especially when it came to imposing royal taxes on church property. Repeated confrontations arose between King Philip the Fair of France (1285–1314) and Pope Boniface VIII (1294–1313) over these issues and in the end the French king prevailed.[27] The outcome of this well-known crisis created a precedent for general direct taxation by central governments, which remains to this day one of the most significant governmental powers.

Just as the crusades furnished medieval popes with justification for general taxation, so monarchs likewise relied upon defence of the realm as justification for impositions upon their subjects. Nor was the need for additional revenue to finance warfare a trivial matter or solely a result of self-aggrandizement by rulers. Changes both in military technology and in social organization during the thirteenth, fourteenth, and fifteenth centuries transformed warfare from the intermittent occupation of noble landholders and chivalric knights into a far more complex business than it had been earlier. The new military technologies required the services of engineers,

26. Christopher Tyerman, *England and the crusades, 1095–1588* (Chicago, 1988), pp.111–23.
27. Charles T. Wood, ed., *Philip the Fair and Boniface VIII* (New York, 1967).

construction experts, bombardiers, artillerymen, and other specialists. This, together with the employment of mercenary troops who became increasing necessary to augment, and ultimately to replace, the older levies of feudal cavalry, cost money; increasingly vast sums of it, far more than traditional revenue sources could provide.

Even in peacetime, moreover, the routine costs of government operations grew, as trained functionaries, many of them products of the law schools, increasingly displaced feudal counsellors and ad hoc appointees from the corridors of palaces, the offices of royal administration, and the benches of the law courts. The thirteenth century saw the dawn of the age of modern governmental bureaucracy, and the bureaucrats expected to be paid, usually in cash, for the administrative efficiencies that they achieved.[28]

These developments combined to augment royal ambition as well as royal power and drew public finance to the centre of the political stage in a way that earlier styles of government had not often done. Royal taxation and other revenue-related matters, such as the public debt, inevitably raised moral questions and theoretical issues, together with policy considerations, and these interested canon lawyers as much as royal administrators. 'Church and treasury walk in step with each other', wrote the great jurist Bartolus (ca. 1313–57). The treasury, like the church, was immortal and, once it had grasped property, rarely let it go.[29] The church was also a major property-holder in every European kingdom and monarchs naturally yearned to be able to tax ecclesiastical property in the same way and for much the same reasons that they taxed property held by the laity. Governments could and did argue that churchmen benefited from the protection that governments offered against foreign enemies just as much as laymen did and that the church accordingly had the same

---

28. Ellen E. Kittell, *From ad hoc to routine: A case study in medieval bureaucracy* (Philadelphia, 1991) furnishes a detailed analysis of this process in medieval Flanders and argues that the Flemish model may have influenced developments elsewhere.

29. Bartolus, *Commentary* to Dig. 11.62(61).4 §1, quoted by Kantorowicz, *King's two bodies*, pp.177, 192.

equitable obligation to contribute to the costs of the defence of the realm. Churchmen, for their part, understandably resisted these claims. Church property, they maintained, was dedicated to serving the spiritual needs of everyone in Christian society and alienating that property to meet the needs or desires of temporal rulers would violate both the canons of the church and the intentions of the donors. Church authorities seem to have perceived, in addition, that allowing temporal powers to tax church property could readily lead to control or even confiscation of the material resources that gave the church its independence from secular control. They were implicitly aware that, as a great modern jurist put it, 'The power to tax involves the power to destroy'.[30]

Canon lawyers and ecclesiastical practices also played a leading role in the development of medieval diplomacy. Governments, both royal and papal, had long possessed means of communicating their policies, positions, and intentions to one another in times of crisis. During the early Middle Ages and up to the mid-thirteenth century they usually did so by appointing special ad hoc messengers (*nuncii*) or legates to carry messages and replies back and forth between heads of state when some special problem seemed to make communication desirable. These messengers, sometimes described as 'living letters', simply transmitted the information confided to them and had no power to modify the position that their principal enunciated, or to negotiate on his behalf. During the latter part of the twelfth century, however, popes and bishops occasionally began to use a different type of representative, a proctor (*procurator*), for this purpose and to grant their proctors full power (*plena potestas*) to negotiate on their behalf. Gradually monarchs and other rulers also commenced to dispatch representatives plenipotentiary (i.e., with full powers) to negotiate and conclude treaties and other agreements on behalf of their principals. During the thirteenth century plenipotentiary representatives emerged as the favoured intermediaries to facilitate relationships among rulers. In the course of the fourteenth

---

30. Chief Justice John Marshall, in McCullouch v. Maryland (1819), 17 US 316 at 431; 4 L ed 579 at 607.

and fifteenth centuries princes increasingly found it useful to keep one or more such representatives stationed permanently abroad so that they could advise their principals quickly about problems and crises as they arose and could even deal with critical situations on the spot. This marked the beginning of the practice of maintaining resident ambassadors at the seat of foreign governments and empowering them to conduct diplomatic relations on behalf of the principals whom they represented.[31]

The rules that developed during the later Middle Ages to govern diplomatic practice and the conduct of international relations drew heavily from canon and civil law alike. So, too, did the laws that governed the 'continuation of diplomacy by other means', namely war. Although at first glance the 'laws of war' may seem to be an oxymoron, the apparent contradiction is not difficult to resolve. Military action almost invariably damages property, for example, and societies need rules to determine when and under what conditions those damages may create an obligation to make restitution and what process should be used to deal with war damage claims. Similarly medieval warfare, like modern warfare, routinely resulted in the capture by at least one party (and usually by both parties) of combatants from the opponent's side. Rules for the release, ransom, or exchange of prisoners were obviously essential. Again, war often results in the capture not only of persons but of property. Orderly settlement of the conflict required some agreed-upon standards for determining the ownership of captured property – under what circumstances, for example, may a soldier rightfully keep the personal effects of a slain enemy? Who becomes the owner of land and houses captured in combat? The soldier who seizes them? His unit commander? The victorious monarch? A case could be made for each of those answers, and mutually agreed rules were necessary to resolve the competing claims. Similarly rules were needed to deal with numerous other matters, such as disciplinary problems within an army, the rights of non-combatants in a war zone, the formalities necessary to initiate hostilities or to declare

31. Donald E. Queller, *The office of ambassador in the Middle Ages* (Princeton, 1967), esp. pp.26–84.

a temporary truce, as well as the procedures required to bring a state of war to an end.[32]

The medieval laws of war depended in large part upon practices customary among military men, but these were changeable, often loosely defined, and not always and everywhere agreed upon. Men trained in canon and civil law saw this situation both as an intellectual challenge and as a practical problem of considerable significance. Canonists and civilians, accordingly, sought to impose order on the vague, conflicting, and variable rules that custom had devised. They proceeded to apply principles and analytical techniques familiar to them from Roman civil law to fashion mechanisms for settling the conflicting claims to property and compensation that warfare inevitably produced. This approach appears clearly in the treatises *On war, reprisals, and the duel* and *On peace* written by Giovanni da Legnano (ca. 1320–83).[33] Giovanni was not only a professor of canon law at Bologna, but also an experienced diplomat, who appeared frequently as a negotiator for various Italian city-states and the papacy amid the stormy, often violent, crises that rocked fourteenth-century Italian politics. He thus brought to the study of war and peace not only a strong legal training but also a wealth of practical experience in the problems that arose from international conflicts.

Giovanni da Legnano's work synthesized a great deal of earlier legal thought and reflection on the consequences of violent confrontations between powers. War, violence, and the legal problems that they created had featured prominently, after all, in Gratian's *Decretum,* with the result that by the fourteenth century canonistic teachers and writers had a long tradition of commentary and reflection upon these matters to draw upon.[34]

32. Maurice Keen, *The law of war in the late Middle Ages* (London, 1965).

33. Giovanni da Legnano, *Tractatus de bello, de represaliis et de duello,* ed. and trans. Thomas E. Holland (Oxford, 1917); part of his *De pace* is edited by G. Ermini, 'I trattati della guerra e della pace di Giovanni da Legnano', *Studi e memorie per la storia dell'Università di Bologna* 8 (1923), 5–41.

34. Frederick H. Russell, *The just war in the Middle Ages,* Cambridge studies in medieval life and thought, 3rd ser., vol. 8 (Cambridge, 1975).

Giovanni da Legnano was the first to synthesize the doctrines of these earlier writers into a coherent treatment not only of warfare, but also of the legal basis for relationships between sovereigns. His treatise on war dealt, to be sure, with numerous mundane but important problems, such as, for example, the wages of mercenary troops and when they should be paid, whether a mercenary was entitled to payment while disabled, rules concerning the ransom of prisoners, and the division of the spoils of war among members of a victorious army. In addition, however, Giovanni dealt with the grander diplomatic problems of declaring war and making peace, as well as the moral and ethical principles that he believed should govern these matters in a Christian society.

The influence of medieval canon law was thus not limited to matters that affected the internal organization and structure of ecclesiastical institutions, nor was it solely concerned with matters of doctrine and church discipline. The sharp line that modern conceptions perceive between secular affairs, temporal government, and public policy on the one hand and the religious issues, practices, and institutions of the church on the other was exceedingly dim and blurry to the eyes of those who taught, wrote, and thought about such issues in the Middle Ages. The speculations and hypotheses that medieval canonists pursued in reality had a direct and immediate bearing on the origins of much that we usually consider modern and secular. In their writings one can find traces of the early history of numerous modern ideas about corporation law, tax law, or public finance and even the germ of concepts basic to the constitutional state, the notion that the power of governments must be defined by law, and the conceptual foundations of parliaments and similar legislative assemblies.

Chapter 6

CANONICAL COURTS AND PROCEDURE

The ecclesiastical courts brought ordinary people into contact with the norms and doctrines that academic canonists expounded in their classrooms and the flood of decretals that threatened to overwhelm canonical judges and practitioners. Those courts, which in England were sometimes called Courts Christian, used canonical rules to settle the disputes that litigants brought before them and to impose disciplinary sanctions upon those who infringed the church's rules of behaviour. Like the law itself, canonical courts in the early twelfth century remained ad hoc affairs and had not yet developed a systematic structure. They also lacked a corps of trained personnel to dispatch their business in an orderly and systematic way.

At the local level, bishops and synods usually treated dispute resolution as simply one duty among many that they dealt with in the ordinary course of business. Although canonical rules were numerous and sometimes bewilderingly complex, bishops and their advisers coped with them as best they could, learning as they went along. A few bishops, notably Hubert Walter, archbishop of Canterbury (1193–1205), could afford the luxury of having resident canonical experts in their households to guide them through the legal maze. Indeed, bishops themselves sometimes became formidable legal experts as a result of long experience in dealing with the problems that came before them almost daily.

Bishops who faced a particularly delicate or perplexing legal problem had the option of convening a synod to deal with the matter. Synods were general assemblies of the clergy within a diocese or region. Their meetings provided a forum where clerics and their bishop could consult one another about current issues. Although in principle bishops were supposed to assemble synods at frequent and regular intervals, observance of this rule tended to be haphazard.

The synod furnished a forum for discussion of local issues and could adopt legislation, in the form of synodal canons or decrees, when that seemed indicated, to cope with recurring problems. It could also conduct judicial hearings when the bishop needed or wanted the clergy of his diocese to participate in settling particularly difficult or important controversies. It thus could double as a court to which the bishop could refer legal issues of general interest or great importance – or matters for which he did not wish to bear sole responsibility.

Bishops and synods remained the principal agents for the adjudication of canonical issues during the twelfth century and continued, in some places, to play judicial roles well beyond that period. Such arrangements became increasingly unsatisfactory, however, as canon law itself grew ever more complex and voluminous. Bishops, busy with other administrative and political concerns, could not readily find either the time or the patience to sit in judgment hour after hour, day after day, on routine disputes among members of their flock. Synods were expensive and time-consuming, since holding one required dozens or even hundreds of clerics to absent themselves from their regular duties, often for considerable periods of time, to make the journey, participate in the synod, and then return home. The situation was equally frustrating from the viewpoint of litigants. They might have to follow the bishop for days or weeks on his peregrinations from one parish to the next while waiting for him to find time to deal with their complaints. Summoning a synod compounded the problem and exposed litigants to even greater delay and expense.

By the closing years of the twelfth century, and increasingly thereafter, bishops in many parts of Christendom began to delegate most of their judicial duties to legal specialists, usually men who had formal training in law. These trained and often full-time judges functioned as the bishop's *alter ego* for most legal matters. The bishop's judicial delegate was often described as the bishop's official.

Since most bishops' households included numerous persons who could be styled 'officials', the chief judge-delegate was sometimes distinguished from the rest by the title 'official-principal'. By the latter part of the thirteenth century the officials-principal in many dioceses presided over a judicial bureaucracy, with a staff of clerks who produced and copied documents, a registrar who directed the work-flow and managed the judicial calendar, and one or more apparitors or bailiffs who notified parties when and where they must appear before the judge. This judicial establishment sometimes included, as well, a number of other judges and judicial examiners, who took the depositions of witnesses and to whom the official-principal might assign cases that he could not conveniently hear himself. The official-principal, in short, presided over a regularly constituted court, often known as the bishop's consistory court. That title distinguished it from the occasional judicial sessions at which the bishop presided in person, which often bore the designation 'court of audience'.

Lesser prelates, such as archdeacons and occasionally rural or urban deans, in many regions developed additional courts of their own. These tribunals exercised jurisdiction over petty infractions of church law and heard lawsuits in which the property or other disputed issues seemed not sufficiently important to warrant taking them to the bishop's consistory court. Much of the business of the lower courts involved enforcement of the church's disciplinary rules concerning sexual misbehaviour, drunkenness, marital disputes, infractions of the church's prohibition of work on Sundays and feast days, and the like. The archdeacon's courts touched matters of personal conduct and morality in particularly intimate ways and lay people often resented this intrusion into their daily lives and domestic relationships. People further suspected (perhaps with good cause) that local bigwigs and men of means could persuade archdeacons to overlook their own misdemeanours by a judicious use of gifts, bribes, and other inducements. Suspicions of venality and corruption contributed further to the unpopularity of archdeacons and other minor prelates who exercised jurisdiction at the local level. Since archdeacons, like bishops, were often men of importance with numerous other demands on their time, they, too, sometimes appointed an official of their own – often men with formal legal training – to exercise their judicial functions.

Beyond the level of the diocese the larger units of ecclesiastical administration also maintained courts. Archbishops (also known as metropolitans) had provincial courts, which could hear appeals from the local courts in the various dioceses that made up an ecclesiastical province. Provincial courts further claimed first instance jurisdiction over a few matters, in addition to their appellate jurisdiction. Archbishops, moreover, had their own consistory and audience courts to hear controversies that arose within the boundaries of the diocese over which they presided.

At the highest level of the ecclesiastical court system stood the pope, who exercised both original and appellate jurisdictions over controversies from every part of Western Christendom. Popes, like other bishops, for centuries exercised their judicial functions in person and routinely spent numerous hours almost every day attending to the complaints of litigants, the arguments of advocates, and the advice of their own legal counsellors. This was not entirely a disinterested attention to duty. The bishop of Rome's standing as the ultimate appeals judge of the Latin church was one of the principal sources of papal power. In addition, the fees and costs collected from litigants furnished an important source of revenues for members of the curia and accounted for a large part of the prosperity of medieval Rome.[1]

By the mid-twelfth century, however, the pope's judicial duties threatened to overwhelm the rest of his responsibilities. Concerned churchmen urged that he cut back on this part of his duties and delegate all but the most essential judicial tasks to others. Thus St Bernard of Clairvaux (1090–1153) admonished his former pupil, Pope Eugene III (1145–53):

---

1. I. S. Robinson, *The papacy, 1073–1198: Continuity and innovation*, (Cambridge, 1990), p.3.

I ask you, what is the point of wrangling and listening to litigants from morning to night? And would that the evil of the day were sufficient for it, but the nights are not even free! ... One day passes on litigation to the next, one night reveals malice to the next; so much so that you have no time to breathe, no time to rest and no time for leisure. I have no doubt that you deplore this situation as much as I, but that is in vain unless you try to remedy it ... Patience is a great virtue, but I would hardly have wished it for you in this case.[2]

Despite entreaties such as these, late-twelfth-century popes continued to contend with a rising tide of litigation. They secured a measure of relief by appointing ever-greater numbers of men with legal training to the college of cardinals and relying increasingly upon the advice of the cardinals who assisted them in hearing cases in what came to be called the Roman consistory. The consistory replaced the old synod of the Roman clergy, which under Gregory VII (1073–85) had become primarily a court of justice. In the new judicial structure, the pope met daily with the cardinals and other advisers in consistory. There the whole group heard arguments and appeals, which the pope then decided in consultation with the cardinals. The consistory was thus a judicial body in which the cardinals sifted through the arguments and issues that litigants raised and advised the pope about his options in disposing of the matter before them. This arrangement shifted the burden of the preliminary analysis of disputes from the pope to the cardinals, but still left the final determination of each case in the pope's hands.[3]

Although the consistory eased the burden of the pope's personal involvement in the judicial processes, it still required a massive commitment of papal time. A few popes clearly relished this part of their duties. Innocent III (1198–1216), for example, seems to have enjoyed verbal fencing with the advocates who appeared before him and

2. St Bernard of Clairvaux, *De consideratione* 1.3.4–1.4.5, in Bernard's *Opera*, ed. Jean Leclercq, C. H. Talbot, and H. M. Rochais, 8 vols in 9 (Rome, 1957–77), iii, pp.397–9. The translation is by John D. Anderson and Elizabeth T. Kennan, *Five books on consideration: Advice to a pope*, Cistercian Fathers Series, no 37 (Kalamazoo, MI: Cistercian Publications, 1976), pp.29–30.

3. Robinson, *Papacy*, pp.106–39.

was quick to reprove them when their view of the law differed from his own. Thus, for example, Thomas of Marlborough reported concerning one such episode during an English lawsuit at Rome:

> And our opponent said, 'Holy Father, we teach in the schools and it is the opinion of our masters that prescription does not run against episcopal rights'.
> And the lord pope rejoined, 'Really? Both you and your masters were drinking too much English beer when you taught this'.[4]

Not all popes, by any means, shared Innocent III's taste for forensic rough-and-tumble. Even if they had, spending hours each day on knotty legal problems was a luxury that popes could no longer afford to indulge. Other papal business – political, diplomatic, financial, and even religious – urgently demanded attention. By the mid-thirteenth century the flood of judicial business at the curia had become so overwhelming that the popes could no longer postpone wholesale delegation of all but a few pressing or delicate lawsuits. Earlier popes in the late-twelfth century had, when hard-pressed, occasionally designated one or another of the cardinals as a hearing officer (*auditor*) and referred a few cases to him for disposition. By Innocent IV's pontificate (1243–54) popes had cut back radically on their own judicial duties and appointed general hearing officers (*auditores generales causarum sacri palatii apostolici*) to deal with the great mass of routine legal business. After the pontificate of Boniface VIII (1294–1303), when the popes relocated to Avignon, the auditors-general settled there as well and conducted their hearings in a special round courtroom within the papal palace. The shape of this room, perhaps coupled with the auditors' practice of taking turns in hearing cases, suggested the nickname of 'the Wheel' (*Rota*) for the court

---

4. *Chronicon Abbatiae de Evesham ad annum 1418*, sub anno 1206, ed. William Dunn Macray, Rolls Series, no 29 (London, 1863), p.189. Cf. X 2.26.15. See also Kenneth Pennington, 'Pope Innocent III's views on church and state: A gloss to *Per venerabilem*', in *Law, church, and society: Essays in honor of Stephan Kuttner*, eds Kenneth Pennington and Robert Somerville (Philadelphia, 1977), pp.49–67 at 52–3.

itself. The label stuck and the Holy See still uses it for its chief tribunal.[5]

Other, more specialized courts also developed at the papal curia during the thirteenth and fourteenth centuries. The *Audientia litterarum contradictarum* screened the issuance of papal mandates and regulated the activities of the proctors who represented clients and managed their business at the curia, while the papal penitentiary had his own court to sift through petitions for dispensations. The pope's chief fiscal officer, the chamberlain (*camerarius*), appointed a hearing officer (*auditor*) to adjudicate disputes that arose out of financial operations and eventually to deal also with disciplinary problems among members of the papal curia. The *referendarii signaturae* were another group of curial officials who also came to have important judicial functions. In the twelfth century the *referendarii* were simply a group of clerks of the papal consistory who prepared documents for the pope's signature. Over the course of time, however, they acquired additional duties, such as drafting replies to petitions and determining which appellate cases were sufficiently important or meritorious to warrant the pope's personal attention. It was a short step from doing that to sitting as judges themselves and by the late Middle Ages the *signatura iustitiae* had become the highest-ranking papal appellate court.[6]

5. Emil Göller, 'Zur Geschichte der Rota Romana: Ein Verzeichnis päpstlicher Rota-Auditoren vom Ende des 14. bis zur Mitte des 16. Jahrhunderts', *Archiv für katholisches Kirchenrecht* 91 (1911), 19–48; Egon Schneider, 'Über den Ursprung und die Bedeutung des Namens Rota als Bezeichnung für den obsersten päpstlichen Gerichtshof, *Römische Quartalschrift* 41 (1933), 29–43' Charles Lefebvre, 'Rote romain, in DDC vii, pp.742–71; Gero Dolezalek and Knut Wolfgang Nörr, 'Die Rechtsprechungssammlungen der mittelalterlichen Rota', in *Hanbuch der Quellen und Literatur der neueren europäischen Privatrechtsgeschichte*, ed. Helmut Coing, vol. 1, Mittelalter (Munich, 1973), p.849.

6. Peter Herde, *Audientia litterarum contradictarum: Untersuchungen über die päpstlichen Justizbriefe und die päpstlichen Delegationsgerichtsbarkeit vom 13. bis zum Beginn des 16. Jahrhunderts*, 2 vols, Bibliothek des Deutschen historisches Instituts in Rom, vol. 31–32 (Tübingen, 1970); Daniel Williman, 'Summary justice in the Avignonese Camera', in *Proceedings of the sixth international congress of medieval canon law*, MIC, Subsidia, vol. 7 (Vatican City, 1985), pp.437–49; R. Naz, 'Signature apostolique, Tribunal de la', in DDC vii, pp.1012–18.

For the vast majority of litigants throughout Western Christendom, however, the cost of pursuing an action all the way to the papacy's central courts was prohibitive. Only the wealthy and determined could afford the expense of travelling to Rome, accompanied by their witnesses, legal advisers, and the bushels of parchment that the earlier stages of an action were likely to have produced. Once at the curia, moreover, they were likely to encounter months or even years of delay and to face massive additional expenditures for local proctors and advocates to pilot their case through the warrens of the papal bureaucracy. Each stage of the process predictably brought numerous demands for further fees, 'gifts' to officials, and countless additional outlays, many of them no doubt unforeseen. No wonder that litigants, even successful ones, sometimes found themselves penniless at the conclusion of the process and that they occasionally had to slip away from the curia furtively and at night to evade the importunate demands of their creditors and the imminent possibility of bankruptcy.

Legal counsellors could suggest ways to circumvent all this, however, and still secure a papal decision on a client's problem without incurring the daunting expense of an appeal to the curia. The alternative mechanism involved a petition for the appointment of papal judges-delegate to hear the case.

Popes experimented occasionally with mechanisms for delegating their judicial authority to local officials from as early as the time of Paschal II (1099–1118). Use of this expedient became increasingly common during the twelfth century, notably during the pontificate of Alexander III (1159–81). This system of using local churchmen as the pope's representatives to hear and determine disputes from their own region was useful to the papacy, since it allowed the popes to cut back on the time that they and their officials needed to spend on judicial matters, while at the same time it helped to reinforce the principle that the pope possessed a universal jurisdiction throughout all of Christendom. From the litigant's viewpoint the use of judges-delegate made it easier and less costly to secure a ruling on their dispute from the highest authority in the Christian world. And from the standpoint of local prelates, appointment as a judge-delegate of the pope conferred unquestionable prestige. These appointments required the commitment of a substantial amount of time and effort, but bishops and abbots, although they might grumble from time to time, usually accepted judicial commissions gladly since they reaffirmed their own power and testified to their distinction and importance.

Petitions for the appointment of judges-delegate were what lawyers call *ex parte* statements, that is, they set forth the situation from the petitioner's point of view, described the problem as he saw it, as well as the solution that he desired, and suggested the name or names of the judges he wished to hear the matter. The petitioner's legal advisers usually prepared these petitions and practitioners, in turn, made heavy use of formulary books that provided models that they could adapt to the particular needs of each new case or situation.[7] When the pope or, more commonly, an official in his chancery directed a papal clerk to draft a reply to one of these petitions, the clerk normally turned to the elaborate guides and formularies kept in the various departments of the chancery to find the most appropriate model for the reply.[8] Already by the thirteenth century, in other words, the process was well on its way to becoming routinized and bureaucratized.

The commissions, or mandates, issued to papal judges-delegate normally recited the facts and issues as the petitioner presented them, empowered the judges to summon and question the petitioner, the defendant and other witnesses, to view the relevant documents, and to take any further steps necessary to discover whether the alleged facts were true as stated. The mandate directed the judges to decide the dispute on its merits as shown by the evidence and prescribed the remedies that the judges might grant if the petitioner proved his case to their satisfaction.

7. Dorothy M. Owen, *The medieval canon law: Teaching, literature and transmission* (Cambridge, 1990), pp.30–42 describes these formularies and their uses.
8. Peter Herde, *Beiträge zum päpstlichen Kanzlei- und Urkundenwesen im 13. Jahrhundert*, 2d edn, Münchener historische Studien, Abt. Geschichtl. Hilfswissenschaften, vol. 1 (Kallmünz, 1967), pp.57–78. *Briefsteller und Formelbücher des elften bis vierzehnten Jahrhunderts*, ed. L. Rockinger (Munich, 1863).

Upon receipt of the letters of delegation, the plaintiff, or more likely his proctor, transmitted the mandates to the judges and requested that they initiate proceedings by summoning the defendant to appear before them. From that point onward the process worked in much the same way that a hearing before auditors at Rome would have done, with the important difference that it usually involved considerably less travel, delay, and expense.[9]

Canonical civil procedure (the *ordo iudiciarius*) was already complex and technical by the turn of the thirteenth century and it became increasingly sophisticated and demanding during the century. A litigant (or, if the litigant was prudent and could afford it, his legal agent or proctor) initiated an action by a petition to the appropriate judge – say, for example, the bishop's official-principal. The initial petition might be oral, but early in the proceedings it was bound to be reduced to writing, since canonical procedure consisted, at least from one point of view, largely of compiling a written dossier, which would ultimately furnish the basis for determination of the case. If the petitioner convinced the judge (or in busy courts more likely the judge's clerk) that the complaint was legitimate, that a legal basis for action existed, and that the court had jurisdiction over the matter, the judge cited the defendant to appear before him (usually within ten days) and either to make satisfaction to the petitioner or else explain, if he could, why he was not obliged to do so.[10] The judge normally permitted defendants to take their time in answering, but if a defendant failed to appear after a second citation, the third demand for his appearance became peremptory – in effect the judge warned the defendant that if he failed to respond to this summons the complaint would be tried in his absence. The three citations in effect gave the defendant up to 30 days or thereabouts to prepare his answer to the complaint. If he failed to appear, or to offer a legitimate excuse for his non-appearance after the third

9. Jane E. Sayers, *Papal judges-delegate in the province of Canterbury, 1198–1254: A study in ecclesiastical jurisdiction and administration*, Oxford historical monographs (Oxford, 1971), pp.54–95.
10. Tancred, *Ordo judiciarius* 2.2, ed. Bergmann, p.131; *Ordo iudiciarius*, 'Scientiam' §1, ed. Ludwig Wahrmund, p.2.

summons, the defendant might be declared contumacious. The consequence of this was that the court might proceed to make a summary investigation of the plaintiff's claims and, if it found them justified, give an interim judgment in his favour. If the defendant still failed to respond, that interim judgment became final at the end of a year. A contumacious defendant might, in addition, be excommunicated for failure to appear.[11]

If the defendant did appear, the plaintiff had to submit his formal complaint, known as the libel (*libellus*). The opening clauses of the libel named the plaintiff, defendant, and judge, while the following sections described the grounds the plaintiff alleged for his lawsuit and the remedy he sought to obtain. The closing section of the document invariably reserved the plaintiff's right to amend, withdraw, or enlarge any of the preceding statements.

Once the defendant received the libel he could either answer on the spot or ask for a twenty-day delay to decide whether to defend against the plaintiff's claims and, should he choose to defend, to frame his formal reply. During this period the defendant also had the option of proposing exceptions to points raised in the libel. He had his choice of two kinds of exceptions: peremptory and dilatory. A peremptory exception called into question some essential element, either legal or factual, in the plaintiff's case and, if the judge ruled against the plaintiff on the issue, the case was closed and the defendant was discharged. A dilatory exception alleged some procedural error in the plaintiff's case – the defendant might, for example, challenge the jurisdiction of the court over the matter at issue, assert that the plaintiff's proctor lacked authority to act in the case, or claim that the judge named by the plaintiff was biased or otherwise inappropriate to handle the matter. If the judge chose to allow one or more of the defendant's exceptions, the issue that the exception raised must then be adjudicated before the main issues in the case could come to trial. Should the ruling on an exception go against the defendant, he was compelled to pay both his own and the plaintiff's costs immediately for that phase of the action.

11. Tancred, *Ordo iudiciarius* 2.3.1, ed. Bergmann, pp.132–9; Johannes Andreae, *Processus iudiciarius* (Nürnberg, 1572), fol. 2v.

The intent, presumably, was to deter frivolous exceptions and the consequent delays by making defendants pay for them. Even so, frivolous exceptions were common, particularly in hotly contested cases, and often may have served the defendant well by delaying the proceedings, sometimes for many months, when, for instance, a ruling on an exception was appealed to the papal court. Since delay often worked in the defendant's favour, it was common to enter numerous exceptions in the hope that one or more of them might hold up trial of the case and perhaps induce the plaintiff to retract some of his claims or settle the entire matter out of court. Hearings and determinations on exceptions might also serve to sharpen and clarify the issues that the judge would eventually have to deal with.

Once exceptions had been disposed of and the issues had been defined, the trial of the case (*litis contestatio*) could begin. Once again the plaintiff repeated his claims (by now usually amended and made more specific) and the defendant repeated his specific denial of them. The litigants then swore the calumny oath: the plaintiff called upon God to witness that he had not brought his action simply to harass the defendant and that he intended to prove his claims honestly. The defendant likewise swore that he would offer an honest defence to the plaintiff's claims and that he was not doing so out of malice. The proctors or legal representatives of the parties might take the oath on behalf of their clients, for from this point onwards the proctors were in charge of the proceedings, although they acted in the name of the principals whom they represented.

Now the proctors must begin to prove the claims that their clients had asserted. The burden of proof lay upon the plaintiff; that is he (or his proctor) must produce trustworthy and credible evidence that would support the assertions he had made. The defendant, for his part, sought to produce evidence that would convincingly contradict or undermine his opponent's claims. His task was less demanding, at least in the sense that he did not have to produce positive proof of his claims, but simply show that the plaintiff's assertions lacked adequate foundation in fact or in law.

Judges relied primarily upon the oral testimony of the witnesses produced by the two sides and secondarily on written documents. Each side in the dispute furnished the judge with a list of the names of the witnesses it wished to call, together with a list of questions that the judge was to put to each of them. Parties often brought their witnesses with them when they appeared in court. If any witnesses were not immediately available, however, the judge's clerks drew up a summons for the missing witnesses, appointing a time and place for them to appear for judicial examination. The judge's bailiff or apparitor served the summonses. Witnesses who failed to appear could be declared contumacious and excommunicated.

When witnesses appeared on the appointed day they were first placed under oath. Each of them was then called separately for questioning by the judge or a judicial examiner in private. The judge asked the questions submitted by the parties and supplemented those by any further questions he deemed relevant or appropriate. A notary was also present to record the questions and answers. If the witness list called for testimony from a person who lived far away, the judge might appoint a commissary, or hearing officer, from the witness's place of residence to conduct the examination, make a notarized record of the deposition, and dispatch it in due course to the trial court.

The standard of oral proof was extremely high. Full proof required either that the defendant confess or that the plaintiff substantiate his complaint by the sworn testimony of at least two credible witnesses who had both seen and heard the critical episode or event that was at issue.[12] Lest litigants draw out proceedings unnecessarily, Innocent III limited the number of witnesses who might be produced to 40.[13] Literal proof, that is evidence from documents, was often important as well, but opinions differed as to whether it should carry as much weight as

12. Charles Donahue, Jr, 'Proof by witnesses in the church courts of medieval England: An imperfect reception of the learned law', in *On the laws and customs of England: Essays in honor of Samuel E. Thorne,* ed. Morris S. Arnold et al. (Chapel Hill, NC, 1981), pp.127–58.
13. X 2.20.37 *Cum causam.*

oral testimony.[14] Forgery of charters and other documents, including papal mandates and decretals, was commonplace and judges had good reason to be sceptical of written instruments. Canon lawyers had rules designed to detect forgeries,[15] but application of these rules was far from infallible, even at the hands of a pope. Thomas of Marlborough, the advocate for Evesham Abbey, for example, described how Innocent III carefully examined two papal bulls that Thomas produced in the course of a lawsuit and pronounced them genuine, although we now know that they were certainly forgeries.[16] Innocent III's ruling on a case in 1206 set forth guidelines for the evaluation of written and oral evidence that furnished judges with a set of standards to apply in situations where documents were challenged, but canonists continued to be wary of the evidence of written instruments.[17] It seemed contrary to nature, Innocent IV declared, to trust the skin of a dead animal more than the voice of a living man.[18]

When the judge was satisfied that he had all the relevant evidence in hand, he 'published', or authorized disclosure, of the record of the testimony to the parties and their counsel. At the same time he also set a day for counsel to present their arguments. The proctors and advocates for both parties now examined the depositions of witnesses and framed arguments (*positiones*) intended to call to the judge's attention the strength of the evidence for their client's case and the contradictions and other flaws in the evidence that their opponents had produced. Advocates for the parties also prepared arguments in law (*allegationes*), in which they directed the judge's attention to the canons that supported their theory of the case and those that told against their opponent's position. Judges preferred that the oral arguments be kept brief. When arguments were

---

14. Michael T. Clanchy, *From memory to written record: England, 1066–1307*, 2nd edn (Oxford, 1993), pp.260–3, 272–8, 295–9.
15. A whole title (X 2.22) of the *Liber extra* dealt with these rules.
16. Clanchy, *From memory to written record*, pp.323–7.
17. X 2.22.10 *Cum Ioannes*.
18. Innocent IV, *Apparatus* to X 2.22. 15 §1 (Frankfurt, 1570), fol. 279vb-180ra. See also Jean-Phillipe Lévy, *La hiérarchie des preuves dans le droit savant du moyen-âge depuis la renaissance du droit romain jusqu'à la fin du XIVe siècle* (Paris, 1939), p.102.

especially complex and lengthy, counsel might submit written *positiones* and *allegationes*, which the judges could study when reaching their decision.[19]

Once the judge had heard oral argument and had the written versions in hand he then appointed a day for the parties to appear to hear his decision and sentence. Judges normally announced their decisions orally. Protocol required that they do so while seated and that the announcement be made during the daylight hours. The oral decision was also committed to writing and the survival of draft decisions confirms what one might have expected, namely that these documents were carefully composed, reviewed, and revised prior to publication.[20] The decision normally gave a brief statement of the judge's findings in fact. Unlike modern English and American judicial decisions, medieval canonical judges rarely discussed in any detail the legal reasoning that underlay their conclusions.[21]

Not all lawsuits, by any means, ended with a judicial decision. Indeed, in the records of local consistory courts most cases typically lack a final decision. Sometimes parties simply abandoned their cases part-way through the proceedings and in many instances they no doubt settled the matter out of court. It is not unusual to find this indicated in a terse note by the recording clerk stating simply, 'settled peacefully' (*pax est*) or 'by agreement' (*concordia est*).

The fourteenth-century records of the bishop's consistory court for the diocese of Ely can give us some idea of how ecclesiastical courts of this type functioned.[22] While the see

19. Tancred, *Ordo iudiciarius* 3.4.2 and 3.15, ed. Bergmann, pp.208–9, 261–8.
20. Jane E. Sayers, *Papal judges delegate*, pp.321–2, prints a fine example of a draft decision from Egerton Charter 409 in the British Library.
21. Donahue, 'Proof by witnesses', pp.142–3; an exceptional instance from 1271 where a judge did provide a reasoned decision appears in *Select cases from the ecclesiastical courts of the province of Canterbury, c. 1200–1301*, eds Norma Adams and Charles Donahue, Jr, Selden Society Publications, vol. 95 (London, 1981), pp.88–9.
22. For descriptions of the workings of other courts see Brian Woodcock, *Medieval ecclesiastical courts in the diocese of Canterbury* (London, 1952); Richard M. Wunderli, *London church courts and society on the eve of the Reformation* (Cambridge, MA, 1981); Colin Morris, 'The commissary of the bishop in the diocese of Lincoln', *Journal of ecclesiastical history* 10 (1959), 50–65, and 'A consistory court in the Middle Ages, *Journal of ecclesiastical history* 14 (1963), 150–9.

of Ely was one of the smallest English dioceses, it was also one of the wealthiest and its episcopal consistory was relatively busy. Unlike most consistory courts the Ely consistory did not meet in the bishop's cathedral city, but instead usually held its sessions a few miles away in Cambridge, where the bishop's official-principal normally resided. The presence of a university at Cambridge meant that the consistory had ready access to the services of trained canonists and consequently that the legal standards of this court may have been a shade more sophisticated than those in other dioceses.

The Ely consistory held public sessions on Thursdays and Fridays approximately once every three weeks. The court thus met on average only fourteen or fifteen times each year, since it typically took a recess of six or eight weeks during August and September. Public sessions were usually held in the official's home parish church, although in emergencies, when immediate action on some matter was imperative, the court might sit in the official's private home. The consistory's formal sessions comprised only a small part of the court's activities, however, and it transacted the bulk of its business in private during the intervals between public sessions. Examiners used those intervals to interrogate witnesses and take their depositions individually and in secret, for example, while legal consultations between the judges and advocates also took place outside of the court's formal sittings. Plaintiffs submitted their written complaints and defendants filed their written denials during the periods between public sittings, while the court registrar and his clerks also used the intervals between sittings to draw up records of actions, dispatch summonses, and maintain the bulky files of documents that litigation produced.

The bar of the Ely consistory court consisted of three categories of men trained or experienced in canon law: advocates, proctors, and notaries. The advocates comprised the elite lawyers of the consistory. They were legal experts who often boasted advanced degrees in canon or civil law and sometimes in both. Advocates advised clients about technical questions of law, prepared the formal submissions that procedural law required, and presented legal arguments on behalf of their clients. Between 1373 and

1382 at least nine advocates practised in the consistory court, although not all of them were active at the same time. The bishops of Ely usually appointed their officials-principal from the ranks of their consistorial advocates, while other advocates commonly received appointments as commissary judges to preside over routine hearings and as judicial examiners to interrogate witnesses. The officials-principal and other judges regularly sought legal advice from the court's advocates before rendering their formal decisions.

Several advocates at the Ely consistory in the late fourteenth century were well-connected men who later secured high offices in church and state. One such was Richard le Scrope, doctor of civil and canon law, who first practised as an advocate, then became official-principal and presiding judge of the consistory, as well as chancellor of Cambridge University. Scrope later left England for Avignon, where he became a papal chaplain and an auditor of the Rota in 1381. In 1385 he was named bishop of Chichester. He was subsequently translated to the see of Coventry and Lichfield and finally in 1398 became archbishop of York. As archbishop, Scrope became entangled in the murky politics of the reign of Henry IV, led an unsuccessful rebellion against the king, and subsequently was beheaded for treason in 1405.

Scrope's successor as archbishop of York was Henry Bowet, another former advocate of the Ely consistory. Bowet was also a doctor of both civil and canon law and, in addition to his legal work in the consistory, he secured a series of ecclesiastical benefices, which no doubt supplemented his legal fees quite handily. His success in securing these appointments was enhanced by his connections at the royal court, where he had served as a clerk before embarking on practice at the consistory. In 1382 Bowet quit his legal practice at the Ely consistory to join the household of Henry Despenser, bishop of Norwich. A year later Bowet became the king's proctor at the papal curia, and soon secured new appointments as a papal chaplain and as a judge of the Apostolic Camera. In 1396 he returned to the service of the English king as chief justice of Aquitaine and constable of Bordeaux. Bowet seems to have been a cagey bird – certainly he led a charmed career. Although a political miscalculation landed him in serious trouble in 1399, when he was sentenced to death *in absentia*, he managed to have the sentence revoked within a few months and in 1401 Henry IV named him bishop of Bath and Wells. In 1407 he became archbishop of York, a post he held until his death in 1423.

Yet another Ely advocate contemporary with Bowet and Scrope was John Newton, who was admitted to practise at the consistory in 1375. In addition to his active legal practice, Newton also sat from time to time as a commissary judge and examiner of witnesses. He received his doctorate in civil law at Cambridge in 1378. The following year he was appointed official-principal of the bishop of Ely, and in addition served as master of Peterhouse. In 1390 he was named vicar-general of York, where he also held the post of treasurer of York Minster and remained a power in the ecclesiastical administration of York under his former colleagues at the Ely consistory, Scrope and Bowet, until his death in 1414.

Thus three out of the nine advocates who practised at the Ely consistory during the 1370s and early 1380s became figures of considerable note in church administration in their later careers. And while the remaining six advocates contemporary with these men enjoyed less prominence and visibility, they were nonetheless important local worthies, men of influence and authority in the smaller world of Cambridgeshire and the Isle of Ely.

The proctors who practised at the Ely consistory were about as numerous but considerably less distinguished than the advocates. Of the eight or nine proctors in practice during the period under review, only two or three seem to have had university degrees. The rest presumably either learned their profession as apprentices in the courts or had studied law for a time without taking degrees, as medieval students often did.[23] Unlike the advocates, proctors were not expected to be legal experts and hence depended less

23. On the social history and career patterns of medieval university students see especially Rainer Christoph Schwinges, 'Student life, student education', in *A history of the university in Europe*, vol. 1, *Universities in the Middle Ages*, ed. Hilde de Ridden-Symoens (Cambridge, 1992), pp.195–243.

on academic credentials and more on their practical ability to manage litigation and to guide litigants successfully through the procedural and bureaucratic labyrinths of the court. Proctors literally represented a client by making court appearances on the latter's behalf. They could introduce motions or exceptions, plead defences, or amend complaints, and take other legal actions for the client with the same force and effect as if the client had done so in person. Once issue had been joined and a matter went to trial, the proctor became 'the owner of the case' (*dominus litis*) in his client's place and spoke in court on the client's behalf. The proctor's statements were binding on his client, unless the client happened to be present and immediately disavowed his proctor's words.

A third group of functionaries who clustered around the consistory consisted of notaries. They were the primary producers of legal documents. Notaries differed from mere scribes or copyists in that they usually drafted the documents they produced. Notarial documents had the standing of public instruments and judges normally accepted them as *prima facie* evidence that the transactions they recorded had taken place as described. Both civil and criminal procedures in the ecclesiastical courts required floods of notarized records and the courts furnished a continuous market for notarial services. The registrar of the court was also a notary, who employed clerks to copy documents and maintain the court's records. The registrar also had charge of the court's calendar, docketed hearings and appearances, and supervised the rest of the court's staff. The apparitors or summoners functioned as the court's bailiffs. They served summonses and other legal papers upon witness and parties to litigation. Since they habitually dealt with people who would have preferred to avoid them, apparitors had to exercise a degree of ingenuity and also needed to be able to defend themselves from those who would have preferred the court not to intrude into their affairs.

As happens in every system of dispute resolution, at least half of the parties who appeared before the bishop's consistory were displeased with the outcome of the litigation in which they were involved. For those who were sufficiently unhappy to pursue the matter further, the conclusion of proceedings in a bishop's consistory court frequently marked the beginning of a new, and usually costlier, phase of litigation. Litigants had numerous potential avenues for appeal to higher canonical courts. The losing party might, for example, appeal from the bishop's consistory court to the provincial court of the metropolitan. Alternatively the aggrieved litigant could appeal to the papal courts, either after or in place of appealing to the metropolitan's court. If the appellate judge accepted the matter for review, the lodging of an appeal had the effect of postponing execution of the lower court's decision. That in itself might well seem to the losing party to justify the expense of embarking upon the appellate process.

By 1300, and indeed well before then, demands for a simplified and speedier procedure had become insistent. This is scarcely surprising. Protests against inordinate delays and excessive costs caused by flaws in the reigning procedural system have been commonplace in the history of every highly developed legal system, from antiquity to the present.[24] Already in the thirteenth century the papal chancery from time to time directed judges-delegate to settle the cases assigned to them 'summarily, simply, and directly, without the clamour of advocates and judicial niceties' (*summarie, simpliciter et de plano, sine strepitu aduocatorum et figura iudicii*). This formula allowed judges considerable freedom to abbreviate or omit features of the standard civil procedure that seemed to them unnecessary in the circumstances of a particular case, so long as the parties and their legal advisers agreed. Such wide latitude, however, also opened the way for possible abuse of their discretionary powers by careless or partisan judges and for humiliating reversals upon appeal against the decisions of judges whom the appellate tribunal thought excessively flexible. Pope Clement V (1305–14) therefore agreed to a proposal made by Giovanni d'Andrea (d. 1348) that he append to the constitutions of the Council of Vienne

---

24. For an illuminating discussion of the antecedents of this problem see Charles Lefebvre, 'Les origines romaines de la procédure sommaire auz XIIe et XIIIe siècles', *Ephemerides iuris canonici* 12 (1956), 149–97.

(1311–12) a further constitution, *Saepe contingit*, which specified what could be omitted in summary process and what could not.[25] This constitution defined the elements of canonical summary procedure, although it still left judges and litigants latitude to tailor a specific process to suit the circumstances of the problem before them.

By the early fourteenth century canonical judges had received authority to employ summary process whenever they found it appropriate in a broad range of disputes over issues that involved marriage, usury, tithes, heresy, benefices, or the election of an abbess or prioress by a convent of nuns.[26] Summary procedure further allowed judges to hear cases and take testimony during some periods when the conduct of formal judicial business was normally forbidden, and to curtail the use of dilatory exceptions and appeals by the parties. These measures allowed the judge to save additional time and speed the conclusion of litigation, which, as Justinian had noted eight centuries earlier, showed an alarming tendency to become virtually immortal when lawsuits exceeded the life span of the original litigants.[27]

Criminal procedure, both in secular courts and church courts also experienced fundamental changes during the thirteenth century. The most basic of these were the abolition of judicial ordeals in secular courts and the introduction of inquisitorial procedure in ecclesiastical tribunals. In 1215 the Fourth Lateran Council, presided over by Pope Innocent III, forbade clerics in future to take part in ordeals. Since both the rituals and the rationale for judgment by ordeal demanded formal participation by clergymen, this conciliar constitution effectively made it thenceforth impossible to conduct a judicial ordeal without violating canon law.[28]

The motives that underlay this startling departure from centuries-old practice in secular courts have been the subject of investigation, speculation, and disagreement

---

25. Clem. 5.11.2. See also Kenneth Pennington, *The prince and the law, 1200–1600: Sovereignty and rights in the Western legal tradition* (Berkeley and Los Angeles, 1993), pp.132–64, 188–90.
26. VI 1.6.43 and 5.2.20, as well as Clem. 2.1.2.
27. Cod. 3.1.13 pr.
28. 4 Lateran (1215) c. 18.

among scholars.[29] One purpose that the council's action certainly served was to bring home to monarchs and other lay authorities the lesson that their capacity to govern depended upon the cooperation of church authorities. The action illustrated in a dramatic and concrete way Innocent III's famous simile that the power of the church compares to the power of the state as the light of the sun compares to the light of the moon.[30]

The ban on clerical involvement in ordeals reflects not only papal claims to authority, but also intellectual fashions in the late twelfth and early thirteenth centuries, which produced increasing disenchantment with old-fashioned methods of arriving at judicial verdicts. The professors in the burgeoning law schools disdained the ordeal as crude and unsophisticated. Its use might be hallowed by long tradition, to be sure, and its drama might appeal to a credulous public, but it was hardly consistent with the learned and rational methods of the schools. Logical analysis of the evidence of witnesses and the mute testimony of charters and contracts suited the schoolmen better than the inspection of scars and pustules with a view to inferring from them the mind of God.[31]

The ordeal, however, did not vanish overnight.

29. See especially Robert Bartlett, *Trial by fire and water: The medieval judicial ordeal* (Oxford, 1986); Paul Hyams, 'Trial by ordeal: The key to proof in early common law', in *On the laws and customs of England: Essays in honor of Samuel E. Thorne*, ed. M. S. Arnold et al. (Chapel Hill, NC, 1981), pp.90–126; Richard H. Helmholz, 'Crime, compurgation and the courts of the medieval church', *Law and history review* 1 (1983), 1–26; Richard M. Fraher, 'The theoretical justification for the new criminal law of the high middle ages: "Rei publicae interest ne crimina remaneant impunita', *University of Illinois law review* (1984), 577–95, and 'Conviction according to conscience: The medieval jurists' debate concerning judicial discretion and the law of proof', *Law and history review* 7 (1989), 23–88.
30. Innocent III, *Register* 1.401, eds Othmar Hageneder and Anton Haidacher, et al., Publikationen der Abteilung für historische Studien des Österreichischen Kulturinstituts in Rom, 2nd ser., sect. 1 (Graz, 1964–); also in PL ccxiv, p.377. A translation appears in Brian Tierney, *The crisis of church and state, 1050–1300* (Englewood Cliffs, NJ, 1964), p.132.
31. John W. Baldwin, 'The intellectual preparation for the canon of 1215 against ordeals', *Speculum* 36 (1961), 613–36.

Cumbersome communications and inefficient enforcement mechanisms both contrived to make its disappearance a slow and gradual process, while the need to devise alternative procedures in royal and other secular courts further delayed compliance with the conciliar decree. The withering of the ordeal, moreover, proceeded at a different pace in different regions. It held on considerably longer in Germany and southeastern Europe, for example, than it did in France, England, or Spain. But inexorably it faded from use and by 1300 the ordeal had ceased to be a regular feature of legal systems anywhere in the West.

The procedural system preferred by the church courts at the end of the twelfth century was, and had long been, the accusatory procedure.[32] The canons of the early church had borrowed their main features from Roman procedure, and augmented them with some peculiarly ecclesiastical practices. The result was a criminal procedure that suffered from grave defects. In the first place it required a private individual to come forward with a complaint in order to initiate a criminal action. At the same time, however, the system tended to discourage individuals from bringing complaints, for the action proceeded at the expense of the accuser, who was responsible for all the costs incurred. Further, if the accuser failed to prove his charges, he was liable for damages to the defendant, who could sue him for bringing a false accusation.

Beyond this, the standard of proof in accusatory proceedings was extraordinarily high, for the accuser must provide 'full proof' (*plena probatio*) of his charges.[33] He could do this only by furnishing evidence that was 'clearer than the mid-day light'. In practice that meant that the accuser must either induce the defendant to confess to the crime, or else produce two credible eyewitnesses who would testify that they had seen and heard the accused commit the offence. The rationale behind this exceptionally high standard of proof rested upon the scriptural admonition

32. See above, pp.93–4.
33. On full and partial proof see the interesting discussion by James Franklin, 'The ancient legal sources of seventeenth-century probability', in *The uses of antiquity* ed. Stephen Gaukroger (Dordrecht, 1991), pp.123–44 at 126–39.

that 'the evidence of two or three witnesses is required to sustain any charge'.[34] Crimes, then as now, occasionally occurred in public, where two eyewitnesses to the deed might sometimes have been present and willing to testify. Save for crimes of passion and some varieties of fraud or deceit, however, medieval criminals usually preferred when possible to operate furtively and to conceal their offences so far as possible from the public gaze. And while offenders, when discovered and haled before a tribunal, sometimes broke down and confessed, the determined and obdurate criminal often resisted successfully any urge that he might feel toward self-incrimination.

Also available, but not often used in practice, was an alternative criminal procedure by denunciation. This, too, had its basis in the gospel admonition that 'If your brother does something wrong, go and have it out with him alone, between your two selves . . . But if he refuses to listen . . . report it to the community . . .'.[35] From the accuser's point of view this had the decided advantage that it relieved him of any liability to the defendant for false accusation. The prospect of first confronting the offender and delivering a 'charitable admonition' to him in private, however, cannot often have been pleasant to contemplate. The standard of proof in a proceeding by denunciation, moreover, was as high as that under the accusatory procedure and conviction of the obdurate criminal was therefore far from easy to secure.

A further mechanism for securing criminal convictions supplemented the accusatory and denunciatory procedures and provided a limited avenue for prosecuting suspected criminals. This was the procedural device known as the *exceptio criminis*, which parties to a lawsuit could use to disqualify the testimony of an opponent or a hostile witness. A party to a legal action could invoke the *exceptio criminis* by objecting to the other person's appearance in the case on the grounds that the person named had been guilty of some specified crime and hence could not legally bring an action or testify in an action brought by another. If the person named in this exception had not been

34. Matt. 18:16; cf. Deut. 19:15, 2 Cor. 13:1.
35. Matt. 18:15–17; cf. Lev. 19:17.

convicted of the alleged crime, the procedural hearing on the merits of the exception became, in effect, a criminal trial to determine whether that person was guilty of the offence as charged. If the person against whom an *exceptio criminis* was taken should be found guilty, however, he or she was simply barred from participation in the main lawsuit and suffered no further criminal sanctions.[36]

None of these procedures proved very effective, even when wrongdoing was well-known. Consequently clear and open offences against canon law often went unpunished because the established procedure, the *ordo iudiciarius*, crippled effective action against the culprits. The entrenched procedures were particularly unsatisfactory in penalizing the perpetrators of 'occult crimes', who took the precaution of hiding their nefarious conduct from public view.

During the closing decade of the twelfth century and the opening years of the thirteenth, accordingly, the papacy began to experiment with alternative approaches to the problem of punishing crime. One novel strategy for dealing with canonical crimes was procedure *per notorium*. The rationale for this procedure lay in what may be called the 'common sense' approach to criminal justice, which held that where the fact of a crime and the identity of the offender were both obvious and well-known throughout the community, the niceties of the conventional *ordo iudiciarius* were irrelevant and need not be applied. This was (and for that matter still is) an approach to the problem of crime that enjoyed considerable popular appeal, since it seemed well calculated to punish offenders swiftly and cheaply and at the same time avoided the dodges and delays of lawyers (a group always suspected of aiding and abetting wrongdoers). Advocates of this approach could even point to respectable canonical authority for their position, since Gratian, when commenting upon a passage from St Ambrose, had remarked that a judge need not observe

---

36. The *exceptio criminis* could also be used to prevent an alleged criminal from receiving ordination, as well as from instituting a lawsuit or testifying in one; X 2.25.1; Hostiensis, *Summa aurea* 5.2, *De exceptionibus* §§1–2 (Lyon, 1537; repr. Aalen, 1962), fol. 228va.

all the procedural steps of conventional judicial procedure.[37] Building upon this observation, Popes Lucius III (1181–85) and Innocent III authorized courts to employ an abbreviated and much simplified criminal procedure when they dealt with cases in which a priest was openly living in sin with a concubine or patronizing prostitutes. Not only was no accuser or denunciation required in these situations, the pontiffs declared, but in addition the courts could also relax the strict standard of proof that the *ordo iudiciarius* demanded.[38] If 'full proof' by the evidence of two credible eyewitnesses was not available, then partial proof, that is the testimony of one witness supported by circumstantial evidence, would do.

Thus conviction in proceedings *per notorium* simply required that the judge establish that numerous members of the community in which the defendant resided believed that he was guilty of some crime. No eyewitnesses need be produced. The judge could proceed *ex officio* against a defendant to establish whether he was notoriously suspect of a crime. He need only find two witnesses prepared to testify that the defendant was generally believed by members of the community to have committed the crime. Once they had done so, the judge could forthwith find the defendant guilty and impose punishment. Conservative jurists, to be sure, abhorred this course of action, which they considered far too summary to warrant punishment. They insisted that the judge must at least summon the defendant and question him about the allegations before pronouncing judgment, but that seems to have been the limit of the defendant's rights under this procedure.[39]

Procedure *per notorium* promised a quick and easy solution to the problem of punishing flagrant crimes that outraged a community. It seemed calculated to be especially useful in the papacy's war against concubinage and other types of sexual misconduct by clerics, crimes that were extremely difficult to prove according to the rules of the reigning *ordo iudiciarius*. Jurists could and did construct

37. Gratian, C. 2 q. 1 d.a.c. 15 and d.p.c. 17.
38. X 3.2.8.
39. Tancred, *Ordo iudiciarii* 2.7.1, ed. Bergmann, pp.151–2.

a rationale for employing this procedure on the grounds that the public interest required that crimes must not go unpunished.[40] Authorities claimed that 'the public interest' (of which they naturally assumed they were the arbiters) thus legitimized this new procedure.

Procedure *per notorium* needed all the legitimacy its defenders could muster. On its darker side this procedure stripped defendants of nearly all the protections that the conventional *ordo iudiciarius* afforded them. This opened the way for abuse of the church's criminal justice system, because proceedings *per notorium* could easily be manipulated or contrived in order to brand as criminals persons whose real crime was to be disagreeable to their superiors or unpopular among their neighbours. Punishment of notorious crimes in this summary fashion also suffered from an inherent intellectual flaw. Although *per notorium* procedure no doubt did facilitate punishment of flagrant offenders, and in that sense served the public interest, its apologists never quite managed to produce convincing answers to the counter argument that if the crime and the identity of the offender really were so widely known as to be notorious in a rigorous sense of that term, then a judge ought to be able to find witnesses to prove it. If no witnesses could be produced, according to this reasoning, then the charge should be classed as merely 'manifest', that is, widely believed, rather than 'notorious', that is, widely known. Because *per notorium* procedure was such a slippery, and hence potentially dangerous, tool, authoritative law teachers and writers warned future advocates and judges that they should employ it rarely and with great caution.[41] William Durand (ca. 1230–96), the most eminent of the thirteenth-century procedural writers, went so far as to declare that in order to warrant conviction *per notorium* it was not even sufficient for an offender to commit his crime in the presence of the judge. To ensure a proper conviction, the determined malefactor must

---

40. Fraher, 'Theoretical justification', develops this argument in detail.
41. Hostiensis, *Summa aurea*, tit. 5 De criminibus sine ordine puniendis (Lyon, 1537 edn, fol. 230va-vb); Durandus, *Speculum iudiciale*, lib. 3, partic. 1, rubr. Quid sit pene occultum §7 (Basel, 1574 edn), p.48.

perform his dastardly deed at a time when the judge was acting in his official capacity and in the presence of a large enough crowd to make the offence public knowledge. Under these circumstances an offence was indeed 'notorious' in the full rigour of the term. Otherwise, however, Durand maintained that a conviction *per notorium* would not be justified, so long as the defendant denied guilt.[42]

The reservations that academic jurists voiced about this procedure presumably account for the introduction in practice of defence by compurgation. Once common knowledge of an offence had been established, judges could, and often did, require defendants who denied the allegations against them under oath to purge themselves of the accusation by producing a stipulated number of oath-helpers or compurgators who were prepared to swear that they believed the defendant's sworn denial.[43]

A further, and more widely employed type of criminal procedure appeared quite abruptly during the opening years of the pontificate of Pope Innocent III. As part of the continuing papal campaign against clerical concubinage, fornication, and simony, Innocent in a decretal of 1199 authorized judges to use a new form of action *per inquisitionem*, besides the traditional ones.[44] This novel form of action seems to have been Innocent III's own creation. The pope described the new process more fully in a decretal of 1206[45] and it was firmly established as a regular type of criminal procedure by the Fourth Lateran Council in 1215.[46]

Innocent III claimed, as reformers and revolutionaries often do, that his procedural innovation was no recent

---

42. William Durandus, *Speculum iudiciale*, lib. 3, partic. 1, rubr. De notoriis criminibus §9, and rubr. Notorium quid sit (Basel, 1574 edn), pp.44–5, 49–52. See also Pennington's discussion of *per notorium* procedure in *The prince and the law*, pp.229–30, 247–8, 256–7, 264–6.

43. Richard H. Helmholz, 'Crime, compurgation and the courts of the medieval church', *Law and history review* 1 (1983), 1–26, repr. in his *Canon law and the law of England* (London, 1987), pp.119–44.

44. X 5.3.31.

45. X 5.1.17.

46. 4 Lat. c. 8, later incorporated in X 5.1.24; and see above, pp.94–6.

creation. He asserted instead that a long tradition of utmost respectability lay behind it. According to the pope, God himself had employed procedure *per inquisitionem* when he inquired into the shameful doings at Sodom and Gomorra before he destroyed them.[47] Innocent further claimed that Jesus had also approved of this form of procedure, as shown by his parable of the master who investigated the actions of his steward.[48] These assertions disguised what was in fact a radical novelty behind a reassuring cloak of scriptural authority. Although Innocent's rationalizations had little to do with the juristic lineage of inquisitorial procedure, a subject that has been the subject of prolonged debate among modern scholars,[49] they did invest it with a comforting aura of legitimacy.

Like the process *per notorium*, procedure *per inquisitionem* allowed a judge to take action against a suspected offender *ex officio*, without any accusation or denunciation. A judge could initiate proceedings *per inquisitionem* on the basis of persistent, widespread belief that an individual had committed an offence. In this it resembled a process *per notorium*, in that ill-fame (*mala fama*) constituted an adequate basis for judicial investigation and hence could be deemed to take the place of an accuser. It was not necessary for the judge to produce a written complaint, nor did he need to admonish the defendant informally, as in a process *per denunciationem*, before commencing the action. The whole conduct of a proceeding *per inquisitionem* – determining when and if to initiate the procedure, deciding what charges to prefer and against whom, producing witnesses, taking their testimony, responding to the claims and arguments of the defendant, arriving at a decision, and pronouncing sentence – rested in the hands of the judge, who thus combined the functions of investigator and prosecutor with his judicial role. This concentration of functions in the hands of a single

47. Gen. 18:20–21.
48. Lk 16:1–8; cf. Mt 18:23–35, 25:14–30.
49. See most recently Winfried Trusen, 'Der Inquisitionsprozeß: Seine historischen Grundlagen und frühen Formen', *Zeitschrift der Savigny-Stiftung für Rechtsgeschichte*, kanonistische Abteilung 74 (1988), 168–230.

investigator/prosecutor/judge obviously placed the defendant at an enormous disadvantage and left more than ample room for judicial bias to prejudice the outcome of the case. To make matters worse, a defendant in any canonical criminal proceeding was not permitted to engage a proctor to serve as his representative before the court, nor was he usually entitled to have legal advice from an advocate.[50]

Once a judge had determined that *mala fama* existed and that the information was sufficiently serious and specific to warrant formal charges against a defendant, however, the evidentiary requirements of the standard *ordo iudiciarius* came into play and this afforded the defendant some modest degree of protection. The defendant must be cited before the judge, he must be informed of the charges against him, and he had the right to offer a defence, unless he wished to plead guilty. William Durandus, the preeminent procedural authority among thirteenth-century canonists, insisted that full proof of guilt according to the prescriptions of the *ordo iudiciarius* was essential before a

---

50. Johannes Teutonicus, *Glos. ord.* to C. 2 q. 6 c. 40 v. *exploratores* and C. 3 q. 6 c. 10 v. *de expulsis*; Bernard of Parma, *Glos. ord.* to X 5.1.15 v. *criminale*; Albertus Gandinus, *Tractatus de maleficiis*, ed. Kantorowicz 2:111–20. Although denial of access to legal representation and counsel strikes modern sensibilities as inherently unfair, it is important to keep in mind that this was the common law rule as well. Not until 1696 were English criminal defendants in treason cases allowed to see a copy of the indictment against them, to call witnesses on their behalf, or to have legal advice. Defendants in felony cases were not allowed counsel until 1837; Theodore F. T. Plucknett, *A concise history of the common law*, 4th edn (London, 1948), p.410, citing statutes of 7 & 8 Will. III, c. 3 (1696) and 6 & 7 Will. IV, c. 114 (1837). The United States was slightly speedier to assure criminal defendants a right to counsel – but not by much. No such assurance appeared in the seven original articles of the Constitution; it was only added in the Bill of Rights, Art. VI, which came into effect in 1791. Even so the exercise of the right to counsel remained effectively available only to defendants with the means to afford to avail themselves of it. Indigent defendants only gained the means to exercise this right effectively as a result of a decision by the U.S. Supreme Court in 1963; Gideon v. Wainwright, 372 US 335, 83 S Ct 391, 9 L ed 2d 799.

judge proceeding *per inquisitionem* could declare a defendant guilty.[51]

Others were not so sure that maintaining a high standard of proof was entirely justified as a matter of public policy. Their argument (one that is still familiar) held that insistence upon stringent proof would allow guilty defendants to escape just punishment for their transgressions. This, in turn, they maintained, worked against the interests of the whole community in repressing crime. At the very least, some believed, the judge in an inquisitorial proceeding was entitled to menace defendants and even to torture them, in order to extract an admission of guilt and to deter other potential offenders.

The issues that church authorities and canonists confronted in dealing with criminal procedure reflected tension among medieval jurists between two conflicting values. A safe and just society requires reasonable certainty that those who break the law will, at least most of the time, be apprehended and punished. At the same time, however, a safe and just society also requires some assurance that its members will not be convicted and punished for crimes they have not committed. Authorities at the beginning of the thirteenth century concluded that the stiff standard of proof that the *ordo iudiciarius* required allowed excessive numbers of criminals to escape the punishment they deserved. In an effort to repair the deficiency they perceived in the legal system, they introduced alternative forms of action *per notorium* and *per inquisitionem*. Academic authorities, however, concluded that procedure *per notorium* sacrificed too many of the procedural safeguards built in to the *ordo iudiciarius*. Hence they taught their students that this procedure should be used sparingly and sought to hedge it about with limitations that made it fundamentally unworkable. Academic lawyers likewise considered inquisitorial procedure seriously flawed and insisted that here, too, defendants should enjoy at least some of the formal protections of the conventional *ordo*. This furnishes an instructive example of what might be called 'jurist nullification', whereby academic law teachers taught the

---

51. Durandus, *Speculum iudiciale*, lib. 3, partic. 1, rubr. Manifestum quid sit, pr., v. *Licet aperta* (Basel, 1574), pp.47–8.

church's future lawyers to modify or even ignore certain parts of the canon law that they considered poorly conceived or simply wrong.[52]

Canon law characteristically gave judges broad discretion to fit the punishment both to the crime and to the circumstances of the criminal. In part, certainly, this reflected what is sometimes called the medicinal approach to sentencing, that is, a belief that the primary goal of punishment ought to be rehabilitation of the criminal. Medicinal punishment was the norm in canonical penal law up to the late eleventh century. The application of canonical rules during the early Middle Ages tended to be episodic and reactive: church authorities in that period commonly took action only when offences became so glaring and public that they were likely to cause scandal and lead others astray. For the rest, early medieval churchmen were inclined to leave the detection and punishment of secret offenders to the private, individual ministry of their confessors, rather than to insist on public correction by a judge. Their first goal was to try to save the sinner, rather than to pursue delinquents and subject them to formal disciplinary action.

The reformers who occupied the papal throne from the end of the eleventh century onward, however, tended to be more aggressive in these matters. They and their supporters accordingly set in motion an energetic and vigorous approach to penal law. Bishops and other prelates, the reformers believed, should seek out offenders against orthodox belief and behaviour. Once detected, offenders ought to be put on public trial for their misdeeds and, when convicted, their punishment should likewise be public and ferocious enough to make other potential offenders think twice before imitating the miscreants. Penal

---

52. The allusion here is to 'jury nullification' in England and American common law. This occurs when what lawyers and judges call a 'runaway jury' refuses to find a defendant guilty, despite the evidence and the judge's instructions on the law. For an instructive treatment of this topic see Thomas A. Green, *Verdict according to conscience: Perspectives on the English criminal trial jury, 1200–1800* (Chicago, 1985), esp. ch. 2.

law, according to this view, must serve deterrent as well as corrective purposes.[53]

The menu of penalties from which a judge might choose when sentencing a convicted defendant was accordingly rich and varied. The judge, at least in theory, should compound a mixture of punishments appropriate to each case. Uniform sentencing was far less important, in this view, than the fit between a particular crime and the retribution that followed. The list included coercive penalties such as excommunication, interdict, or suspension from office.[54] These were designed primarily to bring pressure on the miscreant to comply with the law and make his peace with church authorities. Retributive penalties, such as fines, restitution of ill-gotten gains, deposition from office, degradation from clerical status, confinement in a monastery, or other types of imprisonment deprived the guilty party of status, income, or freedom as punishment for his misdeeds. Purgative penalties, such as pilgrimages, the donning of penitent's garb, participation in processions, the public offering of gifts to repair damages, ritual flogging, fasts, and abstinence from meat, wine, or sex for prescribed periods served to humiliate the penitent while at the same time they purified him of the guilt he had incurred.

53. The growing divergence between the internal forum of confession and private penance and the external forum of the church's courts also reflects the process whereby theology and canon law gradually became distinct disciplines during the second half of the twelfth century. One classic treatment of this theme is Joseph de Ghellinck, *Le mouvement théologique du XIIe siècle: Sa prépration lointaine avant et autour de Pierre Lombard, ses rapports avec les initiatives des canonistes*, Museum Lessianum, section historique, no 10, 2nd edn (Bruges, 1948; repr: Brussels, 1969). More recently see also Gérard Fransen, 'Derecho canónico y teología', *Revista española de derecho canónico* 20 (1965), 37–46, as well as Rudolf Weigand, 'Ein Zeugnis für die Lehrunterscheide zwishcen Kanonisten und Theologen aus dem 13. Jahrhundert', *Revue de droit canonique* 24 (1974), 63–71, and Herbert Kalb, 'Bemerkungen zum Verhältnis von Theologie und Kanonistik am Beispiel Rufins und Stephanus von Tournai', *Zeitschrift der Savigny-Stiftung für Rechtsgeschichte* kanonistiche Abteilung 72 (1986), 338–48.

54. See Elisabeth Vodola. *Excommunication in the middle ages* (Berkeley and Los Angeles, 1986).

The most horrendous canonical crimes, especially heresy, might even merit 'relaxation to the secular arm', which involved turning the convicted defendant over to civil authorities who could inflict upon the convict the more bloodthirsty measures available in their courts (such as amputation of limbs, branding, beating, and various forms of execution, some of them extremely savage).[55]

By the fourteenth century, then, the authorities of the Latin church had created a formidable apparatus for law enforcement and adjudication. Canonical courts furnished civil litigants with a forum for resolving their disputes on a wide variety of matters, while the church's criminal justice system took cognizance of a broad spectrum of canonical offences that ranged from petty aberrations from behavioural norms to crimes of the utmost gravity. Canonical procedural law also grew increasingly sophisticated, technical, and complex, as persons with formal legal training became increasingly available to operate it. The relatively informal, and sometimes ad hoc, procedures that characterized actions heard by diocesan synods or bishops with little systematic legal training gave way between the twelfth and fourteenth centuries to processes that bristled with technicalities and required the skills of an increasingly professionalized body of legal experts. Under these circumstances it is scarcely surprising to discover that canon lawyers also became progressively more concerned with problems of legal philosophy and jurisprudence.

---

55. See F. Donald Logan, *Excommunication and the secular arm in medieval England: A study in legal procedure from the thirteenth to the sixteenth century*, Studies and texts, vol. 15 (Toronto, 1968).

Chapter 7

CANONICAL JURISPRUDENCE

Canonists from Gratian's generation onward came increasingly under the influence not only of scholastic methodology, which they helped to create, but also of some of the abstract philosophical speculations that dominated the intellectual interests of contemporary teachers of the liberal arts. Given the intellectual climate that prevailed during the late twelfth and thirteenth centuries, it is scarcely surprising that canonists of that age showed keen interest in analysing the relationship between law, justice, and equity.

Gratian himself devoted the first four Distinctions of his *Decretum* to a discussion of the types, varieties, and sources of law that earlier authorities had described.[1] Law sprang from two basic sources, Gratian declared: natural law and customary practices. He identified natural law with divine law, that is the teachings found in scriptural revelation, and he equated this in turn with 'what is right' (*ius*). What is right, he believed, was unchangeable.[2] Law also included human law (*lex*), however, which is variable.[3] Human laws, Gratian concluded, must be reasonable and must conform to the practices of a community if they were to be valid and

1. Gratian, D. 1 pr.
2. On natural law theory among the canonists see Rudolf Weigand, *Die Naturrechtslehre der Legisten und Dekretisten von Irnerius bis Accursius und von Gratian bis Johannes Teutonicus*, Münchener theologische Studien, ser. 3, kanonistische Abteilung, vol. 26 (Munich, 1967).
3. Gratian, D. 1 c. 1 and d.a.c. 2; Jean Gaudemet, 'La doctrine des sources du droit dans le Décret de Gratien', *Revue de droit canonique* 1 (1950), 5–31, reprinted with original pagination in his *Formation du droit canonique médiéval* (London, 1980).

effective. Gratian accordingly maintained that when laws no longer responded to a community's current behaviour, they ceased to be effective and lost the validity that they once enjoyed.[4] He also declared that equity, or fairness, was the mother of justice and hence of every valid law. A law that was unfair therefore had no legitimate claims to command obedience.[5]

Among the decretists, Huguccio (fl. 1180–1210) identified equity and justice as inseparable, for both sought to give to everyone what was due to them.[6] He also distinguished between natural justice and positive justice. Natural justice for Huguccio meant the benevolence that arises from natural human affections, such as, for example, the love of a mother for her children, and its origin is ultimately divine. Positive justice is of human origin. Positive justice, he continued, aimed to punish offenders and to make good the losses that victims suffered. Human law, according to Huguccio, differs from justice, for law in this world is an art that tries (not always successfully) to achieve goodness and fairness.[7] Huguccio further maintained that laws derive their authority from reason. An unreasonable law cannot be valid, he concluded, no matter what authority decrees it. God, who personifies reason, could not possibly make an unreasonable law; and while human legislators might perversely attempt to do so, any unreasonable legislation they might enact was *ipso facto* void.[8]

Hostiensis (d. 1271), writing in the mid-thirteenth century, saw matters rather differently. While he agreed

4. Gratian, D. 4 d.p.c. 3.
5. Gratian, C. 25 q. 1 d.p.c. 16.
6. Huguccio, *Summa* to D. 50 c. 25 v. *ut constitueretur*, quoted in Le Bras, Lefebvre, and Rambaud, *L'âge classique*, p.357, n. 4. Huguccio was referring, of course, to the definition of justice by the classical jurist Ulpian: 'Iustitia est constans et perpetua uoluntas ius suum cuique tribuendi'; Dig 1.1.10 pr.
7. Huguccio, *Summa* to D. 50 c. 25 v. *iubeo*, quoted in Le Bras, Lefebvre, and Rambaud, *L'âge classique*, p.358, n. 1. Huguccio was again alluding to a classical definition of justice, also formulated by Ulpian; Dig. 1.1.1 pr.
8. Huguccio, *Summa* to D. 4 d.p.c. 3, quoted by Kenneth Pennington, *Pope and bishops: The papal monarchy in the twelfth and thirteenth centuries* (Philadelphia, 1984), pp.21–2.

that the notions of equity, justice, and law were related to one another, he distinguished equity from justice. He saw justice as a strict, unswerving effort to secure retribution for wrongs, while equity for him meant justice moderated by compassion for the offender.[9] Hostiensis therefore admonished canonical judges that, although they had no authority to alter the law, they must nevertheless strive to apply the law's provisions equitably: 'Where a definite penalty is not assigned, or where he is investigating *ex officio*, the judge ought to proceed keeping equity in mind, always choosing the more humane course, as the persons, places, situations, and times may seem to require.'[10]

Fourteenth-century writers further elaborated the distinctions between justice, equity, and law. Giovanni d'Andrea and Giovanni da Legnano saw justice as a moral virtue, an ideal that mere human beings can never attain properly in this world. Law was at best an approximation of justice within the limits of humankind's finite capacities, they thought, and inevitably it fell short, often distressingly short, of the ideal. These writers regarded equity as a principle of mitigation, which adjusted the rigours of strict law to the varied needs of individual situations and thus made it possible for law to approach more closely to the virtue that inspired it.[11]

Medieval canonists also employed the late ancient taxonomy of law that they found at hand in Justinian's *Digest*. As happened with their notions of justice, equity, and law, so also their ideas about the classification of law and the relationship between its various types changed and matured over time. Gratian, for example, did not distinguish sharply between divine law and natural law. His opening reference to natural law cited a scriptural passage as its authority and then immediately quoted a murky excerpt in which Isidore of Seville (ca. 560–636) ascribed a

9. Hostiensis, *Summa aurea* 5.56 De dispensationibus §1 (Lyon, 1537 edn, fol. 289rb).

10. Hostiensis, *Summa aurea* 1 De officio ordinarii §4 (Lyon, 1537 edn, fol. 54vb). This in part paraphrases a decretal of Honorius III in X 1.36.11; see below, p.171.

11. For a more detailed discussion see Le Bras, Lefebvre, and Rambaud, *L'âge classique*, pp.362–6.

divine origin to natural law.[12] The early decretists sought to draw clearer and tighter distinctions between the two categories. They identified natural law with an innate human inclination to do good and avoid evil, while they reserved the term divine law to designate the rules enunciated in the Scriptures.[13] Most decretalists paid scant attention to the theoretical problem of the classification of laws, and tended to leave such issues to theologians.

Hostiensis was a prominent exception to the rule, however, and he devoted a large part of the prologue of his *Summa* (or *Golden Summa*, as it was later styled) on the titles of the *Liber extra* to these problems. In that discussion he distinguished between the common natural law that Ulpian and other classical jurists discussed, and the law of natural reason, which produced the classical 'law of nations' (*ius gentium*). Hostiensis's saw the divine law contained in the Scriptures as an extension of rational natural law and this led him to declare that human laws or judicial decisions that violated rational natural law were untenable and lacked any binding force.[14] Hostiensis's construction of the taxonomy of laws represented a synthesis between the views of the classical Roman jurists and the theological opinions current in his own generation.

A further significant change in terminology appeared in the vocabulary of the early thirteenth-century decretalists. This was the substitution of the term 'positive law' for the older term 'human law'. The significance of the new usage lay in its emphasis upon the notion that human authorities could create law by the express or positive action of a person or group that possessed legislative authority. The new term appeared in one of Gregory IX's decretals in the *Liber extra*, and this gave it official standing.[15] A further refinement of this usage differentiated between positive laws that were 'constituted' and those that were 'unconstituted.' A constituted positive law meant one expressly proclaimed by a pope, monarch, or other

12. Gratian, D. 1 pr. and c. 1.
13. For example, Rufinus, *Summa* to D. 1 pr., ed. Singer, pp.6–7; *Summa 'Elegantius in iure diuino'* 1.4–5, eds Fransen and Kuttner, i, 2.
14. Hostiensis, *Summa aurea* §§5–6 (Lyon, 1537 edn, fol. 2va).
15. X 1.4.11.

authority, while unconstituted positive law referred to laws that originated in the customs of a community and thus derived their force from the implicit assent of the community to a particular practice, rather than from a legislative command by a ruler.[16]

The role of custom as a source of law had puzzled Roman jurists and has continued to vex their medieval and modern successors.[17] Gratian maintained, as Roman jurists and Church Fathers had long done, that custom could be treated as law, but only under certain conditions. In order to acquire the force of law a custom must not run counter to truth, reason, the Christian faith, or natural law.[18] A custom that met these criteria must further be in use within a community for a sufficient time to acquire legal standing by prescription.[19] The decretists accepted these premises, as well, but qualified some of Gratian's assertions and pursued questions that Gratian had either not considered or had dismissed inconclusively. Rufinus, for example, emphasized that in order for a custom to become legally binding it must have been known to and tolerated by the authorities who had the power to abrogate it.[20] Later decretists generally accepted this position and it thus became 'the general opinion of the learned' (*communis opinio doctorum*), to which canonical courts paid respectful heed.[21] Other questions were less readily resolved. Canonists found it difficult, for example, to agree on the minimum size of the group necessary to create a legally binding custom. It seemed clear that customs observed throughout the

---

16. Gratian, D. 1 c. 5; see further Le Bras, Lefebvre, and Rambaud, *L'âge classique*, pp.388–96.
17. C. K. Allen, *Law in the making*, 6th edn (Oxford, 1968), pp.64–152; Alan Watson, *Sources of law, legal change, and ambiguity* (Philadelphia, 1984), pp.22–4, 27–8, 68–75, and *The evolution of law* (Baltimore, 1985), pp.43–65.
18. Gratian discusses these and other criteria for legitimate customs in D. 11 and 12 of the *Decretum*; note also Bernard of Pavia, *Glossa ordinaria* to X 1.4.11 v. *naturalis iure* and *rationabilis*.
19. Gratian, C. 16 q. 3 d.p.c. 15; Bernard of Pavia, *Glos. ord.* to X 1.4.11 v. *legitime sit praescripta*.
20. Rufinus, *Summa* to D. 4 c. 4, ed. Singer, p.13.
21. Johannes Teutonicus, *Glossa ordinaria* to D. 4 d.a.c. 4 v. *abrogatae* and D. 8 c. 7 v. *consuetudinem*. On the *communis opinio doctorum* see Le Bras, Lefebvre, and Rambaud, *L'âge classique*, p.459.

Western church had the force of law, but what about the customary practices of smaller groups? Most writers agreed that customary practices within administrative units, such as ecclesiastical provinces, dioceses, and even parishes could acquire legal force. The same was true for the usages of institutional groups and corporations, such as cathedral chapters and monasteries. A single family, however, seemed too small and intimate a group for the courts to recognize its habitual practices as legally binding upon its members.[22] Consent of the community was also essential to endow a custom with legal force and this in turn raised still further questions for canonists to debate.[23] In addition customs could become binding only if people throughout the community knew about them, and their practice remained uninterrupted and unchallenged throughout the period required for prescription to run its course.[24]

Another source of law in canonistic jurisprudence was the rescript. The term 'rescript' means in general a conclusive reply or judicial decision given by a pope, bishop, prince, or other legitimate authority to a petition, request, or other motion from a subject. Although rescripts were applicable in strict law only to the parties in the case that raised a specific issue, judges in other situations where the same issues arose might well deem it prudent to apply the rules of law or interpretation that a relevant rescript contained.[25] It is important to note, however, that medieval canonical judges did not think of rescripts in the same way that common law judges think of precedents. Roman and canon law acknowledged no *stare decisis* doctrine of the sort that prevails in England, the United States, and other common law jurisdictions. Indeed, Justinian flatly forbade judges to follow the opinions of other courts and commanded them to be guided only by the texts of the law contained in his *Corpus.*[26] The authority of rescripts did not result from any precedent that they established, but rather

---

22. Le Bras, Lefebvre, and Rambaud discuss these opinions in *L'âge classique*, pp.538–9.
23. Johannes Teutonicus, *Glos. ord.* to D. 8 c. 7 v. *consuetudinem.*
24. Le Bras, Lefebvre and Rambaud, *L'âge classique*, pp.545–6.
25. Dig. 1.4.1.2; X 5.33.9; VI reg. jur. 74.
26. Cod. 7.45.13.

from the authority of the ruler who issued them.[27]

Papal rescripts, usually described as decretals, were by far the most important source of new canon law between the late twelfth and the fifteenth centuries. Although they had marginal importance for Gratian, he gave them only cursory notice.[28] This situation soon changed. From the pontificate of Pope Alexander III (1159–81) onward the popes of the generation that immediately followed Gratian's lifetime used decretals as the primary vehicle for legislative innovation. In principle any Christian could seek a papal ruling on any matter under ecclesiastical jurisdiction in which he had standing to petition or appeal. Once the ruling had been made, it was communicated to the originator in the form of a papal decretal letter and he must receive and accept it before it became operative. Because these rulings were not generally published, their contents were often known only to the parties who received them. Since decretals frequently decided issues of considerable general interest, however, practising canonists, law teachers, and judges soon began to assemble collections of the decretals that happened to come to their notice. In this way private decretal collections soon emerged as important reference works for canon lawyers who wished to keep abreast of current law.[29]

Medieval canonists treated privileges and dispensations as further sources of law, alongside of customs and decretals.[30] A privilege meant a variation from the general rules of law that granted a favour to some particular person or class of persons.[31] Thus licences to teach or to practise law or medicine, for example, are legal privileges, since they confer upon recipients the right to perform certain

---

27. On these issues see especially W. W. Buckland and Arnold D. McNair, *Roman law and common law: A comparison in outline*, 2nd edn by F. H. Lawson (Cambridge, 1965), pp.6–10; F. H. Lawson, *A common lawyer looks at the civil law* (Ann Arbor, 1953; repr. Westport, CT, 1977), pp.83–6; and John P. Dawson, *The Oracles of the Law* (Ann Arbor, 1968), pp.119–21, 374–502.
28. Gratian, C. 25 q. 2 c. 16.
29. See also pp.53–5.
30. See generally Le Bras, Lefebvre, and Rambaud, *L'âge classique*, pp.487–532.
31. Gratian, D. 3 c. 3.

functions for pay, which the rest of the population is not allowed to do. Dispensations resemble privileges since both involve exceptions to the ordinary operations of the law, but there is a significant difference between the two. Privileges bestow a positive favour not generally enjoyed by most people, while dispensations exempt some person or group from legal obligations binding on the rest of the population or class to which they belong. Canonical privileges might be acquired by prescription, as a special type of custom and subject to the normal limitations upon customary prescription, while dispensations ordinarily could not. Neither privileges nor dispensations could be given legitimately without just cause.[32] Some decretists, notably Huguccio, maintained that a dispensation must be granted only for the common good, not simply for the benefit of the person who received it, but the decretalists largely ignored this opinion.

One among many fundamental rules of Roman law that medieval canonists adopted involved a presumption still in force: although in principle no one can be obliged to obey a law that he does not know about, nonetheless the law presumes that everyone does know what the law demands of them.[33] As a matter of ordinary experience, of course, that presumption is certainly untrue for most people in most places most of the time. Despite that, however, such a presumption is practically necessary to make a legal system workable. Without it, a profession of ignorance would be sufficient to exculpate virtually everyone from almost every kind of misbehaviour – save, perhaps, professors of law and the legislators who framed the law at issue. Convention, both in Roman law and in the Middle Ages, exempted several large classes of persons from this presumption: minors, madmen, soldiers, and, in most circumstances, women were commonly believed to lack the capacity (in the case of minors and the insane) or the opportunity (in the case of soldiers and women) to know and understand the law. Ignorance of fact, however, unlike ignorance of law

---

32. Johannes Teutonicus, *Glos. ord.* to C. 1 q. 7 d.a.c. 6, v. *ut plerisque.*
33. Dig. 22.6.9 pr. The classical jurist, Paul, distinguished in this passage between ignorance of the law, which must be presumed, and ignorance of fact, which could not necessarily be presumed.

could not necessarily be presumed. Everyone was presumed to be aware of his own actions, to be sure, but it seemed unsafe and unfair to presume that one individual would necessarily know what others have done, unless he had actually witnessed their actions.

Canonists again borrowed from the Roman juristic tradition when they discussed the limits within which law operates. They adopted as a basic premise the principle of the third-century jurist Modestinus, who asserted that 'Law has the power to order, to forbid, to permit, and to punish'.[34] Laws, in addition, must deal with future actions and events, not past ones. Hence laws have no retroactive force: they cannot order, forbid, permit, or punish actions, no matter how wicked or undesirable, that occurred before the law was created.[35] Nor can a law revoke prior transactions, save under exceptional circumstances, when the matter at issue had not been completed at the time of the law's creation and when in addition the legislator expressly provided that the new law encompassed ongoing transactions.[36]

One important limitation on the scope of canon law disappeared during the classical period of its development. Early canonists had generally accepted the premise that canon law was binding only upon Christians. Thus, for example, Jews, pagans, and other non-Christians under Christian rule were not obliged to observe canonical marriage rules that forbade persons related by blood or by legal ties (such as in-laws, for example) to marry one another. Christians, moreover, were not allowed to baptize unwilling pagans or to coerce them into paying the tithes that Christians paid (however grudgingly) to support the church. These still remained standard teachings in Innocent III's time.[37]

Later thirteenth and fourteenth-century canonists found

---

34. Dig. 1.3.7; see, for example, Gratian, D. 3 d.p.c. 3; Rolandus, *Summa*, proem., ed. Thaner, p.3; *Summa 'Elegantius in iure diuino'* 1.24a, ed. Fransen and Kuttner, i, 6.
35. This again was a Roman law principle; see Cod. 1.14.7; also *Summa 'Elegantius in iure diuino'* 1.26, ed. Fransen and Kuttner, i, 7, as well as X 1.2.2.
36. X 1.2.13.
37. X 4.19.8.

it necessary to reconsider these positions and ultimately to abandon them. European Jewry had furnished the model upon which earlier canonists had formed their views about the legal relationship between non-Christians and canon law.[38] Jewish populations, however, tended to be relatively small, stable (save when one ruler or another decided to expel them from his territories), and peaceful. They certainly posed no military threat to Christian rulers and only an occasional fanatic could seriously maintain that they menaced the Christian religious establishment.

Muslims in the Mediterranean basin and pagans along Latin Christendom's eastern frontiers, however, were an altogether different matter. Many Christians considered them a serious threat to Christianity's goal of converting the world and this seemed to justify a policy of encouraging attacks along the frontiers where Christian territories adjoined lands under non-Christian rule. Christian authorities portrayed these incursions as defensive actions designed (so they claimed) to prevent potential infidel aggression. As Europeans pushed further to the east and south during the thirteenth century – this was, after all, the era of crusades in the eastern Mediterranean, the *Reconquista* in Iberia, and Germanic invasion and colonization in central Europe and the Baltic – canonists needed to adapt their treatment of relations with non-Christians to novel situations. They needed in particular to fashion a rationale for Christian conquest and expropriation of infidel property. This in turn required reconsideration of previous positions.

Pope Innocent IV, for one, asserted that although infidels were of course not part of Christ's church, they were nonetheless part of Christ's flock and accordingly subject to Christ's vicar.[39] The pope also insisted, however, that non-Christians could legitimately own property, for the right of ownership, he believed, was an element of the natural law. Hostiensis, on the other hand, rejected

---

38. On this complex and difficult topic see Walter Pakter, *Medieval canon law and the Jews*, Abhandlungen zur rechtswissenschaftlichen Grundlagenforschung, vol. 68 (Ebelsbach, 1988).
39. Innocent IV, *Apparatus* to X 3.34.8 §4 (Frankfurt, 1570; repr. 1968), fol. 430ra.

Innocent IV's argument. The incarnation, Hostiensis claimed, had irreversibly altered world history. One consequence of this was that those who failed to accept Christ's faith lost any legitimate right to power, whether over government or over property.[40] The diametrically opposed positions of Innocent IV and Hostiensis on this issue defined the context within which discussion of Christian expansion and the property rights of the unconverted was to continue for half a millennium.[41]

By the beginning of the fourteenth century most canonists had come around to the view that the pope, as Vicar of Christ, possessed the power to make laws that applied even to non-Christians. Although historians usually refer to Pope Boniface VIII's well-known bull, *Unam sanctam* (1302), in the context of the power struggle between the papacy and the French king Philip the Fair, *Unam sanctam* in fact summed up rather neatly the new papal claims to jurisdiction over non-Christians.[42]

The thirteenth century was an age of spectacular innovation in nearly every department of Western life. The century witnessed the birth and flowering of the mendicant religious orders, the first appearance of universities, the development of scholastic theology and philosophy, the burgeoning of sophisticated poetry in the vernacular languages, and the invention or improvement of numerous scientific, technical, and mechanical devices. It also produced massive amounts of new law and new legal doctrines nearly everywhere in the Latin West. In England, for example, the thirteenth century was an age rich in legislation, from Magna Carta (1215) to the Statutes of Mortmain (1279), Westminster II (1285), and *De tallagio non concedendo* (1297). It was also the age of Bracton and of court reports in the Year Books. Thirteenth-century France likewise witnessed a great wave of legal innovation, including a long string of royal *Ordonnances*, the

40. Hostiensis, *Lectura* to X 3.34.8 §14 (Venice, 1581; repr. Turin, 1965), lib. 3, fol. 128rb-va.
41. On these issues see particularly James Muldoon, *Popes, lawyers, and infidels: The church and the non-Christian world, 1250–1550* (Philadelphia, 1979).
42. *Extrav. comm.* 1.8.1. For a translation see Brian Tierney, *The crisis of church and state* (Englewood Cliffs, NJ, 1964), pp.188–9.

establishment of the Parlement de Paris, and the appearance of Beaumanoir's *Coutumes de Beauvaisis.* Similarly in thirteenth-century Germany we have the *Sachsenspiegel,* in Spain the *Siete partidas* and the *Fuero real,* and in Italy the *Liber Augustalis,* as well as an astonishing wealth of municipal statutes.

Canon law, too, grew enormously in volume and complexity during this period. The thirteenth-century *ius novum* comprised thousands of papal decretals, the hundreds of constitutions adopted by three great general councils (the Fourth Lateran in 1215, the First Council of Lyon in 1245, and the Second Council of Lyon in 1274), as well as the canons that countless provincial and local councils and synods adopted.

This tremendous expansion of available law further complicated the technical problems of interpreting law. Legal texts are notoriously much easier to read than to understand. A superficial, uncritical glance through many legal texts can, and often does, produce the illusion that their statements are straightforward and that the casual reader has grasped its meaning without great effort. If the reader pauses for a moment and tries to formulate some concrete situations to which a given section or paragraph might apply, however, it soon becomes apparent that applications will often raise issues that the text does not clearly or specifically address. Legal texts are typically couched in general terms and abstract language, since they enunciate rules meant to be applied generally. But analysis of the fit between the general rule and specific situations often reveals troublesome gaps and bulges. This is why law teachers have for centuries employed hypothetical questions, based on notional situations, as tools for legal analysis and instruction. The task of legal interpretation is to fill in the gaps between legal texts and human situations so far as possible.

How this works will become clearer if we examine some specific problem, such as for example the question of coerced consent to marriage. Gratian raised the issue in question two of case thirty-one in the *Decretum,* where he posed the question: 'Can a daughter be given to anyone against her will?' He then examined the discussions of this problem by four authorities and concluded: 'These authorities clearly show that no one is to be married to another save by free will.'[43] That seems a simple, straightforward rule and no doubt will strike most people as a reasonable and fair conclusion to the issue.

But what precisely does 'free will' mean here? Suppose, for example, that a young man and a young woman are frolicking in bed with each other, when suddenly her father flings open the door, surprises the couple in the act of intercourse, and demands that the man marry his daughter immediately, then and there. Pope Alexander III (1159–81) had to address precisely that situation and ruled that even if the bridegroom had been somewhat disconcerted and frightened under the circumstances, nevertheless he had consented to marry 'by free will', unless, the pope added, he had acted in response to fear so great that it 'would move a constant man'.[44] The 'constant man' was a mythical creature invented by classical Roman jurists as a benchmark against which to measure degrees of coercion.[45] They described this fictitious figure as 'constant' in the sense that he was courageous, resolute, and steadfast in character; one who was not easily frightened and who was fully capable of standing up against idle threats or bullying tactics. In short the 'constant man' stood for the kind of person that Roman patricians liked to think that they were, or at least that they ought to be.[46]

What precisely did the 'constant man' criterion mean for real people in actual situations? In another decretal Alexander III held that a child whose parents had induced him 'with violence' to agree to a betrothal was not bound to honour the agreement because he had been forced to consent.[47] From this case it appears that when adult

43. C. 31 q. 2 d.p.c. 4.
44. X 4.1.15 *Veniens ad nos*.
45. Dig. 4.2.6 (Gaius).
46. The 'constant man' bears a close resemblance to his much younger cousin, the 'reasonable man', who figures so prominently as a benchmark in the common law of torts. On this 'excellent but odious character' see William L. Prosser, *The law of torts*, 5th edn by W. Page Keeton et al. (St Paul, MN, 1984), pp.173–85 and the classic description in the fictional case of Fardell v. Potts, reported in A. P. Herbert, *Uncommon law* (London, 1977), pp.1–6.
47. X 4.2.9 *De illis qui*.

authority figures inflict actual violence upon a minor child, that constitutes 'fear sufficient to move a constant man'. But what about violent menaces against a child without actual implementation of those threats? Urban III (1185–87) instructed the archbishop of Pisa that consent given by a nine or ten-year-old girl, 'compelled by threats from her parents' was invalid.[48] The implication here was that the 'fear that would move a constant man' need not necessarily involve actual physical mistreatment. A decretal of Gregory IX (1227–41) confirmed that impression. Pope Gregory ruled that the threat of a grave penalty for failure to consent might induce sufficient fear to invalidate consent so given.[49] Persons who had consented to marriage under duress must take timely action, moreover, if they wished to contest the marriage successfully. A woman who lived with a man for eighteen months after their marriage could no longer expect the courts to believe that she had consented unwillingly, according to a decretal of Clement III (1187–91).[50]

These decretals brought the question a long way from Gratian's statement that marital consent must be given 'by free will'. They established a standard, namely that of the 'constant man' and specified in some circumstances what that meant. Even so, the precise limits of permissible pressure remained undefined. Here judges must resort to interpretation to determine just where the situation before them fell within this web of rules. Obviously the court must take into account the age, gender, and status of complainants. In one case when a father threatened to disinherit his daughter should she refuse to marry a prospective husband, the father was held to have exceeded the permissible limits of paternal coercion. Similarly when a widow's brother threatened to strip her of her property unless she agreed to marry a suitor he had chosen, a judge held the marriage invalid. These seem to have been situations in which the complainant was economically so dependent that refusal to submit to the threat would have

---

48. X 4.2.11 *Et literis.*
49. X 4.1.29 *Gemma.*
50. X 4.1.21 *Ad id.*

been likely to lead to penury. But a threat to deprive a family of 'a certain portion of land', while it might entail economic loss, did not carry the same potential for disaster and hence a judge held it insufficient to warrant a nullity decree. Actual violence, such as beating a young woman with staves to force her to consent, might nullify the marriage. But an implicit threat of beating, such as when members of the bridal party turned up carrying staves – which they claimed they needed to vault over ditches on their way to the wedding – was deemed inadequate to instil fear in a 'constant man'.[51]

Canonical judges, therefore, constantly had to analyse the texts of Gratian and the *Liber extra* to determine whether the situation they dealt with fell within the assigned limits. Teachers in the law schools prescribed in considerable detail the criteria that judges should use in making these determinations when the law left them room for discretion, as it did, for example, in dealing with coerced marital consent.

Interpretation of law rested upon a basic premise, known to canonists from Roman law, that judgments about the application of a law should be guided by its *causa*, that is the legislator's reason for making the law.[52] Where the legislator's purpose was clear, it was improper to twist the terms of the law in order to avoid compliance with it. Interpretation became far more difficult, however, where the law was ambiguous or expressed in such a way that the legislator's purpose was uncertain.[53]

Medieval legal analysis also relied in part upon rules derived from then current grammatical theory concerning the properties and signification of words. Among these were rules such as the ones that taught that general terms should be understood to apply to every member of the

51. These cases are all taken from Richard H. Helmholz, *Marriage litigation in medieval England*, Cambridge studies in English legal history (Cambridge, 1974), pp.90–4.
52. Gratian, C. 22 q. 5. c. 11; C. 25 q. 1 d.p.c. 16 §2; cf. Dig. 1.3.25 (Modestinus).
53. Bernard of Parma, *Glos. ord.* to X 1.4.8 v. *nec iure communi*; cf. Dig. 14.1.20 and 32.15.1.

designated group,[54] and that indefinite expressions should be read as universal terms.[55] Interpretation of statements in legal texts must also be guided by the context within which the law appeared. Judges should not focus their attention so sharply on the individual words of a legal text that they lost sight of the meaning of the text as a whole. Instead judges needed to consider the meaning of an entire sentence or passage to determine its proper sense.[56]

Other principles of juristic interpretation sought to distinguish between situations in which a narrow or restrictive interpretation was appropriate and those that called for a broader, more expansive application of the law's provisions. One key principle held that broad interpretation was appropriate in situations that would maintain a person's juridical status, while strict interpretation was in order for actions that would alter it.[57] Thus, when the resolution of an issue was unclear, the judge was obliged to extend the benefit of the doubt to defendants rather than plaintiffs, since doing so would maintain the *status quo ante*. Similarly, if property rights were at issue, the judge ought to favour the possessor; and when the validity of a contract was questioned, the judge should resolve uncertain evidence in favour of validity. In marriage cases, likewise, doubtful issues ought to be resolved in favour of the marriage; and when the validity of a will was disputed, doubts should also work in favour of validity.

Canonists further resorted in many situations to analogical reasoning as an interpretative strategy. When the meaning and intent of a law taken by itself seemed impenetrable, a judge could legitimately try to clarify the matter by comparing it with parallel passages, not only in the *Decretum* and the *Liber extra*, but also in the *Digest* and

---

54. 'Verba generalia generaliter sunt intelligenda': Johannes Teutonicus, *Glos. ord.* to D. 19 c. 1 v. *dicendo*; Bernard of Parma, *Glos. ord.* to X 5.40.17 v. *nomine terrae*; Accursius, *Glos. ord.* to Dig. 37.4.1 v. *in infinitum*; cf. Dig. 1.3.8 and 50.17.147.

55. 'Indefinita locutio aequipollet universali': Bernard of Parma, *Glos. ord.* to X 1.29.37 v. *vices suas*.

56. 'Non verbum ex verbo, sed sensum ex sensu transferri, quia plerumque dum proprietas verborum attenditur, sensus veritatis amittitur,' X 5.40.8; cf. Dig. 1.3.24.

57. VI reg. jur. 15: 'Odia restringi et favores convenit ampliari'.

Code of Justinian. Thus passages where there was no doubt about the meaning of a term or a phrase might help to explain its usage in other passages where it seemed ambiguous. This practice, incidentally, explains why canonistic commentaries and treatises so often cite lengthy strings of parallel passages in other parts of the law. Indeed some early canonistic glosses consisted almost entirely of cross-references to parallel or related passages elsewhere in the law books.

The date of a law might be another significant element in its interpretation, especially where two laws seemed inconsistent with one another. If one of the conflicting laws was later than the other, the judge could presume that the more recent law derogated the earlier one – but only if the later law expressly referred to the earlier law. If no such reference appeared in the text, then the judge must somehow try to reconcile the apparent conflict. Where two laws were of the same age, the special law derogated the general law, unless the special law stated explicitly that its provisions constituted an exception to the rule.[58] Thus, for example, a general law required Christians to pay one-tenth of their annual wheat harvest to their parish priest.[59] A later decretal, however, exempted properties farmed by members of the Cistercian order from this requirement.[60] Here we have a special law, in the sense that it confers an exemption from the general law on a specific group, namely the Cistercians. This special law, however, must be strictly interpreted, so that other religious communities, such as the Cluniacs or the Franciscans to whom the decretal made no reference, cannot claim the exemption. The decretal expressly stated that it was granting an exception to the general requirement to pay tithes and thus did not derogate the general law that obliges all Christians to pay tithes on the grain they harvest. A related rule of law likewise provided that when a law granted a favour to a broad class of persons, judges must allow that class of persons to enjoy only those benefits that the legislator can

58. Johannes Andreae, *Glos. ord.* to VI reg. jur. 34 v. *generi.* Canon law borrowed this rule from Dig. 50.17.80.
59. Gratian, C. 16 q. 7 c. 4.
60. X 3.30.10.

reasonably have intended to include.[61] Thus the Cistercians' exemption from tithes, for example, cannot be interpreted to allow them exemptions from other ecclesiastical taxes.

Other basic principles of canonical interpretation included the rule that where a law's meaning was unclear, it should be applied as narrowly as possible.[62] Here again canonists preferred in doubtful situations to leave the existing situation unchanged. Above all, canonical doctrine exhorted judges and other interpreters of the law to aim at maintaining a fair balance between parties to the disputes that came before them. One decretal counselled: 'In matters that the law does not expressly cover, proceed with equity ever in mind, always choosing the more humane course, as the persons and cases, times and places may seem to require'.[63]

Medieval canon lawyers also introduced a new and revolutionary approach to criminal law, one that lies at the root of most modern theories of criminal justice. This was the canonical theory of culpability, which taught that the intentions of the offender must be an essential element in determining guilt or innocence. Earlier approaches to criminal law had centred on determining what harm the offender had caused and the appropriate compensation that the victim and the community ought to receive. Canonical teachers and writers in the late twelfth and early thirteenth centuries, however, based their ideas about criminal law upon the church's penitential tradition, in which the degree of guilt was primarily a function of the mental and moral intent of the sinner, while the harm that his sinful actions caused became a secondary consideration. Under this theory, what the sinner actually did might be morally neutral, but his reasons for doing it could readily convert a morally indifferent act into a grievous offence.

---

61. 'In generali concessione non veniunt ea quae quis non esset concessurus'; VI reg. jur. 81; cf. Dig. 20.1.6, as well as VI 5.10.2.
62. 'In obscuris minimum est sequendum', VI reg. jur. 30. This was a well-established principle in classical Roman law; Dig. 50.17.9.
63. Pope Honorius III, in X 1.36.11: 'In his vero super quibus ius non videtur expressum, procedas aequitate servata, semper in humaniorem partem declinando secundum quod personas et causas, loca et tempora videris postulare'. See above, p.156.

Thus, for example, if I buy an axe, the purchase of the tool is in itself neither good nor bad. But if I buy an axe in order to silence my noisy neighbour once and for all, my murderous intention converts the purchase into a serious sin, even if I fail to follow through and actually never use the axe for anything except chopping firewood. Approached in this way, guilt resides primarily in the internal, subjective attitude that exists in the mind and will of the actor, rather than in some external, objective action or event in which the actor participates. Canonists who started from these premises inevitably constructed a criminal jurisprudence that differed radically from the traditional approach, which considered the act first and foremost, and either ignored the actor's intent or assigned only secondary importance to it. Medieval canonistic theories of culpability underlie the modern criminal law's concern with determining whether an event was voluntary or involuntary, whether it was premeditated or impulsive, whether it was an isolated offence or part of a habitual pattern of behaviour, whether the outcome of the offender's deeds resulted from deliberate, purposeful action or was accidental and unforeseen.[64]

Laws are no more immortal than other human artifacts and medieval canonists needed to define the circumstances under which a law ceased to remain in force. The most straightforward way to achieve this was through formal repeal. The author of a law, or his successor in office, or his ecclesiastical superior had the power to revoke a law that he had made.[65] These authorities could accomplish this in any of three ways. The first and most obvious was to revoke the law directly by a decree that expressly repealed it. It was also possible to achieve the same effect by indirect revocation, that is by adopting a new law that contained provisions contrary to the old law and also included an abrogation clause, such as 'previous provisions to the contrary notwithstanding', or some similar formula. The

---

64. The classic study of the history of canonistic culpability theories is Stephan Kuttner, *Kanonistische Schuldlehre von Gratian bis auf die Dekretalen Gregors IX.*, Studi e testi, vol. 64 (Vatican City, 1935). See also R. C. Van Caenegem, *An historical introduction to private law*, trans. D. E. L. Johnston (Cambridge, 1992), p.67.
65. X 1.6.2 and 5.4.1.

third possibility was simply to adopt a new law that contained provisions contrary to an old one. This constituted a tacit revocation of the old law, although it carried with it the danger that people, including judges, might fail to notice the contradiction and this in turn could potentially lead to erroneous judgments and other undesirable consequences.

Canonists, unlike Roman lawyers, also taught that laws ceased to have effective force when the reason that had prompted them ceased to exist. Gratian enunciated this principle in his *Decretum* and Innocent III affirmed it explicitly in a decretal of 1206.[66]

This principle, which seemed simple enough in the abstract, proved extremely complex in practice. It certainly offered canonistic writers ample room for discussion and interpretation, and they took advantage of the opportunity with enthusiasm. They soon concluded that this principle evidently could not apply to natural law or divine law, which are by definition unchanging. It must therefore apply exclusively to positive law. Further debate centred on the meaning of 'cause' in this context. In Aristotle's fourfold classification of 'causes', did the term refer here to the material, the efficient, the formal, or the final 'cause' of the law? Jurists soon discovered that the Aristotelian classification was inappropriate for discussion of the issues that concerned them and distinguished instead between the 'impulsive cause' and the 'final cause' of a law. By 'impulsive cause' they meant the situation or problem that had induced the legislator to adopt the measure at issue. By 'final cause' they meant the aim or objective that the legislator intended the law to achieve. Ultimately a consensus of sorts emerged that in case of doubt it was preferable to assume that the 'impulsive cause' rather than the 'final cause' was at issue.[67]

The issues raised in discussions of the principles of

---

66. C. 1 q. 1 c. 41; the same principle also appears in several other passages, including D. 61 d.a.c. 9 and C. 1 q. 7. c. 7. Innocent III's decretal appears in X 2.24.26.
67. See H. Krause, 'Cessante causa cessat lex', *Zeitschrift der Savigny-Stiftung für Rechtsgeschichte*, kanontistische Abteilung 46 (1960), 81–111.

canonistic jurisprudence were not solely matters of theoretical interest. Unlike the metaphysical speculations of philosophers or the dogmatic problems that often preoccupied theologians, the musings of academic lawyers on the nature of law and the methods of determining its meaning often had direct relevance to specific human problems and situations. The distance between canonical ideals and practical applications of canonistic theories was relatively short. Teachers of canon law and their students bridged that gap when they practised in the canonical courts, which brought jurisprudential theories face to face with the problems and troubles of ordinary Christians.

Chapter 8

CANON LAW AND WESTERN SOCIETIES

Canon law was simultaneously a product of and an integrating component within medieval religion and politics. There was virtually no way to escape its influence. Canonical rules were all-pervasive. They reached, as we have seen, into virtually every nook and cranny of human conduct, both public and private. Even when people flouted canonical norms, as nearly everyone did occasionally, they were often conscious that the rules existed and took pains to disguise, or at least to rationalize, significant departures from them.

Knowledge, however vague, of what those rules required reached down through every level of society – at least that appears to have been true by the high Middle Ages. When issues of consanguineous marriage arose, for example, even ordinary peasants and villagers, although usually illiterate, could often testify in minute detail about their family's marital history back through four or five generations, a feat that presupposes more than a casual acquaintance with the canonistic rules on the matter – and one that few of their modern descendants could probably manage. Literate witnesses in such cases (usually persons from the higher end of the social scale) frequently produced written records of the genealogies that their families maintained as a matter of course.[1] This interest was not entirely prompted by familial piety or antiquarian curiosity. It was shaped, at least in part, by widespread awareness of canonical

---

1. On the transition from oral tradition to written documents see generally Michael T. Clanchy, *From memory to written record: England, 1066–1307*, 2nd edn (Oxford, 1993).

regulations concerning consanguinity and affinity. Court records likewise reflect a surprisingly high level of popular knowledge, even among people of quite humble social status, about canonical doctrines concerning such things as marital consent, usury, the observance of feasts and fasts, and the formalities required for valid wills and testaments.[2]

This was, of course, even more likely to be true among kings, princes, and other worldly potentates, as well as wealthy laymen in general, than it was among tavernkeepers, millers, and peasant farmers. Persons of ample means among the influential classes could, when necessary, secure the services of expert legal advisers to pilot them through the labyrinth of canonical rules. Rulers and other powerful persons, both lay and clerical, as well as religious communities, municipalities, and other institutions, found it prudent either to maintain a resident canon lawyer in their households or, more commonly, to grant pensions to one or more of them as a long-term retainer. Trained canonists routinely served as ambassadors, spokesmen, and negotiators for both great and small corporations, cities, and individual potentates. Use of canonists for these purposes became especially common during the thirteenth and early fourteenth centuries. After the mid-fourteenth century men trained in civil law gradually began to displace canonists in many of these roles.

The boundaries between canon law and civil law remained highly permeable throughout the Middle Ages and well into modern times. The *ius commune* on the Continent, which drew upon both of the learned laws, provided the underlying platform upon which many secular legal systems rested until the nineteenth century, and in some respects even into the twentieth century. The two learned laws depended so heavily upon one another that it

2. Richard H. Helmholz, *Marriage litigation in medieval England* (Cambridge, 1974), pp.79–85 and Daniel Waley, *Siena and the Sienese in the thirteenth century* (Cambridge, 1991), pp.140–2, 147–50 provide examples of this. For popular guides to elementary canon law see also Roderich von Stintzing, *Geschichte der populären Literatur des römisch-kanonischen Rechts in Deutschland am Ende des fünfzehnten und im Anfang des sechszehnten Jahrhunderts* (Leipzig, 1867; repr. Aalen, 1959).

is often difficult or misleading to classify one or another legal scholar or commentary as civilian or canonist. Although university curricula and degrees distinguished sharply between civilians and canonists, the symbiosis between them was close, if not always cordial.

This tight intertwining of canon law with secular law, and of both with ecclesiastical and royal politics, had marked consequences for relations between the church and civil authorities. Major medieval conflicts between ecclesiastical interests and the interests of civil rulers – such as the investiture contest, the Becket controversy in England, the conflict between the Hohenstaufen emperors and the popes, the struggle between Boniface VIII and Philip the Fair, to mention only a few dramatic examples – invariably had conflict-of-laws issues at their very core. In trying to make sense of those issues, academic canonists in the thirteenth century had to explore the legitimacy and the limits of both papal and royal power. The conclusions of those investigations turned out to have broad implications. Canonistic speculations about the relationship of head and members in ecclesiastical corporations suggested to political writers a rationale for limiting the power of monarchs over their subjects through the parliamentary institutions that appeared in civil societies nearly everywhere in Western Europe during the thirteenth and fourteenth centuries. Theologians and others during the fifteenth-century conciliar crisis also drew upon those same canonistic sources for arguments to support their project of limiting papal power by making popes responsible to general councils.

Medieval canon law was thus a good deal more than simply a set of religious regulations with which pious persons might choose to comply. Rather, the canons embodied a system of law often parallel to, sometimes in conflict with, and occasionally victorious over, the competing civil jurisdictions of kings and princes. Canon law offered litigants in many civil controversies an alternative forum in which to air their disputes and seek relief from wrongs. For persons accused of crimes, the canonical courts offered a system of justice that demanded more rigorous proof than secular jurisdictions frequently did before pronouncing guilt; and even (perhaps especially) for the convicted, canonical tribunals provided a potential haven from the savage vindictiveness that was so common in royal and customary law courts.

Canonical courts also had their less benign side. Their procedures were intricate and formal and readily became protracted and costly as well. Judges and other court officials were often accused of venality and while those charges may have exaggerated the frequency and scope of corruption, there can be little doubt that many complaints were well-founded. Canonical judges were empowered to inquire into the most intimate and personal corners of people's lives and in consequence acquired a reputation for intrusiveness and censoriousness. This odious reputation was enhanced by the development of inquisitorial procedures for detecting and punishing 'occult' crimes. Inquisitorial procedure stripped the accused of most of the safeguards that earlier church authorities had devised to protect defendants against convictions on inadequate evidence. The rationale for this change of policy asserted that the older procedural safeguards resulted in ineffective administration of the judicial system. The conventional rules, according to partisans of the new criminal procedure, too often allowed the guilty to escape unpunished and thereby undermined the general welfare of Christian society. In effect they argued that the end – punishing criminals – justified the means, that is, disregarding defendants' rights. This is an argument that is still heard, for these issues, like the poor, are always with us. Inquisitorial procedure allowed church courts to pursue rumours and complaints, not only concerning the actions and behaviour of the faithful, but about their beliefs, thoughts, and opinions as well. Indeed, church courts often penalized persons convicted of harbouring unorthodox ideas far more harshly than those whose actions deviated from the canonical norms.

For all its limitations and shortcomings, however, medieval canon law played a central role in medieval political, economic and social life. It was also a significant element in the intellectual ferment of the high Middle Ages. Canonists devised new solutions to problems, old and new, originated fresh approaches to the analysis of institutions, and contributed novel ideas to what has since become the common stock of Western tradition. Canonists, in short, formed one major creative component of the intellectual as well as the practical life of the European Middle Ages.

Canon law regularly attracted a large share of the most talented minds in each of the six or seven generations that lived between the mid-twelfth and the mid-fourteenth century. Theologians, philosophers, and teachers of the liberal arts deplored the worldly lures of the law. Furiously they denounced the ambition and greed that, they claimed, enticed so many bright young men to desert their own schools in favour of the schools of the lawyers. Critics grumbled about the moral and personal shortcomings of lawyers, their penchant for sophistry, their dishonesty, their lack of firm principles. Above all detractors resented the offices, wealth, and power that so many canonists accumulated with apparent ease. It is easy to see this reaction as simple envy, which no doubt did inspire much of the vituperation directed at lawyers. But there was more to the criticisms than jealousy.

The theologians and philosophers had some legitimate points to make in their denigration of the lawyers. The ascendancy of law-trained men within the church had widespread and not always benevolent consequences for the church's leadership. Canon lawyers were trained in large part to analyse problems and to deploy appropriate techniques for coping with them. Practising canonists were expert at finding ways for their clients to achieve their goals without actually breaching the law. With equal aplomb they could devise defences for clients who crossed the legal boundaries, and discover ways to smash through those same defences should their opponents happen to erect them. Practitioners were not apt, one suspects, to spend a great deal of their time worrying about the larger theoretical and moral issues implicit in their day-to-day work – they were content to leave those problems to theologians and the academics in the law faculties.

The worldliness and careerism so evident among the leadership of the Western church during the fifteenth and early sixteenth centuries stemmed in part from the fact that so many bishops, cardinals, and even popes rose from the ranks of the canonists. It seems all too likely that the apparent insensitivity of late medieval popes and their advisers to moral and ethical issues, and their obsession with worldly techniques rather than spiritual goals, owed quite a lot to the predominance of canonical practitioners at the curia. Such episodes as, for example, the campaign to exploit the demand for indulgences to finance the building of the new Basilica of St Peter reflected the pragmatic turn of mind that canonical practitioners often cultivated.[3]

Not all the later medieval canonists who attained high office in the church were shallow, unreflective careerists, to be sure, just as not all canonists of the classical period had measured up to the intellectual calibre of Huguccio, Hostiensis, or Innocent IV. Scholarly and thoughtful writers such as Peter of Ancharano (ca. 1330–1416), Cardinal Zabarella (1360–1417), and Panormitanus (1386–1445), for example, continued to appear and to enunciate fresh ideas, new insights into old questions, and novel solutions to the problems of their age.

As the law itself became increasingly intricate and technical, however, styles of investigation and genres of canonistic writing also experienced a transformation. Ambitious attempts at synthesis gave way to small-scale treatises upon increasingly minute technical problems. Canonistic *summae* in the style of the classical age became increasingly rare in the fourteenth and fifteenth centuries, although those that did appear showed a marked increase in size and complexity, since they had to take account of an ever-growing volume of canonical scholarship. A characteristic genre of canonical writing in this period was the monograph on some specialized topic, such as arbitration techniques, the taxation of litigation costs, intestate succession, provision to benefices, precedence in liturgical processions, or the privileges of academic rank.[4] Another favourite genre was the *consilium*, which analysed in great detail the law relevant to a some highly specific

3. Harold J. Grimm, *The reformation era, 1500–1650*, 2nd edn (New York, 1973), pp.89–90.
4. A vast array of these was collected and published under the auspices of Pope Gregory XIII (1572–85) in the *Tractatus universi iuris*. 22 vols in 28 (Venice, 1584–86).

situation. Some late medieval legal experts compiled collections of replies that they or others had written in response to inquiries in real cases, while others simply used the *consilium* as a literary vehicle for discussion of complex legal problems. Late medieval canonists also produced numerous aids to legal scholarship, such as dictionaries and digests or epitomes, that were increasingly necessary to locate relevant material within the vast body of legal literature – 'the ocean of law', as some described it.

António Agustín (1517–86) inaugurated an approach to the study of canon law quite different from the conventional one. A Spanish canonist, trained at Padua and Bologna, he became the first major scholar to apply to canon law the techniques of philological and linguistic analysis that had become fashionable among French humanist jurists a generation earlier.[5] Agustín was interested in restoring the texts of the classical canon law to their original state. He devoted his scholarly career to a painstaking comparison of early legal manuscripts in an effort to clear away the additions and errors that generations of manuscript copyists had introduced into the original texts. This humanistic style of jurisprudence won the favour of several sixteenth-century popes. In 1566 Pope Pius V (1566–72) appointed a commission of cardinals and scholars to prepare more reliable texts of the classical law. The Roman Correctors (*Correctores Romani*), as they were called, completed their task in 1580 and in 1582 Pope Gregory XIII (1572–85) gave official papal approval to their labours and ordered that all subsequent editions of the *Corpus iuris canonici* should reproduce their text of the law.[6]

As the numbers of canonists multiplied and canonistic expertise became an increasingly reliable path to positions of dignity, power, and generous emoluments, it is scarcely surprising that many canonists should have identified their professional interests and prerogatives with maintenance of the status quo. Canon law became a bastion of conservative,

---

5. On this see Donald R. Kelley, *Foundations of modern historical scholarship: Language, law, and history in the French Renaissance* (New York, 1970).
6. Alfons M. Stickler, *Historia iuris canonici latini* (Turin, 1950), pp.214–15; see also the *Prolegomena* of Emil Friedberg to his edition of the *Corpus*, vol. 1, cols LXXVI–LXXX.

and at times blatantly reactionary, sentiment within the late medieval church. Critics of the Roman church frequently identified what they most disliked about the medieval religious establishment with canon law and canonists. It was certainly not by chance, for example, that when Martin Luther (1483–1546) wanted a symbol in 1520 to represent his rejection of Roman authority, he chose to pitch a copy of the *Liber extra* into the fire.[7] Likewise when King Henry VIII (1510–47) broke with Rome, the immediate subject of dispute was a fine point of canonical marriage law and both monarch and pope defended their positions with ample citations of canon law and canonistic opinions.[8]

In the aftermath of the Protestant Reformation, canon law experienced renewed growth and importance in those parts of Europe that retained their allegiance to the Roman church. The Council of Trent (1545–63) made numerous significant changes in the church's substantive law, in response to criticisms from both Catholics and Protestants. Perhaps even more fundamental, the council revamped the processes whereby Roman canon law was created, interpreted, and applied. The council erected a formidable bureaucracy of specialized Roman congregations. Each congregation or permanent commission was headed by a cardinal assisted by other members of the curia. The congregation employed a staff of specialists, many of them trained canonists, who handled the bulk of its day-to-day business. The cardinal in charge of a congregation was in effect a department head within the curial bureaucracy, while the other members of the congregation acted as his advisers and administrative officers. Each congregation was responsible within its sphere of jurisdiction both for determining how existing canons should be implemented and also for tailoring and, when necessary, reshaping the law to fit the problems and circumstances that it had to deal with. The consequence of this transformation of the Roman church's central government was to concentrate power and responsibility for creating law and implementing policy in the curia. The decrees of the various

---

7. Grimm, *Reformation era*, pp.108–9.
8. Henry Ansgar Kelly, *The matrimonial trials of Henry VIII* (Stanford, 1976).

congregations amounted to a body of new statute law, while their decisions constituted for most practical purposes a supplementary body of case law that bishops everywhere adopted as guides for dealing with similar matters in their own dioceses.[9]

Although protestant Christians in principle rejected the canon law of the medieval church, they often retained a substantial part of its regulations and policies. This was particularly evident in the Anglican church, where medieval canon law remained a notable force long after the break with Rome. Various sixteenth-century projects for the creation of a reformed English canon law foundered, with the result that a substantial part of the law of the early modern Anglican church remained virtually identical with medieval canon law. Historians have only begun to explore the causes and consequences of this remarkable continuity.[10]

Evangelical Protestants on the Continent typically cast off a good deal more of the heritage of medieval canon law than did their Anglican brethren in England. Even so, marked elements of continuity remained between the older law and the new discipline of the established protestant churches, perhaps most notably within the German Lutheran tradition.[11] Nonconformist protestant groups, however, vehemently rejected not only the rules embodied in the canon law of the medieval church, but the very idea of canon law itself. Baptists and Quakers, for example, believed that the Scriptures and the Holy Spirit were the only authentic Christian guides to salvation. Medieval canon law, in their view, was an all-too-human invention that had led countless men and women into religious error.

9. Early modern historians have barely begun to explore the thousands of decrees and decisions these Roman Congregations published, to say nothing of their vast archives of unpublished documents. One study that does make use of this material is John T. Noonan's *Power to dissolve: Lawyers and marriages in the courts of the Roman curia* (Cambridge, MA, 1972), which demonstrates the wealth of evidence that these sources can yield.

10. Richard H. Helmholz, *Roman canon law in Reformation England* (Cambridge, 1990).

11. For an overview see Peter Landau, 'Kirchenverfassungen' in *Theologische Realenzyklopädie* xix, pp.110–65 at 147–55.

Other protestant groups, such as Congregationalists, maintained that the autonomous local churches described in the Acts of the Apostles and the Pauline letters were the proper models for Christians to imitate. Individual congregations, they believed, must be responsible for making and enforcing whatever rules their members deemed necessary and appropriate for their community.

Despite fierce disagreements in post-Reformation Europe and the Americas over the role of religious law in Christian life, numerous elements of the medieval canonistic tradition remain embedded in the civil laws of modern national states. Laws concerning marriage, family relationships, inheritance, sexual conduct, and other types of personal behaviour, for example, often retain substantial elements of medieval church law at their core. Western societies to this day vigorously resist efforts to displace those core elements. The history of divorce laws in the nineteenth and twentieth centuries demonstrates this with particular clarity.[12] The tax treatment of churches and other religious bodies in most Western nations, to cite another obvious example, is predicated on the medieval canonical policy that exempted church property from the usual fiscal obligations that governments impose on other corporate groups.

. . .

CONCLUSIONS

Christian canon law began, as we have seen, as a relatively modest body of regulations that prescribed norms for the conduct of worship and the exercise of authority within the Christian communities that dotted the Mediterranean world during the first three centuries of the common era. From the reign of Constantine onward, the church's legal system grew and flourished under the patronage of Christian emperors. As the church acquired property, converts, and prestige, its leaders also acquired new powers of coercion and control. Under these circumstances, the church's laws inevitably multiplied as well. As new problems

---

12. Roderick Phillips, *Putting asunder: A history of divorce in Western society* (Cambridge, 1988); Lawrence Stone, *Road to divorce: England, 1530–1987* (Oxford, 1990).

presented themselves and new opportunities appeared, canon law responded, with the result that the church's regulatory system became increasingly voluminous and more complex.

The 'German' invasions of the fifth century, the settlement of the newly-arrived peoples on former Roman soil, and ultimately the replacement of Roman government by the Germanic kingdoms, momentarily stripped the church and its leaders of much of the power and many of the privileges they had amassed under the Christian Empire. Within a short time, however, leading churchmen established a *modus vivendi* with the new regimes. As Germanic rulers converted to Christianity or, in a few cases, abandoned allegiance to the Arian Christian faith for the catholic version, bishops and other church authorities reasserted claims to judge the moral behaviour of all Christians and, where necessary, to impose sanctions upon those who fell short of the prescribed standards.

The new rulers, like their Roman predecessors, saw the church's hierarchy as a useful, indeed a nearly indispensable, adjunct to their own regimes. Germanic kings found it politic to shower gifts and favours, property and privileges upon the church. In return, the rulers expected support, both moral and political, from the church's leaders. Shrewd rulers also endeavoured to ensure the loyalty of bishops and other ecclesiastical dignitaries by influencing, or, when possible, even dictating the selection of those who filled key offices within the church.

Clerical objections to such interference in churchly business by laymen, even royal or noble laymen, surfaced vigorously, however, and took the form of a powerful church reform movement whose members had secured control of the papacy by the mid-eleventh century. Reformers looked upon canon law as an essential tool in their efforts to rescue the church from what they regarded as the evils of lay control. The results, as we have seen, were renewed efforts to strengthen the church's legal system. These efforts involved making the law itself more accessible through the compilation of authoritative collections of church law and teaching canon law systematically as an intellectual and practical discipline separate from both theology and civil law.

Gratian's *Decretum* in the mid-twelfth century provided the reformed church with a comprehensive textbook of canon law, while the schools where that textbook was studied emerged as powerful engines for reshaping the ecclesiastical establishment to meet the demands of a society that decade by decade became more complex and demanding. By the end of the twelfth century, alumni of the canon law schools had begun to occupy most of the chief seats of power within the church. Armed with a detailed command of the intricacies of substantive law and procedure, trained canon lawyers became indispensable experts upon whom authorities at every level of the hierarchy necessarily relied. Some canonists became popes themselves – Gregory IX, Innocent IV, Boniface VIII, and John XXII are formidable examples – while other canonists secured control not only of the day-to-day operations of the papal judicial system, but also of its diplomatic, financial, and administrative offices as well. Canonists with increasing frequency became cardinals, archbishops, bishops, abbots, or archdeacons in every corner of the Western church. By the mid-thirteenth century canonists dominated a church that was becoming increasingly legalistic with every passing generation.

Reactions against the 'reign of the lawyers'[13] in church affairs proved as inevitable as they were futile. Critics cried out repeatedly that shallow legal opportunists, not wise spiritual giants, complacently occupied the church's thrones of authority, that students preferred to learn lawyerly legerdemain rather than sound theology in the schools, that legalistic sophistry had supplanted fundamental Christian values in church government.[14] The

13. I owe this phrase (as I do much else) to the late Christopher R. Cheney; see *From Becket to Langton: English church government, 1170–1213* (Manchester, 1956), p.5.
14. See, for example, John W. Baldwin, 'Critics of the legal profession: Peter the Chanter and his circle', in *Proceedings of the second international congress of medieval canon law*, MIC, Subsidia, vol. 1 (Vatican City, 1965), pp.249–59; James A. Brundage, 'The ethics of the legal profession: Medieval canonists and their clients', *The Jurist* 33 (1973), 247–58; Walter Holtzmann, 'Propter Sion non tacebo: Zur Erklärung von Carmina Burana 41', *Deutsches Archiv für Erforschung des Mittelalters* 10 (1953), 170–5; Stephan Kuttner, 'Dat

critics protested in vain. Once in command of the church's key institutions, canonists were not prepared to relax their grip readily or soon. Even the stormy fury of the sixteenth-century Reformation failed to shake the canonists' dominance of the Roman establishment and the Counter-Reformation left them, if possible, even more securely in control than before.

Systems of canon law, complete with courts, judges, lawyers, and penal sanctions, still continue to operate in modern Western societies, although in most countries canonical decisions are no longer enforced by civil authorities. Modern canon law relies for its effectiveness on the faithful's voluntary compliance with the determinations of religious tribunals. Members of those Christian communions that maintain systems of canon law – mainly Roman Catholics, Anglicans, and Eastern Orthodox Christians – implicitly agree as a condition of membership in their churches that they will submit themselves and their disputes to canonical judges for adjudication and will comply with their decisions.

In this, of course, the position of modern canon law differs radically from the medieval situation. 'The medieval church was a state,' declared F. W. Maitland, and he added it would be difficult, indeed impossible, to formulate a definition of a state that would not equally well fit the church in the high Middle Ages.[15] True, the medieval

14. (*Continued*)
Galienus opes et sanctio Justiniana', in *Linguistic and literary studies in honor of Helmut A. Hatzfeld*, ed. A. S. Crisavulli (Washington, 1964), pp.237–56, reprinted with original pagination in Kuttner's *History of ideas and doctrines of canon law in the Middle Ages*, 2d edn (London, 1992); John A. Yunck, 'The venal tongue: Lawyers and the medieval satirists', *American Bar Association journal* 46 (1960), 267–70.

15. Frederic William Maitland, *Roman canon law in the Church of England* (London, 1898), p.100, pursues the argument still further: 'The medieval church was a state. Convenience may forbid us to call it a state very often, but we ought to do so from time to time, for we could frame no acceptable definition of a state which would not comprehend the church. What has it not that a state should have? It has laws, lawgivers, law courts, lawyers. It uses physical force to compel men to obey its laws. It keeps prisons. In the thirteenth century, though with squeamish phrases, it pronounces sentence of death. It is no voluntary society. If people are not born into it, they

church shared power with civil governments: in every region canon law operated in tandem with other juridical systems. Royal, regional, and municipal courts each claimed their own spheres of competence, alongside the canonical courts, and each court system had the power to compel the unwilling to conform to its rules. It is also true that canonical jurisdiction and the various civil jurisdictions frequently overlapped one another. This often gave litigants an important tactical tool. By choosing to plead their cases in the courts that seemed most likely to give them the settlement they desired, and to do so speedily and at minimal cost, plaintiffs sought to gain the upper hand over their opponents. Defendants who had the resources and the cunning to manipulate the system could likewise use competing jurisdictional claims to delay and frustrate those who advanced claims against them.[16]

Not only does medieval canon law remain a major source of religious law (at least in those modern churches that identify themselves with the traditions of catholic Christianity), but in addition many vital elements of modern secular legal systems continue to show its influence. The speculations and insights of medieval canonists remain enshrined both within the common law tradition of the English-speaking world and within the civil law heritage of Continental Europeans. This is most obviously true in family law and testamentary law, but canonical tradition is also evident in many other branches of the law – contracts, torts, property law, and corporation law among them. Canonical ideas and techniques even more obviously underlie much of Continental procedure

15. (*Continued*)
   are baptized into it when they cannot help themselves. If they attempt to leave it they are guilty of the crimen laesae maiestatis, and are likely to be burnt. It is supported by involuntary contributions, by tithe and tax. That men believe it to have a supernatural origin does not alter the case. Kings have reigned by divine right, and republics have been founded in the name of God-given liberty.'

16. This situation is in fact reminiscent of the manipulative possibilities inherent in federal systems of government, such as those in the United States and Canada, for example. Here, litigants often have a choice between overlapping court systems, a situation that modern lawyers have also learned to exploit with considerable finesse.

and substantive law as well. Western political thought and, indeed, the idea of constitutional government itself ultimately draw much of their substance and many of their basic premises from debates that raged in the canon law faculties in the twelfth and thirteenth centuries. Medieval canon law, in short, constituted a fundamental formative force in the creation of some of the elemental ideas and institutions that continue to this day to characterize Western societies.

APPENDIX I: THE ROMANO-CANONICAL CITATION SYSTEM

Scholarly treatments of the history of medieval Roman and canon law conventionally employ a system of references to the sources that, when first encountered, may appear mysterious and perplexing, but readily leads to the appropriate texts when properly used and understood. The elements of the citation system are as follows.

. . .

CANON LAW CITATIONS

The Decretum of Gratian

The *Decretum Gratiani*, or *Concordia discordantium canonum*, became the fundamental textbook of canon law in the Middle Ages. The *Decretum* not only comprises a vast repertoire of some 3,945 excerpts or canons drawn from church councils, papal letters, penitentials, and a variety of authoritative writers, such as St Augustine, St Jerome, and other Fathers of the Church, but also attempts (as the work's longer title indicates) to resolve by dialectical reasoning the conflicts and discrepancies between the authorities that it draws upon. Because of its dialectical nature and also because of some oddities in its arrangement, the *Decretum* makes difficult reading for beginners and its train of thought is not always easy to follow. This, in the opinion of some, merely confirms the tradition that Gratian was a law teacher.

Individual sections of Gratian's work usually include two kinds of texts: the canons (*capitula*) themselves and Gratian's comments (*dicta Gratiani*) on the canons. Some *capitula* bear the label *Palea*. These are canons added to the original version of the *Decretum*, perhaps by Gratian's disciple, Paucapalea, or possibly by someone else.

The *Decretum* as a whole consists of three major divisions:

PARS I is divided (perhaps by Paucapalea) into 101 Distinctions (*Distinctiones*), each made up of *capitula* and *dicta* that deal with a single subject or a closely related group of topics. Thus, for example, *Distinctio 1* deals with the species of law in general; *Distinctio 2* deals with the various types of enactments found in Roman law; *Distinctio 3* treats the nature and function of ecclesiastical law, and so-forth. There are all in all 973 canons in *Pars I*.

PARS II consists of 36 *Causae*, or Cases. Each Case describes a situation and then develops one or more questions (*quaestiones*) concerning it. Gratian then discusses each question in turn and cites some authorities that deal with the problem, usually adding *dicta* of his own to address problems raised by discrepancies or conflicts between the canons. *Quaestio 3* of *Causa 33* stands apart from the rest, however, since it is subdivided into seven *Distinctiones* (on the same pattern as *Pars I*) and is known as the *Treatise on penance* (*Tractatus de penitentia*). This awkward arrangement strongly suggests that the *Tractatus de penitentia* may have been added to *Pars II* at some early stage in its history. *Pars II* is by far the longest section of the *Decretum* and comprises some 2,576 *capitula*.

PARS III is known as the *Tractatus de consecratione* and is divided into five Distinctions (*Distinctiones*), with 396 *capitula*. This section of the *Decretum* deals primarily with sacramental and liturgical law. Unlike the first two sections, there are no *dicta* in *Pars III* and this anomaly suggests that it, too, like the *Tractatus de penitentia*, may be a later addition to the primitive text of Gratian's work.

Until fairly recent times it was not usual to cite the canons of the *Decretum* by their numbers – indeed the numbering of the capitula only became uniform in the sixteenth century. Instead, earlier authors generally cited the canons by their opening words. It is not uncommon, however, to find even early commentators referring to the first (and occasionally even the second or third) canon of a *Distinctio or quaestio* as *cap. j* (or *cap. ij,* or *cap. iij*) and the last, next-to-last, or even next-to-next-to-last canon as *cap. fin.* (or *ult.*), *cap. penult.* (or *pen.*, or sometimes just *pe.*), and *cap. antepenult.* respectively. Also, if two or more canons in a given Distinction or question happen to begin with the same word, they may be distinguished, as for example, *c. Si quis i, Si quis ii, Si quis iii.*, etc. Further, when a very lengthy canon is cited, a more precise reference may be given to a portion of it, as *in prin[cipio], init[io], circa med[ium]*, or *in fi[ne]*. Medieval authors commonly introduced citations with a prefatory word, usually *ut* or *ar[gumentum]*. Frequently, too, citations are accompanied by a relational indicator, such as *s[upra]*, or *i[nfra]*, or *in ea[dem] Distinctionem*, [or *Causam*, or *Quaestionem*]. Sometimes, too, a portion of the *Decretum* may be cited by a reference to the topic that it deals with, such as *causa simoniacorum* (= *Causa 1*), *causa monachorum* (= *Causa 2*), or *causa secunda haereticorum* (= *Causa 24*).[1]

CITATION FORMS. Readers will commonly encounter three styles of citation. The first of them may be called the *Obsolete Form*: it was used most commonly by medieval and early modern writers, but since the eighteenth century has gradually fallen out of use. In this form of citation, the major divisions (*Distinctio, Causa, quaestio*) are cited with Roman numerals (although occasionally, even in manuscripts, with Arabic numerals) and the *capitulum* is cited by its opening word or phrase. Thus:

PARS I di. xxxij c. multorum
xxiv § Cum itaque
D. lxxvi § necessario ergo

PARS II C. iii q. i Nulli dubium
xxiii q. viii § hinc datur
iii de pen. totam

PARS III ii de cons. In Christo ii.

A second form of citation is the *Obsolescent Form*. It was commonly employed by writers between the seventeenth

---

1. The *Indices canon, titulorum et capitulorum corporis iuris canonici*, compiled by Xavier Ochoa and Aloisio Diez, Universa biblioteca iuris, Subsidia (Rome, 1964) will be found extremely useful for identifying passages cited according to the older citation forms.

century and the beginning of the twentieth century, although a few authors still use it even now. The obsolescent citation form begins with a reference to the smallest unit (the *capitulum* or *dictum*) usually in Arabic numerals, followed by the largest unit (*Distinctio* or *Causa*), usually in Roman numerals, and then the middle-sized unit (*quaestio*) when required. Citations in obsolescent form look like this:

PARS I   c. 2, D. XXXII
dict. post c. 4, D. XXIV
d. p. c. 8, D. LXXVI

PARS II   c. 5, C. 3 q. 1
dict. p.c. 25, C. XXIII q. 8
c. 24, D. 3 de pen.

PARS III c. 82, D. II de cons.

The third style of citation is the *Modern Form*, which was apparently invented by Edward Gibbon but has become common only during the twentieth century.[2] This citation form proceeds *a maiore ad minorem*, that is, it begins with the largest unit (*Distinctio* or *Causa*), followed by the smaller subdivisions (*quaestio, capitulum,* or *dictum*) in order of size. Citations in the modern style number all units in Arabic numerals. Thus:

PARS I   D. 32 c. 2
D. 24 dict. ante c. 5
D. 76 d. post c. 8

PARS II   C. 3 q. 1 c. 5
C. 23 q. 8 d. p. c. 25
D. 3 de pen. c. 24

PARS III D. 2 de cons. c. 82

---

2. Gibbon makes this claim in *The Decline and Fall of the Roman Empire*, ch. 44, n. 1: 'I have dared to adopt the simple and rational method of numbering the book, the title, and the law.' Gibbon was referring, of course, to Roman civil law texts, whose history he treats in this chapter of *The Decline and Fall*, but the rationale for his citation method applies equally well to canon law.

It is not customary to specify the *Pars* of the *Decretum* in citations, since the citation form itself shows clearly enough which part of the work is meant.[3]

The Quinque compilationes antiquae

Canonists who wrote before 5 September 1234, the date on which Pope Gregory IX promulgated his great decretal collection, often referred to the five earlier decretal collections that were used as textbooks in the canon law schools of the late-twelfth and early-thirteenth centuries. The *Quinque compilationes* fell into disuse soon after 1234 and are rarely cited thereafter by medieval writers. Medieval authors usually referred to the *Compilationes* as *extravagantes* (abbreviated as *ex.* or *extra.*), since the decretals in them circulated outside of the *Decretum*. Each of the five compilations is divided into five books (*libri*) and each book includes canons that deal with more or less homogeneous subject matter. The general topics of the five books were summed up in the mnemonic line: *Iudex, iudicium, clerus, connubium, crimen.*

Each book in turn was subdivided into titles (*tituli*), treating individual aspects of the general topic of the book. Each title, in turn, was composed of chapters (*capitula*), which are arranged in chronological order within the title.[4]

Bernard of Pavia (d. 1213) compiled *Compilatio prima* and probably completed the work in 1191. Medieval writers often referred to it as the *Breviarium Bernardi* or the *Breviarium extravagantium*. It contains 912 chapters arranged in 152 titles. The *capitula* are for the most part papal decretals, although Bernard included some conciliar canons, as well as citations from the Fathers and a few excerpts from Roman and Germanic laws.

Compilatio secunda was the work of John of Wales (Johannes Gallensis), a master and professor of the University of Bologna. He began this work in 1210 and

---

3. Modern scholars usually cite Gratian's *Decretum* from the standard edition by Emil Ludwig Richter, as revised by Emil Friedberg, in the *Corpus iuris canonici*, 2 vols (Leipzig, 1879; repr. Graz, 1959).
4. The standard modern source for these compilations is the analytical edition, *Quinque compilationes antiquae*, ed. Emil Friedberg (Leipzig, 1882; repr. Graz, 1956).

completed it in 1212, so that it was in fact the third of the *Compilationes* in order of composition. Its 331 chapters, arranged in 106 titles, are drawn mainly from the decretals of Clement III (1187–91) and Celestine III (1191–98).

Compilatio tertia was assembled by Pietro Collivacina (sometimes called Petrus Beneventanus), a notary of the Roman curia under Pope Innocent III (1198–1216), who commissioned him to make this collection. Pietro completed it in the summer of 1209 and the pontiff transmitted it formally to the University of Bologna by the bull *Devotioni vestri*. This was the first official papal collection of canon law, for the *Decretum* and the first two *Compilationes* were private collections, even though they formed the basis of the teaching of canon law in the schools and were often used in the courts. All of the 482 chapters in the 122 titles of *Compilatio tertia* are drawn from the decretals issued by Pope Innocent III during the first twelve years of his pontificate.

Compilatio quarta was the work of an energetic German professor at Bologna, Johann Zemeke, commonly known as Johannes Teutonicus. The canons of the Fourth Lateran Council (1215) formed the nucleus of this collection, to which Johannes Teutonicus added numerous decretals from the last years of the pontificate of Innocent III. The collection contains 189 chapters, arranged in 69 titles, and is thus the shortest of the *Quinque compilationes*.

Compilatio quinta was composed by another influential Bolognese professor, Tancred (ca 1185–1234/36), who was commissioned by Pope Honorius III (1216–27) to undertake it. The collection consists entirely of decretals of Honorius III, save for one imperial constitution of the emperor Frederick II. There are 223 chapters in the 94 titles of this compilation, which Honorius III formally promulgated in the bull *Novae causarum* on 2 May 1226.

CITATION FORMS As with other canonistic sources, three styles of citation to the *Compilationes antiquae* appear in the literature. The *Obsolete Form* normally uses *extra.* or *extrav.* to indicate a citation from one of the decretal collections. Occasionally, but not often, the form *extra. j*, *extra. ij*, etc. will be met, and sometimes the name of the compiler will appear, as for example, *extrav. Tancredi* in a reference to

Compilatio quinta. Medieval authors who use the obsolete citation form usually give an abbreviated form of the *titulus,* followed by the opening words of the *capitulum* cited. Occasionally, too, the number of the book (almost invariably in Roman numerals) will be added. Thus:

> extra. de appellationibus, super eo
> extra. ii. de electione, suffraganeis
> iv. extra v. de iudeis, cum sit nimis

Citations of the *Quinque compilationes* in the *Obsolescent Form* begin with the chapter number, followed by the Compilation (Roman numerals), with the numbers of book and title added in Arabic numerals within parentheses; thus:

> c. 34 Comp. I (2,20)
> c. 1 Comp. II (1,3)
> c. 2 Comp. IV (5,4)

The *Modern Form* proceeds as usual in order from the largest unit to the smallest, that is, Compilation, book, title, chapter. It is also common in modern citations to add in parentheses a reference to the place, if any, where the chapter may be found in the *Liber extra;* thus:

> 1 Comp. 2.20.34 (X–) [for a chapter not found in the *Liber extra*]
> 2 Comp. 1.3.1 (X 1.6.11)
> 4 Comp. 5.4.2 (X 5.6.16)

The Decretales Gregorii IX, or Liber extra

This vast decretal collection was the work of a famous Dominican canonist from Catalonia, St Raymond of Penyafort (d. 1275), who undertook it at the direction of Pope Gregory IX (1227–41). It follows the same division into five books and the same order of subject matter as the *Quinque compilationes antiquae.* The five books of the *Liber extra* comprise 185 titles (*tituli*), within which the individual decretals (or extracts from decretals) are arranged in chronological order. The *Liber extra* was largely a synthesis of the *Quinque compilationes:* 1,796 out of the 1,971 chapters (*capitula*) in the *Decretals of Gregory IX* (or more than 90 per cent of the total) had appeared previously in one or another of the earlier *Compilationes*. In addition to the material from the *Compilationes*, the *Liber extra* includes 195 decretals of Gregory IX, seven decretals of Innocent III, and two other decretals of uncertain origin.[5]

CITATION FORMS Methods of citing the *Decretales Gregorii IX* follow the same principles as those used for the *Quinque compilationes*. A few common abbreviations that often appear in citations from the *Liber extra* include:

c. un. (*capitulum unicum*)
c. fin. (*capitulum finalem*)
de iure. (*de iureiurando* = X 2.24)
de m. et o. (*de maioritate et obedientia* = X 1.33)
de r. j. (*de regulis iuris* = X 5.41)
de spo. et ma. (*de sponsalibus et matrimoniis* = X 4.1)
de v. s. (*de verborum significatione* = X 5.40)
de vi. et ho. (*de vita et honestate clericorum* = X 3.1)
de vo. et vo. (*de voto et voti redemptione* = X 3.34)
qui fi. (*qui filii sint legitimi* = X 4.17)

The three citation styles that we have met before also appear in references to the *Liber extra*:

Obsolete Form	Extra. de serv. non ordi., miramur extra. de vo. et vo., litteraturam in X de furt. c. fures
Obsolescent Form	c. 7 X (1,18) c. 3 X (III, 34) c. 2 X, V de furtis
Modern Form	X 1.18.7 X 3.34.3 X 5.18.2

The Liber sextus (VI)

The *Liber sextus*, compiled by a committee of canonists commissioned by Pope Boniface VIII (1294–1303), was formally promulgated on 3 March 1298 by the bull

---

5. The discrepancy in numbers is explained by differences between X and the *Compilationes* in the arrangement of *capitula*. St Raymond broke up some of the earlier decretals into two or more chapters and united others.

Sancrosanctae Romanae ecclesiae. Like its predecessors, the *Liber sextus* is divided into five books, which comprise 76 titles and 359 chapters. The canons are drawn from the decrees of the first and second general councils of Lyon (1245 and 1274) and decretal letters of Gregory IX, Innocent IV (1243–54), Alexander IV (1254–61), Urban IV (1261–64), Clement IV (1265–68), Gregory X (1271–76), Nicholas III (1277–80), and Boniface VIII himself.

CITATION FORMS The *Liber sextus* is usually designated in citations as VI (sometimes VI°). The usual three forms occur in the literature:

Obsolete Form	VI de prebend. c. mandatum
	li. vi. de sent. excomm., venerabilibus
Obsolescent Form	c. 41 (3,4 in VI)
	c. 7 de sent. excom. (V, 11 in VI')
Modern Form	VI 3.4.41
	VI 5.11.7

The Constitutiones Clementinae (Clem.)

Pope John XXII (1316–34) promulgated this short decretal collection by the bull *Quoniam nulla* on 25 October 1317. The *Clementines* were the last decretal collection to be published officially by a medieval pontiff and the appearance of this collection marked the close of an era of prolific papal decretal legislation. The *Clementines* followed the organizational pattern of the *Liber extra*, with five books, 52 titles, and 106 chapters. The collection includes one decretal of Boniface VIII and one of Urban IV; the remaining decretals are all by Pope Clement V (1305–14).

CITATION FORMS The title of the collection is usually abbreviated *Clem.* Once again there are three citation styles, following the established patterns.

Obsolete Form	Clem. de celebratione missarum, dignum
	Clem de elect. et elect. pot., in plerisque
Obsolescent Form	c. 2 de celeb. missarum (3,14) in Clem.
	c. 5 (I, 3) in Clem.
Modern Form	Clem. 3.14.2
	Clem. 1.3.5

The Extravagantes Johannis XXII (Extrav. Jo. XXII)

This small private collection of 20 decretals was completed between 1325 and 1327 by Zenzelinus de Cassanis (d. 1354), who also wrote glosses on it. Zenzelinus, a former professor of canon and civil law at the University of Montpellier was resident at the Roman curia in Avignon at the time he was working on the *Extravagantes*. At the end of the fifteenth century Jean Chappuis, a licentiate in canon law of the University of Paris, divided this collection into fourteen titles and published it, together with the gloss of Zenzelinus, as part of the edition of the *Corpus iuris canonici* that he prepared for the Paris publishers, Udalric Gering and Berthold Rembolt. The edition first appeared in 1500. Since that time the *Extravagantes Johannis XXII* have regularly been considered a part of the *Corpus*.[6]

CITATION FORMS The two styles of citation used for this collection resemble the ones used for earlier collections, save that this small compilation was not divided into books.

Obsolescent Form	c. 1 de concess. preb. tit. IV in Extrav. Jo. XXII
	c. 2 de verb. sig. tit. XIV in Extra. Jo. XXII.
Modern Form	Extrav. Jo. XXII 4.1
	Extrav. Jo. XXII 14.2

The Extravagantes communes (Extrav. comm.)

In addition to his editorial work on the decretals of John XXII, Jean Chappuis also prepared a further collection of frequently-cited decretals that did not appear in previous collections for his edition of the *Corpus iuris canonici*. In its first edition (Paris, 1500), Chappuis's collection included 69 decretals; to these he added four more in the second edition (Paris, 1503). In this latter form, Chappuis's collection has been reprinted in all subsequent editions of the *Corpus* under the title *Extravagantes communes*. The

6. The critical edition of this work is *Extrauagantes Iohannis XXII*, ed. Jacqueline Tarrant, Monumenta iuris canonici, Corpus collectionum, vol. 6 (Vatican City, 1985).

collection shows signs of haste in its preparation: three decretals of John XXII in this collection also appear in the *Extrav. Jo. XXII*, while two decretals of Clement V and one of Boniface VIII appear in *Clem.*, as well as in the *Extravagantes communes*. In addition, one of the decretals of Benedict XI (1303–4) included by Chappuis had been revoked by Clement V.

CITATION FORMS These follow established patterns:

Obsolescent Form	c. 1 de iudaeis (V, 2) in Extrav. comm.
	c. un. (5,5) in Extrav. comm.
Modern Form	Extrav. comm. 5.2.1
	Extrav. comm. 5.5.un.

The Glosses to the Canon Law

From the time of Paucapalea onward lecturers in the canon law faculties of medieval universities commonly framed their remarks on the legal texts in the form of glosses, that is explanations of individual words and phrases in the text, together with discussions of the applications that students might find for the provision under discussion and cross-references to relevant passages elsewhere in the law. Students and commercial copyists commonly wrote glosses in the margins (or, less frequently, between the lines) of the text itself, so as to create a running explanation and commentary on the text. Glosses of one master might also be incorporated (with or without acknowledgement) among the glosses of another. By the end of the twelfth century large and elaborate apparatuses of glosses begin to appear in manuscripts, side-by-side with the text of the *Decretum*. Ultimately university teachers agreed on a standard gloss apparatus, known as the *glossa ordinaria* (*glos. ord.*) for the *Decretum*, the *Liber extra*, *Liber sextus*, and the *Clementines*.[7] The gloss of Zenzelinus is usually printed alongside the text of the *Extrav. Jo. XXII*, while the *Extrav. comm.* never received an authoritative gloss. With the

---

7. For a convenient sample of the ordinary gloss on Gratian's *Decretum* see *The treatise on laws (Decretum DD. 1–20)*, trans. Augustine Thompson and James Gordley, Studies in medieval and early modern canon law, vol. 2 (Washington, D.C., 1993), which includes an English translation of the *glos. ord.* to the first 20 Distinctions.

appearance of printing, successive editions of the canon law up to the beginning of the seventeenth century normally printed the *glos. ord.* for each book in the margins of the text. The *glos. ord.* was taught as a usual and customary part of the law curriculum in the universities and cited in the courts as an authority almost equal in weight to the canonical texts themselves.

The *glossa ordinaria* to the *Decretum* was first compiled by Johannes Teutonicus (d. 1245/46), who drew heavily from the *Summa* of Huguccio (d. 1210) and the *Apparatus* of Laurentius Hispanus (d. 1248). Johannes Teutonicus completed the first redaction of the *glos. ord.* before 1217. This version was subsequently reworked and expanded by Bartholomew of Brescia (d. ca. 1258), who completed his revision ca. 1245. Early printed versions of the *glos. ord.* frequently incorporate other material as well, notably the *Casus decretorum* of Benencasa (d. 1206) and *additiones* from the gloss apparatus of Guido de Baysio (d. 1313), known as the *Rosarium decreti* (written between 1296 and 1300).

The *glossa ordinaria* on the *Decretales Gregorii IX* is the work of Bernard of Parma (d. 1263), who apparently continued to work on it up to the time of his death. Bernard wrote many of the glosses in this apparatus himself, but he also made liberal use of the work of commentators on the *Quinque compilationes antiquae*, notably Alanus, the elder Bernard of Compostella, Lawrence of Spain, Tancred, and Vincent of Spain. Printed versions of this *glos. ord.* frequently incorporate *Additiones*, drawn mainly from Giovanni d'Andrea, Panormitanus, and Hostiensis. The printed versions also add to the *gloss. ord.* much of the text of Bernard of Parma's *Casus longi* on the *Decretals.*

The *glossa ordinaria* on the *Sext* and *Clementines* were the work of Giovanni d'Andrea. Giovanni finished his *glos. ord.* on the *Sext* in 1304 and his gloss on the *Clementines* in 1326.

Gloss apparatuses often gave credit for individual glosses to their authors, usually by attaching a *siglum*, or abbreviated form of the master's name, to his comments.

CITATION FORMS Glosses may be cited in an anglicized style as 'gloss to' some passage, word, or phrase in a legal text; many writers, however, prefer a latinized citation style.

Thus references may read:

> Ordinary gloss to C. 27 q. 1 c. 41, *legis*
> *Glos. ord.* to C. 17 q. 2 c. 1 pr. v. *beneficia*
> *Glos. ord.* ad D. 82 c. 1 ad v. *Episcopus pauperibus*
> Tancredus, *glos.* ad 1 Comp. 3.19.2 (X 3.34.2) v. *in puerili*

.   .   .

ROMAN LAW CITATIONS

The Codex Justinianus

Justinian's *Code* was first promulgated as the law of the East Roman Empire in 529. A revised edition of the *Code* appeared in 534 and only this second version has survived. The *Code* consists of twelve books, which are divided into titles (*tituli*). Each title consists of individual laws (*leges*), and, save for the shortest laws, these are further divided into numbered sections or paragraphs. When medieval law teachers and glossators referred to the *Code* they usually meant just the first nine books. They taught the last three books separately and referred to them as *the Three Books* (*Tres libri*); manuscript copyists and binders normally included the *Tres libri* together with Justinian's *Institutes* and the *Authenticum* in a single tome, which they referred to simply as *The Volume* (*Volumen*).

CITATION FORMS Two citation styles appear frequently in the literature. Medieval and early modern writers cited passages in the *Codex* by the opening words of the *titulus* and *lex*. It is now customary to cite Justinian's Codex by the numbers of book, title, *lex*, and paragraph in that order. Some modern citations abbreviate the name of the *Codex* as Cod., others prefer C. J. (for *Codex Justiniani*), while still others simply refer to it as C.; of these three options, Cod. or C. J. are preferable, since they are less likely to mislead than C. used alone, which can easily be confused with a citation to *Pars II* of the *Decretum*.

Obsolete Form	C. de episcopis, l. omnes § privilegiis sane
	C. de nup., l. Imperialis § His illud
Modern Form	Cod. 1.3.32.7
	C. J. 5.4.23.5

The Digestum or Pandecta

Justinian promulgated the *Digest* in 533. It contains 50 books, each divided into titles (*tituli*); each title contains one or more fragments (*fragmenta*) from ancient jurists, mainly of the classical period of Roman law. Most fragments in the *Digest* are subdivided into a *principium* (pr.) and numbered paragraphs. The fragments are commonly, if incorrectly, referred to as laws (*leges*). Medieval scribes (and early printers and publishers) usually divided the *Digest* into three parts: The *Digestum vetus* (books 1–24.2); the *Infortiatum* (books 24.3–38); and the *Digestum novum* (books. 39–50). Medieval authors accordingly often cited passages in the *Digest* as *Dig. vet.*, *Infort.*, and *Dig. nov.* respectively. An even more common abbreviation for the *Digest* in medieval usage was *ff.*; this apparently represents a misreading of the Greek letter *pi* (π), which stood for *The Pandects* (πανδεκτα). Modern writers usually refer to the *Digest* either as Dig. or D.; of the two, Dig. is preferable to avoid possible confusion with a citation to *Pars I* of the *Decretum*.

CITATION FORMS These follow the models used for the *Codex*.

Obsolete Form	ff. locati conducti, si quis domum, § si alienam
	Dig. vet., De orig. iuris, necessarium, § his legibus
	Infort. De leg. tutoris, tutela legitima
Modern Form	Dig. 19.2.9.6
	Dig. 1.2.2.5
	Dig. 26.4.3 pr.

The Institutes of Justinian

The *Institutes* of Justinian represent an adaptation and revision by Tribonian of the most successful legal textbook of the classical period, the *Institutes* of Gaius. Justinian promulgated Tribonian's new version of the *Institutes* by an imperial constitution in 533. In that constitution the emperor designated the new work as the officially-sanctioned introductory text for beginning law students and the approved guide to the basic principles of

Roman law. The work consists of four books, which are divided into titles; the titles are subdivided into fragments, each of which consists of an introduction (*principium*) and numbered paragraphs.

CITATION FORMS Medieval references to the *Institutes* usually consist of an abbreviated version of the title followed by the opening words of the fragment. Modern citations follow the same model used for the *Digest* and *Codex*.

Obsolete Form	Inst. de rer. div., riparum
	de ver. ob., omnis, in Inst.
	Inst. de l. aquil., iniuria
Modern Form	Inst. 2.1.4
	Inst. 3.15.2
	Inst. 4.3.2 pr.

The Novels of Justinian and the Authenticum

The *Novellae leges* consist of 168 laws promulgated between 535 and 545 and collected during the reign of Tiberius II (578–82). This collection, however, circulated primarily in the Eastern Empire. Medieval lawyers in the West cited the *Novels* from another collection, the *Authenticum* or *Liber authenticorum*. This collection comprises 134 of the *Novellae leges*, mainly in chronological order and presented in a Latin translation (for many of the original *Novellae* were in Greek). From the eleventh century, Western glossators were accustomed to use a version of the *Authenticum* in which 96 of the *Novellae* were grouped into nine *collationes*, which were divided into *tituli*; the titles were subdivided into *fragmenta*, and these typically consisted of a *prefatio*, numbered paragraphs (or *capitula*), and an *epilogum*.

CITATION FORMS. The usual medieval system of citing the *Authenticum* began with the *titulus*, followed by the opening words of the *fragmentum* or other subdivision, and closed with the number of the *collatio*. Modern usage normally proceeds from the largest to the smallest units, giving in sequence the numbers of the *collatio*, *titulus*, and *fragmentum*. Citations of the *Authenticum* are further complicated by the fact that medieval scribes customarily incorporated summaries of the *Novellae* from the

Authenticum into the relevant sections of manuscripts of the *Codex*, a practice that early printers also adopted. These summaries were known individually as *authenticae* and collectively as the *Corpus authenticorum*. Medieval citations of the *Corpus authenticorum* usually open with the words of the appropriate *titulus* of the *Codex*, followed by the opening words of the particular *authenticum* that is being referred to. Modern citations of the *Corpus authenticorum* normally give the number of the corresponding *Novel*, followed by the number of the specific sub-section in question, the equivalent numbered reference to the *Liber authenticorum*, and a numbered reference to the section of the *Codex* in which the *authenticum* occurs. To complicate still further the problem of locating and verifying medieval citations, the standard modern edition of the *Novellae* by Schöll and Kroll does not furnish a proper concordance of the *Novellae* and the *Authenticum*. In practice, therefore, it is necessary to verify references to the *Authenticum* either from the *Indices corporis iuris civilis iuxta vetustiores editiones cum criticis collatis*, prepared by Ugo Nicolini and Franca Sinatti d'Amico, in the *Subsidia* series of *Ius Romanum medii ævi* (Milan, 1964– ; 3 vols to date) or the *Indices titulorum et legum Corporis iuris ciuilis* compiled by Xavier Ochoa and Aloisio Diez (Roma, 1965). If neither of these is available, it is sometimes helpful to consult the indices of an early printed edition of the *Corpus*, although these are often unreliable.

Obsolete Form	(a) *Liber authenticorum*: Authen. de testibus, neque igitur, coll vii.
	(b) *Corpus authenticorum*: C. de sacrosanctis ecclesiis, auth. Si qua mulier
Modern Form	(a) *Liber authenticorum*: Auth. coll. 7.2.3 = Nov. 90
	(b) *Corpus authenticorum*: Excerptum Nov. 123.38 = Auth.134 coll. 9.15 post Cod. 1.2.13.

APPENDIX II:
MAJOR CANONISTS OF THE CLASSICAL PERIOD: BIOGRAPHICAL NOTES

These brief notes on the lives and careers of a few well-known canonists who flourished during the classical period of canon law (ca. 1140–ca. 1350) are intended primarily to flesh out earlier references to them and to provide a guide to further information about their lives and careers. In addition, these biographical sketches illustrate concretely remarks made earlier concerning the variety of careers open to canonists, as well as their geographical mobility and the diversity of their origins.

[~ is the approximation sign and designates a range of dates within which a person probably lived or an event probably occurred.]

Abbas Antiquus. See Bernard of Montemirat.

Alanus Anglicus (fl. 1208~38). All that is known of Alanus's personal life is that he was an Englishman who taught at Bologna early in the thirteenth century and who seems to have had close connections with the Dominican order. He may later have returned to England as a canon of St Paul's Cathedral. Alanus wrote a gloss apparatus on *Compilatio prima*, which he completed before 1210; and compiled his own decretal collection, which Johannes Galensis (John of Wales) drew upon when he put together *Compilatio secunda*. Alanus was probably the author of the apparatus known as *Ius naturale* on Gratian's *Decretum*.[1]

---

1. Schulte, QL i, 188–9; E. Magnin, 'Alain de Galles' in DDC i, p.361; Stephan Kuttner, *Repertorium der Kanonistik*, Studi e testi, vol. 71 (Vatican City, 1937), pp.316–17, 325–6; Jane E. Sayers, *Papal government and England during the pontificate of Honorius III (1216–1227)*, Cambridge studies in medieval life and thought, 3rd ser., vol. 21 (Cambridge, 1984), p.178.

Baldus de Ubaldis (ca. 1327–1400). Baldus was born into a family with strong academic credentials. His father, Francesco Ubaldi, was a professor of medicine at Perugia and Baldus, who studied both civil and canon law at Perugia and Pisa, later taught at six universities during a long and complex career in which he combined teaching and practice. Two of Baldus's brothers, as well as his son, Francesco, were also well-known jurists. Perhaps the most visible of Baldus's many notable students was Pierre Roger de Beaufort, who became Pope Gregory XI (1370–78). Baldus could also count among his pupils several of the most influential jurists of the succeeding generation, including Peter of Ancharano, Cardinal Zabarella, Johannes ab Imola, and Paulus de Castro. Baldus wrote extensively on both civil and canon law. The most important of his canonistic works was his *Commentary* on the first three books of the *Liber extra*. He also wrote a great number of *consilia*, as well as *additiones* to the *Speculum iudiciale* of William Durand.[2]

Bartholomaeus Brixiensis (Bartholomew of Brescia; d. 1258). Few traces survive of the career of Bartholomaeus Brixiensis. He studied canon law under Tancred at Bologna, where he also attended the lectures of Hugolinus in Roman law. After completing his studies, Bartholomaeus himself taught canon law at Bologna. His principal works include two sets of *quaestiones disputatae* and his revised and updated version of Johannes Teutonicus's *Glossa ordinaria* on the *Decretum* of Gratian. Virtually all glossed manuscripts of the *Decretum* after the mid-thirteenth century reproduce Bartholomaeus's revised form of the ordinary gloss, as do the numerous printed editions that appeared between the fifteenth and the seventeenth centuries.[3]

2. Schulte, QL ii, 275–7; G. Chevrier, 'Baldi de Ubaldi', in DDC ii, pp.39–52; N. Horn, *Aequitas in den Lehren des Baldus*, Forschungen zur neueren Privatrechtsgeschichte, vol. 11 (Berlin, 1968); Hermann Lange, *Die Consilien des Baldus de Ubaldis (†1400)*, Abhandlungen der Akademie der Wissenschaften und der Literatur, Geistes- und Sozialwissenschaftlichen Klasse, 1973, no 12 (Mainz, 1974); J. P. Canning, *The political thought of Baldus de Ubaldis*, Cambridge studies in medieval life and thought, 4th ser., vol. 6 (Cambridge, 1987).

3. Schulte, QL ii, 83–8; Gabriel LeBras, 'Bartholomaeus Brixiensis', in DDC ii, pp.216–17; Kuttner, *Repertorium*, pp.103–22.

Benedetto Gaetani (Pope Boniface VIII; ca. 1235–1303).
Born at Anagni into the powerful Gaetani clan, Benedetto
enjoyed a meteoric ecclesiastical career. Ambitious and
able, Benedetto studied canon law at Bologna and then
immediately entered the papal curia, where he progressed
swiftly into the upper ranks of the papal bureaucracy.
Successive popes entrusted him with numerous diplomatic
missions and in 1281 Pope Martin IV (1281–85) rewarded
his successful performance by naming him a cardinal. A
crisis in papal politics following the death of Pope Nicholas
IV in 1292 left the papal throne vacant for 27 months.
Although the cardinals finally agreed upon a compromise
candidate, Peter Morrone, who became Pope Celestine V in
July 1294, the new pope abruptly resigned his office on 13
December of that same year. Another extended vacancy in
the papacy would have been disastrous and accordingly,
eleven days after Celestine V's resignation, the cardinals
chose Benedetto Gaetani to succeed to St Peter's throne
under the title of Boniface VIII. Boniface's pontificate was
stormy and frequently dramatic. He was not only embroiled
in internal dissension within the ranks of the clergy – such
as the bitter strife between the spiritual and conventual
wings of the Franciscan order – but also with rivalries
between his own family and another powerful Roman
house, the Colonnas. During his 40-year career as a
practising canonist, the new pope had ample experience
with canonists' chronic difficulties in discovering the most
recent law on the problems they had to deal with. Early in
his pontificate Boniface VIII appointed a commission of
prominent canonists to prepare a new official collection of
the decretal law that had accumulated since the publication
of the *Liber extra* by Pope Gregory IX in 1234. On 3 March
1298 Boniface formally promulgated the new decretal
collection that his commissioners had prepared. He
entitled it the *Sixth book of decretals* (*Liber sextus decretalium*),
which signalled that the new work was a continuation of
and supplement to the five books of the *Liber extra*.
Thereafter other problems monopolized the pope's
attention. The greatest of the many crises in Boniface's
pontificate centred on the relationship between papal and
monarchical powers. Boniface's leading antagonist in this
struggle was King Philip IV of France (1285–1314). This

conflict entered a crucial phase in 1301 and the pope's situation deteriorated rapidly thereafter. In 1303 King Philip dispatched Guillaume de Nogaret to Italy to capture and imprison the pope, which Guillaume did briefly after storming the papal castle at Anagni on 7 September 1303. The French forces released Boniface after holding him prisoner for only two days, but the pope returned to Rome a broken man and died on 11 October 1303.[4]

Bérengar Frédol (d. 1323). Bérengar came from the region of Montpellier in the south of France. He studied and later taught canon law at Bologna. As quite a young man he received ecclesiastical appointments, first as a canon of Béziers and succentor of the cathedral there. He subsequently became a papal chaplain, abbot of St Aphrodisius in Béziers, canon of Narbonne and Aix, and bishop of Béziers. Pope Celestine V (July–December 1294) named Bérengar a cardinal. He was a prominent member of the committee that drafted the *Liber sextus* and also composed a treatise on excommunication and interdict.[5]

Bernard of Montemirat (Abbas antiquus; d. 1296). Although born in France, Bernard studied law at Bologna and later taught at Béziers. He wrote a *Lectura* on the *Liber extra* between 1259 and 1266, when he became abbot of the Benedictine monastery of Montmajour. In 1286 he was named bishop of Tripoli in Syria, but the city fell to the Saracens before he could take possession of his see. By 1295 he had become administrator of the abbey of Montecassino. Bernard's cognomen, 'the Old Abbot' (*Abbas antiquus*), by which he is best known, helped later canonists to distinguish him from Nicholas de Tudeschis

4. James Muldoon, 'Boniface VIII's forty years of experience in the law', *The Jurist* 31 (1971), 449–77; Gabriel LeBras, 'Boniface VIII, symphoniste et modérateur', in *Mélanges Louis Halphen* (Paris, 1951), pp.383–94; Walter Ullmann, 'Boniface VIII and his contemporary scholarship', *Journal of theological studies* 27 (1976), 58–87; T. S. R. Boase, *Boniface VIII* (London, 1933); Charles T. Wood, *Philip the Fair and Boniface VIII* (New York, 1967).
5. Schulte, QL ii, 180–2; A. Van Hove, *Prologomena ad Codicem iuris canonici*, 2nd edn, Commentarium Lovaniense in Codicem iuris canonici, vol. 1, pt 1 (Malines, 1945), pp.177, 259; *Le 'Liber de excommunicatione' du Cardinal Bérengar Frédol*, ed. E. Vernay (Paris, 1912).

(1386–1445), who was commonly called 'the Modern Abbot' (*Abbas modernus*). He was also known as 'the Sicilian Abbot' (*Abbas Siculus*) and *Panormitanus*, or 'the man from Palermo'.[6]

Bernard of Parma (d. 1266). Bernard was born close to the beginning of the thirteenth century at Parma and was a member of the locally prominent de Botone family. He studied canon law at Bologna under Tancred and by 1247 had become a canon of the cathedral of Bologna, where he taught throughout his career. The best-known of his students at Bologna was William Durand. Bernard was also a papal chaplain and, in addition to his teaching, conducted a great deal of important business at the papal court. Bernard compiled the *Glossa ordinaria* and the *Casus longi* to the *Liber extra*, as well as a *Summa super titulis decretalium*, which reproduces much of the gloss apparatus of Tancred on *Compilatio prima*. When Bernard died, he was buried next to Tancred in the cathedral of Bologna.[7]

Bernard of Pavia (d. 1213). The early life of Bernard of Pavia, sometimes called Bernard Balbi, is extremely obscure. He was a native of Pavia and first appeared as a student of canon law and theology at Bologna, where he studied canon law with Huguccio. When he had finished his legal studies, Bernard taught for a time at Bologna, then joined the papal curia in Rome, and in 1178 was named provost of Pavia. In 1191 he succeeded another canonist, Johannes Faventinus, as bishop of Faenza. In 1198 Bernard returned to Pavia, this time as its bishop; a position he retained until his death in 1213. Bernard contributed significantly to the intellectual development of canon law as a systematic discipline. He was responsible for

6. Schulte, QL ii, 130–2; Stephan Kuttner, 'Wer war der Dekretalist "Abbas antiquus"?' *Zeitschrift der Savigny-Stiftung für Rechtsgeschichte*, kanonistische Abteilung 26 (1937), 471–89, reprinted with original pagination and additional comments in his *Studies in the history of medieval canon law* (London, 1990).
7. Schulte, QL ii, 114–17; P. Ourliac, 'Bernard de Parme', in DDC ii, pp.781–2; Stephan Kuttner and Beryl Smalley, 'The *Glossa ordinaria* to the Gregorian decretals', *English historical review* 60 (1945), 97–105, reprinted with original pagination and supplementary notes in Kuttner's *Studies in the history of medieval canon law*, no XIII.

assembling and organizing *Compilatio prima*, whose structure became the model for all subsequent decretal collections.[8] He also wrote an influential textbook, the *Summa decretalium*, as well as two specialized treatises, the *Summa de matrimonio* ·and the *Summa de electione*, on particularly complex areas of canon law. In addition he produced glosses on the *Decretum* and on his own decretal collection, as well as several lesser works.[9]

Boniface VIII, Pope. See Benedetto Gaetani.

Gérard Pucelle (1115~20–1184). Gérard Pucelle was a fellow student of John of Salisbury (1115~25–1180) at Paris and by 1156 was teaching philosophy there. He also lectured at times on theology, civil law, and canon law. Ordained by Thomas Becket (1118–70), Gérard became a member of Becket's household during his exile on the Continent. Late in 1165 or early in 1166 Becket sent Gérard on a mission to the court òf the German ruler, Frederick Barbarossa (1152–90), to try to solicit the emperor's support in Becket's dispute with King Henry II (1154–89) of England. Gérard returned to England in 1168 and, to Becket's chagrin, swore allegiance to Henry II. Becket and Gérard were soon reconciled, however, after Gérard's return to France, where he resumed teaching for several years. He subsequently returned to England as a member of the household of Becket's successor at Canterbury, Archbishop Richard of Dover. Not long before his death Gérard was named bishop of Coventry. Gérard seems to have been one of the links between the Paris canon law schools and the canonists who made Cologne the principal centre of the Rhineland school of decretists.[10]

Geoffrey of Trani (d. 1245). Geoffrey, a native of Apulia, studied law in Bologna at the same time as Sinibaldo dei

---

8. See above, Appendix I, p. 194.
9. Schulte, QL ii, 175–82; Gabriel LeBras, 'Bernard de Pavie', in DDC ii, pp.782–89; Kuttner, *Reportorium*, pp.322–3, 387–90, 398–9.
10. Stephan Kuttner and Eleanor Rathbone, 'Anglo-Norman canonists of the twelfth century', *Traditio* 7 (1949), 296–303; Ralph V. Turner, 'Who was the author of Glanvill? Reflections on the education of Henry II's common lawyers', *Law and history review* 8 (1990), 97–127.

Feischi, who later became Pope Innocent IV. After teaching civil law at Naples and canon law at Bologna, Geoffrey entered the papal curia. Honorius III (1216–27) made him a papal chaplain and he also became an auditor, or judge, of the *Audientia litterarum contradictarum*, a position that he apparently retained until his death. He is best known as the author of an early treatise on the *Liber extra*, the *Summa super titulis decretalium*, which Bernard of Parma drew upon heavily when he compiled the *Glossa ordinaria* on the Gregorian decretals. Geoffrey also wrote glosses on the *Liber extra*, as well as some *quaestiones*. Innocent IV named him a cardinal in 1244 and Geoffrey died in the following year while attending the First Council of Lyon.[11]

Gratian (fl. ca. 1140). The life and career of Master Gratian, sometimes called the 'father of scientific canon law' left few traces in contemporary documents. He apparently taught canon law, probably at Bologna, and he may well have been a monk. Beyond those two tentative statements, nothing is reliably known (although a great deal has been surmised) about Gratian's biography. Even the date at which he completed his *Decretum* can be established only approximately from circumstantial evidence.[12]

Gregory IX, Pope. See Hugolinus.

Guido de Baysio ('The Archdeacon'; ca. 1250–1313). Guido de Baysio's family, although long established in Bologna, was forced into exile during Guido's youth because of their Ghibelline connections. Consequently Guido first studied

---

11. Schulte, QL ii, 88–91; Agostino Paravicini-Bagliani, *Cardinali di curia e 'familiae' cardinalizie dal 1227 al 1254*, 2 vols, Italia sacra, vol. 18–19 (Padua, 1972), i, pp.272–8; Jane E. Sayers, *Papal judges-delegate in the province of Canterbury, 1198–1254: A study in ecclesiastical jurisdiction and administration* (Oxford, 1971), pp.22–3.
12. John T. Noonan, Jr, 'Gratian slept here: The changing identity of the father of the systematic study of canon law', *Traditio* 35 (1979), 145–72; Stephan Kuttner, 'Research on Gratian: Acta and agenda', in *Proceedings of the seventh international congress of medieval canon law*, ed. Peter Linehan, MIC, Subsidia, vol. 8 (Vatican City, 1988), reprinted with additional notes in Kuttner's *Studies in the history of medieval canon law*, Gérard Fransen, 'La date du Décret de Gratien', *Revue d'histoire ecclésiastique* 51 (1956), 521–31.

and taught canon law at Reggio, where his family settled and where he became a canon of the cathedral. In 1296 Pope Boniface VIII named him archdeacon of Bologna, which led in turn to his appointment as archchancellor of the university. He taught at Bologna, in addition to his other activities, until 1304, when he joined the papal curia, first at Rome, later at Avignon. Guido is best-known for his *Rosarium*, a rich and scholarly commentary on Gratian's *Decretum*. Several of his *quaestiones* also survive, as does his *Apparatus* on the *Liber sextus*, a treatise on the law concerning heresy, and a procedural manual concerning the practice of the *Audientia litterarum contradictarum*, of which he was an auditor. He was also a master teacher. Among his pupils the most famous was Johannes Andreae, whom Guido took through his doctorate without fee. Guido died at Avignon in the summer of 1313.[13]

Honorius (d. after 1203). Master Honorius was a native of Kent, where he held his earliest benefices. He studied at Paris between 1185 and 1192. Between 1186 and 1190 Honorius wrote a *Summa decretalium quaestionum*, of which seven manuscripts survive. He had returned to England before October 1192, when he appears as *magister* Honorius on a witness list. He may have been teaching canon law at Oxford between 1192 and 1195, when Geoffrey Plantagenet, archbishop of York (1189–1212), appointed him as his official-principal. Honorius was named archdeacon of Richmond in 1198, but the appointment was challenged and Honorius travelled to Rome to participate in the litigation over this matter, which was eventually decided in his favour in 1202. While in Rome, Honorius also acted as proctor for Archbishop Hubert Walter (1193–1205). In 1203, when Honorius returned to England, he became a member of the archbishop's household.[14]

13. Schulte, QL ii, 186–90; G. Mollat, 'Gui de Baysio', DDC v, pp.1007–8; Filippo Liotta, 'Appunti per una biografia del canonista Guido da Baisio, arcidiacono di Bologna (con appendice di documenti)', *Studi Senesi*, 3rd ser., 13 (1964), 7–52.
14. Kuttner and Rathbone, 'Anglo-Norman Canonists', pp.304–16; C. R. Cheney, *English bishops' chanceries, 1100–1250*, University of Manchester, Publications of the Faculty of Arts, no 3 (Manchester,

Hostiensis (Henricus de Segusio; 1190~1200–71). Hostiensis was born at Susa, in the diocese of Turin, shortly before 1200. He became a law student at Bologna at the same time as Sinibaldo dei Fieschi (Pope Innocent IV). Hostiensis's teachers in civil law included Jacobus Balduinus and Homobono, while he studied canon law under Jacobus de Albegna. After completing his legal training, Hostiensis taught canon law in Paris in the early 1230s. In 1234~35 he received an appointment as prior of Antibes. In 1236 he went to England as a member of the household of Eleanor of Provence, spouse of King Henry III (1216–72). He remained in England until 1244, when he became bishop of Sisteron. In 1250 he was named archbishop of Embrun and in 1261 became cardinal-bishop of Ostia, whence the title 'Hostiensis' by which he is usually known. His reputation as an eminent canonist rests chiefly on his *Summa*, which later came to be known as the *Golden Summa* (*Summa aurea*). Hostiensis's *Summa* survives in two versions, the earlier of which he completed in 1250~51. He commenced writing a *Lectura* on the *Liber extra* at the request of his students in Paris, but did not finish it until shortly before his death in 1271. Hostiensis was so highly-regarded a canonistic authority that he warranted an appearance in Dante's *Divina commedia* (*Paradiso*, 12.82–97).[15]

14. (*Continued*)
1950), pp.11–12, 158, and *Hubert Walter* (London, 1967), pp.164–5; Charles E. Lewis, 'Canonists and law clerks in the household of Archbishop Hubert Walter', in *Seven studies in medieval English history presented to Harold S. Snellgrove* (Jackson, MS, 1983), pp.57–64 at 61; Rudolf Weigand, 'Bemerkungen über die Schriften und Lehren des Magister Honorius', in *Proceedings of the fifth international congress of medieval canon law*, eds Stephan Kuttner and Kenneth Pennington, MIC, Subsidia, vol. 6 (Vatican City, 1980), pp.195–212.

15. Schulte, QL ii, 123–30; Charles Lefebvre, 'Hostiensis' in DDC v, pp.1211–27; Noël Didier, 'Henri de Suse en Angleterre (1236?–1244)', in *Studi in onore di Vincenzo Arangio-Ruiz*, 4 vols (Naples, 1953), ii, 333–51, 'Henri de Suse, évêque de Sisteron (1244–50)', *Revue historique de droit français et étranger*, 4th ser., 31 (1953), 244–70, 409–29, and 'Henri de Suse, prieur d'Antibes, prévôt de Grasse (1235?–1245)', *Studia Gratiana* 2 (1954), 595–617; Richard Kay, 'Hostiensis and some Embrun provincial councils', *Traditio* 20 (1964), 503–13.

Hugolinus (Pope Gregory IX; ca. 1170–1241). Hugolinus was born about 1170 at Anagni. He was a relative of Pope Innocent III (1198–1216), although probably not his nephew as was formerly believed. Hugolinus studied at Paris, where he was a classmate of the theologian Peter of Capua. He subsequently studied canon law, probably at Bologna. After completing his legal studies Hugolinus received numerous appointments as a papal legate and soon was named a papal chaplain. Innocent III named him a cardinal in 1198 and employed him as an *auditor causarum* in papal judicial business. Hugolinus was keenly interested in the Franciscan life and contemplated becoming a Franciscan himself, until St Francis advised him not to do so. Hugolinus became instead the first cardinal-protector of the Franciscan order. In 1227 he was elected pope and took the title of Gregory IX. His own experience as a canonist made Gregory IX keenly aware that students, teachers, and practitioners would benefit from a more convenient and systematic collection of decretals. In 1230, therefore, the new pope commissioned Ramón de Penyafort to compile the decretal collection that came to be known as the *Decretals of Gregory IX* (*Liber extra*). As pope, Hugolinus also continued to interest himself in the Franciscans and sought to improve the order's organizational structure. During much of his pontificate Gregory IX was of course deeply involved as well in the papacy's power struggle with the Hohenstaufen emperor Frederick II (1212–50). Gregory IX died, after a turbulent pontificate, in 1241.[16]

Huguccio (d. 1210). Huguccio came originally from Pisa, where he was born at some unknown date during the first half of the twelfth century. After studying the liberal arts and theology (perhaps in his native city), Huguccio received his training in canon law at Bologna and subsequently taught there until Pope Clement III (1187–91) named him bishop of Ferrara in 1190. At Ferrara Huguccio not only engaged in routine diocesan

16. Werner Malaczek, *Papst und Kardinalskolleg von 1191 bis 1216: Die Kardinäle unter Coelestin III. und Innocenz III.*, Österreichischen Kulturinstitut in Rom, Publikationen, Abhandlungen, vol. 6 (Vienna, 1984), pp.126–33; Schulte, QL ii, pp.3–7.

administration, but also received numerous appointments as a papal judge-delegate. Huguccio was particularly busy with these and other missions during the pontificate of Pope Innocent III (1198–1216), who had studied canon law at Bologna while Huguccio was teaching there and who clearly esteemed his abilities. Huguccio was an acute and original thinker, qualities that emerge clearly in the *Summa super corpore decretorum*, which he wrote at the urging of his students at Bologna. It is ironic that Huguccio's *Summa*, which has generally been acknowledged from the twelfth century to the present as one of the most important monuments of canonical jurisprudence, remains unpublished to this day and must be consulted in manuscript versions of markedly uneven reliability.[17]

Innocent IV, Pope. See Sinibaldo dei Fieschi

Johannes Andreae (Giovanni d'Andrea, ca. 1270–1348). Johannes Andreae was illegitimate, the offspring of an informal union between his father, Andreas, and a concubine named Novella. When Johannes was about ten years old his father moved from the boy's birthplace at Rifredo, near Florence, to Bologna and entered the priesthood. Andreas supervised his son's elementary education and prepared him for university studies at Bologna, first in theology, then later in civil and canon law. In 1301 Johannes became Professor of Decretals at Bologna and in 1303 took the canon law faculty's chair in the *Decretum*. In 1307 he briefly took a teaching position at Padua, then after two years returned to Bologna, where he taught until 1319, when he went back to teach at Padua for a year. In 1320 he returned once more to a professorship at Bologna, where he at last formally became a citizen. He remained teaching at Bologna for the remainder of his life, but punctuated his teaching career by conducting a

---

17. Schulte, QL i, pp.156–70; Alfons M. Stickler, 'Uguccio de Pise', in DDC vii, pp.1355–62; Kuttner, *Repertorium*, pp.155–60; Wolfgang P. Müller, 'Huguccio of Pisa: Canonist, bishop, and grammarian', *Viator* 22 (1991), 123–31; C. Leonardi, 'La vita e l'opera di Uguccione da Pisa', *Studia Gratiana* 4 (1956/57), 37–210; Giuseppe Cremascoli, 'Uguccione da Pisa: Saggio bibliografico', *Aevum* 42 (1968), 123–68.

number of diplomatic missions on behalf of the city government. The best-known of these was his embassy in 1328 to Pope John XXII (1316–34), during which he was robbed by highwaymen; he later received reimbursement from the pope, after the city fathers of Bologna refused to indemnify his losses. Johannes Andreae was the second known married layman to become a professor of canon law (the first was apparently Aegidius Fuscarariis, one of his teachers). He had three sons as well as four daughters and several bastard children. One of his sons, Bonincontro, became a law teacher, while his second and third daughters married canonists. Johannes's youngest daughter (named Novella after Johannes's own mother) was said by Christine de Pisan to have lectured as a substitute for her father when he was ill. One of his bastard sons was legitimized by a papal rescript and became a papal chaplain, while a second bastard son became cantor of the cathedral in Ravenna. In addition to all his other occupations, Johannes Andreae was a prolific author. He wrote, among numerous other things, gloss apparatuses on the *Sext* and the *Clementine constitutions*, and the canonistic schools soon adopted these as the *glossa ordinaria* on those two collections. Beyond that, he also produced a lengthy commentary, which he entitled the *Novella*, on the *Liber extra*, a *Summa* on marriage problems and another on consanguinity, another commentary (also called the *Novella*) on the *Sext*, a set of canonistic *quaestiones*, as well as numerous shorter works. Johannes prospered both from his teaching salary and the considerable fees he earned from practising law. He nevertheless lived an industrious, studious life. When he died of the plague in 1348, he divided his substantial wealth between his numerous offspring and various pious and charitable works.[18]

18. Schulte, QL ii, pp.205–29; Sven Stelling-Michaud, 'Jean d'André', in DDC vi, pp.89–92; Stephan Kuttner, 'Johannes Andreae and his Novella on the decretals', *The Jurist* 24 (1964), 393–408, and 'The Apostillae of Johannes Andreae on the Clementines', in *Études d'histoire du droit canonique dédiées à Gabriel Le Bras*, 2 vols (Paris, 1975), I, pp.195–201 (both of these are reprinted, with supplementary notes, in Kuttner's *Studies in the history of medieval canon law*); Guido Rossi, 'Contributi alla biografia del canonista Giovanni d'Andrea', *Rivista trimestrale di diritto e procedure civile* 11 (1957), 1451–1502.

Johannes de Legnano (Giovanni da Legnano; ca. 1320–83).
Johannes de Legnano was a native of Milan, the son of
Count Giacomo degli Oldrendi. After youthful studies at
Bologna in liberal arts, mathematics, medicine, and
astrology, Johannes finally settled on a career in law. By
1350 he had received the doctorate in civil law and in 1351
he was created a doctor of both laws (*Juris utriusque doctor*)
and was lecturing on the *Sext* and the *Clementine
constitutions.* In 1352 he began teaching the ordinary course
on the *Liber extra,* which was then the central subject of the
canonistic curriculum. Johannes de Legnano was active in a
bewildering variety of roles. He conducted diplomatic
missions for the commune of Bologna, acted as protector
for the Bolognese Franciscans, and was a personal friend
and counsellor to the three popes who reigned between
1362 and his own death in 1383 (Urban V, Gregory XI, and
Urban VI). At the beginning of the great schism in 1378
Johannes warmly defended the legitimacy of the Roman
pope, Urban VI. The pope responded by offering him the
red hat of a cardinal, but Johannes declined that honour.
He had earlier accepted another honour from Emperor
Charles IV (1346–78), who created him a Count Palatine in
1368. Through all of this Johannes continued his legal
teaching and writing. In addition to a *Commentary* on the
Liber extra and a *Lectura* on the *Clementine constitutions,* he
wrote numerous specialized treatises on such topics as
ecclesiastical censures, the canonical hours, the laws
concerning pluralism, and marriage impediments, among
other subjects. Johannes is best known, however, for his
treatises on the laws of war and peace. His *De bello*
(completed in 1360) is a grand synthesis of the legal
problems that arise from warfare, while his *De pace* deals
with the legal consequences of making peace between
warring powers. He may be described as the creator of the
juridical doctrine of war and his work on these topics
stands as a precursor of modern international public law.[19]

19. Schulte, QL ii, pp.257–61; Sven Stelling-Michaud, 'Jean de
Legnano', in DDC vi, pp.111–12; J. P. McCall, 'Chaucer and John of
Legnano', *Speculum* 40 (1965), 484–9.

Johannes Galensis (John of Wales; fl. 1210~15). The life of John of Wales is extremely obscure. We know almost nothing about him save that he came from Wales, studied and taught at Bologna, and compiled *Compilatio secunda* sometime between 1210 and 1215. He also wrote glosses on his own compilation and on *Compilatio tertia.* Tancred was one of John of Wales's students at Bologna and John was familiar with the decretals assembled by Alanus Anglicus, for he drew upon them for his own decretal collection.[20]

Johannes Monachus (Jean LeMoine; ca. 1250–1313). Jean LeMoine was born at Crécy and studied philosophy and theology at Paris before turning to legal studies. He took a doctorate in both civil and canon law at Paris and received appointments as a canon at Amiens and then at Paris. He later went to Rome, where he became an auditor of the Rota, then returned to France in 1288 as dean of Bayeux, a post that he held until 1292. While in Italy Jean had become a confidant of King Charles II of Naples (1285–1309), who was influential in the election of Pope Celestine V (July–December 1294) and Celestine, as an act of gratitude, named Jean a cardinal. Under Pope Boniface VIII (1294–1303) Jean became vice-chancellor of the Roman church and was later sent as a legate to the court of King Philip IV of France (1285–1314) in a vain effort to persuade the king to accept the terms of the bull *Unam sanctam.* Although he was unsuccessful in this mission, Jean founded while at Paris a college that bore his name down to its dissolution in 1793. He died at Avignon in 1313. He is now principally known for his *Apparatus* on the *Liber sextus,* which was taught as the *Glossa ordinaria* on the *Sext* at Paris, but not at Bologna. He also wrote a commentary on the *extravagantes* of Boniface VIII, which later found a place in the *Extravagantes communes.*[21]

Johannes Teutonicus (Johannes Zemeke; ca. 1170–1245). A Saxon by birth, Johannes settled in Bologna, first as a law

---

20. Schulte, QL i, p.189; G. Oesterle, 'Jean de Galles', in DDC vi, pp.105–6; Franz Gillmann, 'Johannes Galensis als Glossator', *Archiv für katholisches Kirchenrecht* 105 (1925), 488–565; Kuttner, *Repertorium,* pp.345–6, 355–6.
21. R. Naz, 'Jean le moine' in DDC v, pp.112–13; Schulte, QL ii, pp.191–3.

student, later as a teacher. By far the most influential of his works was the massive *Glossa ordinaria* on the *Decretum*, a commentary that subsequent teachers and judges relied upon as their basic guide to Gratian's work. John made a collection of the later decretals of Innocent III, but the pope, for reasons that are unclear, refused to promulgate it officially, although the schools accepted it as a useful textbook. Johannes also wrote gloss apparatuses on the decrees of the Fourth Lateran Council, as well as on *Compilatio tertia* and his own decretal collection, which is known as *Compilatio quarta*. He completed all of this between about 1210 and 1218, when he went back to Germany. There he was apparently content to settle into the comfortable life of a beneficed ecclesiastic of middling rank at the cathedral of Halberstadt.[22]

John of Tynemouth (d. ca. 1221). We know nothing about this English canonist's early life, nor has any evidence appeared to show where he received his legal training, although his writings make it clear that he had certainly received a thorough grounding in both civil and canon law. John of Tynemouth first appears as a teacher of canon law, lecturing and participating in disputations at Oxford between 1188 and 1198. Hubert Walter, who had been elected as archbishop of Canterbury a few years earlier, persuaded John to join his household as a legal adviser in 1198. John subsequently appeared as the archbishop's counsel in numerous lawsuits. John received so many prebends and other ecclesiastical appointments as rewards for his services that Gerald of Wales (1146–1223) regarded him as a man of great wealth and claimed that his annual revenues exceeded 100 marks, which, if true, would have left him very comfortably well off. In 1214 John succeeded

22. Schulte, *QL* i, pp.172–5; Sven Stelling-Michaud, 'Jean le Teutonique', in DDC vi, pp.120–2; and especially Stephan Kuttner, 'Johannes Teutonicus' in *Neue deutsche Biographie*, x, 571–73, as well as *Repertorium*, pp.93–9, 357, 370–1. See also Kenneth Pennington, 'The epitaph of Johannes Teutonicus', in *Bulletin of medieval canon law* 13 (1983), 61–2 and 'Johannes Teutonicus and papal legates', in *Archivum historiae pontificiae* 21 (1983), 183–94, now reprinted with additional notes in his *Popes, canonists and texts, 1150–1550* (London, 1993).

Walter Map (ca. 1140–ca. 1208) as archdeacon of Oxford, a position that he held for the remainder of his life.[23]

Laurentius Hispanus (Lawrence of Spain; d. 1248). The early life of Laurentius Hispanus is obscure. He was a Spaniard by origin and first appears in the record as a law student at Bologna early in the thirteenth century. He studied civil law under Azo (ca. 1150–1230), as well as canon law, and in due course became a teacher of canon law at Bologna – Tancred and Bartholomaeus Brixiensis were among his pupils. He also gained a reputation as a brilliant advocate and pleaded numerous cases before the papal courts in Rome. Laurentius returned to Spain as archdeacon of Orense, where he was elected bishop in 1218 or 1219. Laurentius was the author of the gloss apparatus '*Jus naturale*' on the *Decretum* and was very likely the author of the *Glossa Palatina* as well. He also wrote glosses on the first three of the *Compilationes antiquae*. Other canonists adopted many of the interpretations and opinions in Laurentius's glosses, which further testifies to the high regard he enjoyed among his contemporaries.[24]

Oldradus da Ponte (d. after 1337). Oldradus was a native of Lodi, near Milan, and studied law at Bologna in the late 1280s and early 1290s. By 1297 he had become a member of the household of cardinal Peter Colonna, who was bitterly at odds with the then reigning pope, Boniface VIII. Oldradus's connection with the Colonna family meant that it was unlikely that he could prosper in the Roman curia and accordingly he soon found other employment, first as a judge in Bologna, then as a law teacher at the University of Padua, where he became a friend and colleague of Johannes Andreae. Shortly after 1310 Oldradus moved to

23. Christopher R. Cheney, *Hubert Walter* (London, 1967), p.165; Charles E. Lewis, 'Canonists and law clerks in the household of Archbishop Hubert Walter', pp.57–64; Kuttner and Rathbone, 'Anglo-Norman canonists', pp.317–27; A. B. Emden, *Biographical register of the University of Oxford to 1500*, 3 vols (Oxford, 1957–59), iii, p.1923.
24. Schulte, QL i, 190–91; Kuttner, *Repertorium*, pp.76–80, 326, 356; Alfons M. Stickler, 'Laurent d'Espagne', in DDC vi, 361–64 and especially 'Il decretista Laurentius Hispanus', *Studia Gratiana* 9 (1966), 463–549.

Avignon, where he rejoined the household of cardinal Peter Colonna, who, after the death of Boniface VIII, was back in papal favour. Cardinal Peter was, among other things, instrumental in securing an ecclesiastical preferment for Oldradus's son John. At Avignon Oldradus seems to have prospered as a consistorial advocate and formed a friendship with the poet Francesco Petrarcha (1304–74), who described him as the most illustrious jurist of the age. Oldradus is usually said to have died in 1335, but since his name appears in Thomas Fastolf's case reports from 1336 and 1337, the conventional date appears to be erroneous.[25]

Ramón de Penyafort, Saint (Raymond of Penyafort; 1180~85–1275). Born in Catalunya, Ramón de Penyafort appeared in Bologna in 1210, first as a law student, then as a teacher. He returned to Barcelona in 1219 as a canon and provost of the cathedral chapter, positions that he resigned at some point between 1223 and 1229, when he entered the Dominican order. In 1230 Pope Gregory IX summoned Ramón to Rome, appointed him a papal chaplain, and commissioned him to compile an official collection of the decretals that had appeared since the time of Gratian, nearly a century before. The pope gave him broad leeway to edit existing decretals and even encouraged him to fill gaps in the law by composing new decretals, which Gregory promulgated under his own name. The pope formally published this collection, known as the *Decretals of Gregory IX*, or the *Liber extra*, on 5 September 1232. It immediately became a core element in the curriculum of the schools of canon law and remained in force among Roman Catholics until 1917. Ramón returned to Catalunya in 1236 and two years later was elected master-general of the Dominican order, a post that he accepted with considerable reluctance. Once installed in this new position, Ramón proceeded to edit and revise his order's constitutions. He did this so expeditiously and

---

25. Schulte, QL ii, pp.232–3; Friedrich Carl von Savigny, *Die Geschichte des römischen Rechts im Mittelalter*, 7 vols (Heidelberg, 1834–51) vi, pp.55–9; Norman Zacour, *Jews and Saracens in the consilia of Oldradus de Ponte*, Studies and texts, vol. 100 (Toronto, 1990), pp.6–9.

successfully that the order's general congregation approved his revised constitutions in 1239 and they remained in force until 1924. In 1240 Ramón resigned as master-general, returned once more to Spain, where he actively encouraged missionary work among Jews and Muslims. In furtherance of these projects, Ramón asked his Dominican *confrère* Thomas Aquinas to compose a basic handbook of Christian doctrine for prospective converts. The result was Aquinas's *Summa contra Gentiles*. Throughout his career Ramón continued to write. The most widely influential of his works (aside from the *Liber extra*) was his *Summa de penitentia*, together with a separate *Summa de matrimonio*. He also produced a brief *Summa iuris canonici*, a *Summa pastoralis*, glosses on the *Decretum*, a few *consilia*, and numerous minor works. When he died in 1275, the presence at his funeral of the kings of Aragón and Castile testified to the high regard in which contemporaries held this extraordinary figure. He was canonized in 1601.[26]

Ricardus Anglicus (d. 1242). Richard de Mores, a native of Lincolnshire, was the first Englishman who is known to have gone to Bologna to teach and study canon law. After first studying logic at Paris, where he came into contact with a group of Anglo-Norman canonists, Richard appeared in Bologna during the pontificate of Celestine III (1191–98). Richard was lecturing on *Compilatio prima* during the last few years of Celestine's pontificate and his gloss apparatus on that collection survives. Richard in fact wrote prodigiously during the closing years of the twelfth century and the opening years of the thirteenth. In that period he produced a *Summa quaestionum*, a *Summa brevis*, an extremely important set of *Distinctiones decretorum*, a

---

26. Schulte, QL ii, pp.408–13; R. Naz, 'Raymond de Pennafort', in DDC vii, pp.461–4; Giulio Silano, 'Raymond of Peñafort, St', in DMA x, pp.266–7; Fernando Valls-Taberner, San *Ramón de Peñafort* (Madrid, 1953; repr. 1986); Stephan Kuttner, 'Zur Entstehungsgeschichte der Summa de casibus des hl. Raymund von Penyafort', *Zeitschrift der Savigny-Stiftung für Rechtsgeschichte*, kanonistische Abteilung 39 (1953), 419–34, and 'Raymond of Peñafort as editor: The "decretales" and "constitutiones" of Gregory IX', *Bulletin of medieval canon law* 12 (1982), 65–80, both reprinted with additional notes in his *Studies in the history of medieval canon law.*

Casus decretalium, an *Ordo iudiciarius* and a collection of *Generalia* or *Brocardica,* in addition to his *Apparatus decretalium.* All of these, save for his procedural *Ordo,* remain unpublished. In 1202 Richard returned to England. There he became prior of the Austin canons at Dunstable, a position that he held until his death in 1242. While ecclesiastical administration consumed much of his time and energy during his 40 years at Dunstable, Richard nonetheless continued to function as a jurist. He received numerous commissions as a papal judge-delegate, as a visitor sent to investigate conditions in various religious institutions, and as a diplomat – King John (1199–1216), for example, dispatched him to Rome to negotiate with Pope Innocent III (1198–1216).[27]

Rolandus, Master (fl. late 1150s). Virtually nothing is known about the career of this intriguing canonist, save that he was teaching canon law, probably at Bologna, during the latter part of the 1150s. He was thus lecturing on Gratian's *Decretum* shortly after its completion and is one of the earliest teachers who is known to have used it as a textbook. Internal evidence in his commentary on Gratian, known as the *Stroma,* hints that Rolandus may have had some connection with Modena. Further internal evidence in a theological tract entitled the *Sententiae,* also ascribed to Master Rolandus, makes it reasonably clear that he was an admirer, perhaps even a student, of Pierre Abélard (ca. 1079–ca. 1142). Master Rolandus was evidently not popular among other canonists of his generation. Stephen of Tournai dismissed his views as of little account, while Rufinus described him far more unkindly as a pompous, lazy drunk. Despite such unflattering references, it was long thought that Master Rolandus was no less a figure than Rolando Bandinelli, who in 1159 was elected Pope Alexander III. Recent scholarship, however, has made it clear that this identification is untenable.[28]

27. Schulte, QL i, pp.183–5; Stephan Kuttner, 'Ricardus Anglicus', in DDC vii, pp.676–81; Kuttner and Rathbone, 'Anglo-Norman canonists', pp.329–39, 353–8.
28. John T. Noonan, Jr, 'Who was Rolandus?', in *Law, church, and society: Essays in honor of Stephan Kuttner,* eds Kenneth Pennington and Robert Somerville (Philadelphia, 1977), pp.21–48; Rudolf

Rufinus (d. 1192). Born in central Italy, probably near Assisi, Rufinus studied at Bologna, where he was styled *magister* and named a canon of the cathedral. He taught canon law at Bologna. Among his pupils he numbered Stephen of Tournai, who modelled his own work on that of his master. Rufinus became bishop of Assisi in 1179, then archbishop of Sorrento between 1180 and 1186. His *Summa* exercised wide influence among later decretists, particularly those who belonged to the French school.[29]

Sinibaldo dei Fieschi (Pope Innocent IV; d. 1254). Sinibaldo dei Fieschi was born at Genoa late in the twelfth century, son of Count Hugo of Lavania, a member of the Fieschi family. He studied both civil and canon law at Bologna: his teachers in civil law included Azo (ca. 1150–1230), Accursius (1185–1263), and Jacobus Balduinus (d. 1235), while he attended the canon law lectures of Laurentius Hispanus, Vincentius Hispanus, and Johannes Teutonicus, among others. After completing his legal studies Sinibaldo taught for a time at Bologna, then became a canon of the cathedral of Parma and in 1226 went to Rome as an auditor (or judge) of the *Audientia litterarum contradictarum* at the curia. Sinibaldo served as an assistant and counsellor to Cardinal Hugolino of Ostia, who later became Pope Gregory IX (1227–41). Further curial assignments followed: Sinibaldo was named papal legate in the Marches, then bishop of Albegna, and vice-chancellor of the Roman church. Gregory IX created him a cardinal during the first consistory of his pontificate. Not long after Gregory's death, following the brief pontificate of Celestine IV (25 October–10 November 1241), Sinibaldo was elected pope in the cathedral of Anagni and was crowned there as Pope Innocent IV in June 1243. The major political and diplomatic focus of his pontificate centred on the struggle

28. (*Continued*)
   Weigand, 'Magister Rolandus und Papst Alexander III', *Archiv für katholisches Kirchenrecht* 149 (1980), 3–44. Modern scholars no longer consider earlier accounts, such as those by Schulte, QL i, pp.114–18, or Marcel Pacaut, 'Roland Bandinelli' in DDC vii, pp.702–26, reliable.
29. Schulte, QL i, 121–30; Robert L. Benson, 'Rufin' in DDC vii, 779–84; Kuttner, *Repertorium*, pp.131–2.

with the emperor Frederick II (1212–50), whom he excommunicated and deposed at the First Council of Lyon (1245). As pope, Sinibaldo was also much involved with the crusading projects to the Holy Land and worked hard, but unsuccessfully, to persuade Eastern Christians to reunite with the Latin church in the West. He was in addition hopeful that it might prove possible to convert the Tartars to Christianity and to that end sought to establish diplomatic relations with the Mongol Khan. It is astonishing, but apparently true, that in the midst of all of these activities Sinibaldo found the time and energy to write a massive and incisive *Apparatus* on the *Liber extra*. In addition, as pope he promulgated three important decretal collections and established a law school in his Lateran palace. Sinibaldo died at Naples on 7 December 1254 and is buried in the cathedral there.[30]

Stephen of Tournai (1135–1203). Stephen was born at Orléans on 19 March 1135. He received his early education from one Master A. and later studied at Ste-Croix in Orléans. He received his legal education at Bologna, where he studied civil law with Bulgarus (d. 1166) and canon law with Rufinus. Among his classmates were the canonist known as Cardinalis, Heraclius, who later became patriarch of Jerusalem, and the future Pope Urban III (1185–87). About 1155 Stephen became a member of the regular chapter of St Euverte in Orléans and later became the abbot of the chapter. He completed his *Summa* during this period at Orléans. In 1176 he became abbot of Ste-Geneviève in Paris. He also served as a counsellor to King Philip Augustus (1179–1223), who made him a godfather to his eldest son, later King Louis VIII (1223–26). Late in 1191 Stephen became bishop of Tournai, in part at least because the French crown needed a loyalist in that position to support its Flemish policy. Stephen's writings include a collection of 240 letters and approximately 30 sermons (only one of which seems to be published), as well

---

30. Schulte, QL ii, pp.91–4; J. A. Cantini and Charles Lefebvre, 'Sinibalde dei Fieschi', in DDC vii, pp.1029–62; Paravicini-Bagliani, *Cardinali*, i, pp.62, 65–6; Gerda von Puttkamer, *Papst Innocenz* IV (Münster, 1930).

as his *Summa* to Gratian's *Decretum,* which shows evidence of the strong influence of Rufinus.[31]

Tancred (ca. 1185–ca. 1236). Tancred's career was a study in constancy. Born in Bologna, he remained there, save for brief periods when professional commitments took him elsewhere, throughout his life. He studied canon law with Laurentius Hispanus and John of Wales and Roman law with Azo. By 1214 Tancred was styled Master of Decrees (*magister decretorum*) and was teaching canon law at Bologna; he apparently continued to teach, at least intermittently, until his death. In later years Tancred secured a few modest ecclesiastical appointments, which no doubt required him to curtail the time devoted to teaching: he became a canon of the cathedral in his native city and in 1226 was named its archdeacon. In addition, three successive popes – Innocent III, Honorius III, and Gregory IX – commissioned Tancred to undertake diplomatic and judicial missions for the Holy See. Tancred also appeared occasionally as an advocate in the papal consistory and other ecclesiastical courts. In the midst of all his other activities, Tancred found time to produce a steady and consistent stream of writings. The most widely influential (and widely imitated) of his works was his procedural manual, the *Ordo iudiciarius,* which he wrote between 1214 and 1216 in response, as he said in its preface, to repeated requests from friends and colleagues. He had earlier produced gloss apparatuses on the first two of the *Quinque compilationes antiquae* and by the time he commenced work on the *Ordo iudiciarius* Bolognese law teachers had already adopted these as the ordinary glosses on the decretal

31. Schulte, QL i, pp.133–6; Herbert Kalb, *Studien zur Summa Stephans von Tournai: Ein Beitrag zur kanonistischen Wissenschaftsgeschichte des späten 12. Jahrhunderts,* Forschungen zur Rechts- und Kulturgeschichte, vol. 12 (Innsbruck, 1983); Kuttner, *Repertorium,* pp.132–6; Ronald G. G. Knox, 'The problem of academic language in Rufinus and Stephan', in *Proceedings of the sixth international congress of medieval canon law,* eds Stephan Kuttner and Kenneth Pennington, MIC, Subsidia, vol. 7 (Vatican City, 1985), pp.109–23; Stephan Kuttner, 'Les débuts de l'école canoniste française', *Studia et documenta historiae et iuris* 4 (1938), 193–204 (reprinted in his *Gratian and the schools of Law*) and *Repertorium,* pp.133–6; G. Lepointe, 'Étienne de Tournai', in DDC v, pp.487–92.

collections. In 1220 he revised his earlier gloss collections and composed a further apparatus on *Compilatio tertia*; Bolognese law teachers adopted that apparatus, too, as the ordinary gloss that they taught in the schools. Bernard of Parma subsequently incorporated a substantial part of Tancred's glosses into the ordinary gloss on the *Liber extra*, thereby assuring that Tancred's name and his ideas would retain a central place in canonistic doctrine throughout the Middle Ages. In addition Tancred produced a *Summa de sponsalibus et matrimonio*, and here again later authors drew freely upon his work for their own purposes. Ramón de Penyafort's *Summa de matrimonio*, to name just one notable example, reproduced verbatim large portions of Tancred's *Summa*.[32]

Vincentius Hispanus (d. 1248). The date and place of Vincentius's birth are unknown, although he was certainly a native of the Iberian peninsula. He studied and taught canon law at Bologna. Vincent wrote glosses on the *Decretum* (1210~12), gloss apparatuses to *Compilatio prima* and *Compilatio tertia*, as well as glosses on the constitutions of the Fourth Lateran Council and a gloss apparatus to the *Liber extra*. He refers in his work to several places in Portugal (Braga, Coimbra, and Lisbon) where he held ecclesiastical positions. In 1226 he was chancellor to the Portuguese king Sancho II (1223–45). Vincentius was elected bishop of Idanha-Guarda in 1229, a post that he held until his death in 1248.[33]

William Durand ('The Speculator'; 1231–96). Born at Puimisson on the Mediterranean coast near Béziers, William Durant the elder became the most distinguished French canonist of his generation. He studied canon law at Bologna under Bernard of Parma and subsequently taught at Bologna and at Modena. He soon found a position at the papal curia, which apparently suited him since he spent

32. Schulte, QL i, pp.199–205; L. Chevailler, 'Tancredus', in DDC vii, pp.1146–65; Kuttner, *Repertorium*, pp.327–8, 346, 358–9.
33. Schulte, QL i, pp.191–3; R. Chabanne, 'Vincent d'Espagne', in DDC vii, pp.1507–8; Gaines Post, ' "Blessed lady Spain" – Vincentius Hispanus and Spanish national imperialism in the thirteenth century', *Speculum* 29 (1954), 198–209; Kuttner, *Repertorium*, pp.326–7, 356–7, 370, 374.

most of the rest of his life in papal service. Early in his curial career, William became a protégé of Hostiensis, whose learning and solicitude impressed him so greatly that he continued throughout his career to refer to Hostiensis as 'my lord'. In 1274 William Durant accompanied Cardinal Simon (later Pope Martin IV) to the Second Council of Lyon and in 1280 Pope Nicholas III (1277–80) named him rector of the patrimony of St Peter. Martin IV (1281–85) appointed him papal vicar, a post that involved responsibility for extensive military operations in 1281–82. In 1284 he climaxed his administrative career as papal rector of the Romagna. He was named bishop of Mende in 1286, but remained in Rome for the next five years and did not actually occupy his see until 1291. In 1296 he returned to Rome and died there on 1 November of that year. His most important contribution to canonistic literature was a treatise entitled the *Speculum iudiciale*, from which he came to be known as 'The Speculator'. The *Speculum iudiciale* was a comprehensive, almost encyclopedic, treatment of romano-canonical procedural law and remained a standard reference work for centuries. William completed his *Speculum* ca. 1271 and later revised it ca. 1287.[34]

William Durand, Junior (ca. 1266–1330). The younger William Durant, like his uncle 'The Speculator', was born at Puimisson. Although no evidence survives to show where he received his legal education, the younger Durant, like his uncle, became a jurist of distinction. Family connections, especially the patronage of the elder William Durant, secured a series of ecclesiastical appointments for the younger Durant. When 'The Speculator' died, Pope Boniface VIII appointed the younger William Durant to succeed his uncle as bishop of Mende. Amid the political turbulence that surrounded the struggle between Boniface VII and King Philip IV, William managed the not inconsiderable feat of keeping on good terms with, and receiving favours from, both sides. His experiences during

---

34. Schulte, QL ii, pp.144–56; L. Falletti, 'Guillaume Durant', in DDC v, pp.1014–75; Constantin Fasolt, *Council and hierarchy: The political thought of William Durant the younger*, Cambridge studies in medieval life and thought, 4th ser., vol. 16 (Cambridge, 1991), pp.64–72.

this conflict convinced William that the church was in pressing need of structural reform. Distressed by the excesses of papal centralization, William elaborated a scheme to limit papal authority by convening regular general councils that would place a check on papal absolutism. After Pope Clement V (1305–14) summoned a general council to meet at Vienne, William spelled out his thoughts on the relationship between pope and council in his *Tractatus maior* (often styled the *Tractatus de modo concilii generalis celebrandi*, although this title is a later concoction). Following the Council of Vienne (1311–12), at which his reform proposals failed to gain a following, the younger Durant sat as a member of the Parlement de Paris and acted as a counsellor to successive kings of France. He was also entrusted with a number of important diplomatic missions. Pope John XXII (1316–34) commissioned him to undertake a mission to Egypt with a view to preparing the way for a future crusade expedition, a matter in which William had a long-standing interest. As he was returning from this mission William Durant, Jr, died on the island of Cyprus in July 1330.[35]

---

35. Fasolt, *Council and hierarchy*, pp.73–100 and *passim*; R. Naz, 'Guillaume Durand le jeune', in DDC v, pp.1013–14.

SELECT BIBLIOGRAPHY

. . .

INTRODUCTION

A single individual, Stephan Kuttner, has towered over the study of medieval canon law in the twentieth century. The *Repertorium der Kanonistik (1140–1234)*, Studi e testi, vol. 71 (Vatican City, 1937), Kuttner's pathbreaking guide to the manuscript sources, revolutionized this field of scholarship. The *Repertorium* not only demonstrated in exquisite detail how much canonistic material survived from the period between Gratian and Gregory IX's decretals, but also showed how little of this evidence had been published and how much needed to be done to make it accessible. The outbreak of World War II, just two years after the appearance of the *Repertorium*, temporarily interrupted the programme of research and scholarship that Kuttner had outlined. Forced into exile himself, Kuttner and his family relocated to Washington, D.C., where the Catholic University of America created a post for him in its canon law faculty.

Ten years after the end of the war, Kuttner organized an Institute of Research and Study in Medieval Canon Law with its headquarters at Washington and with himself as president. The Institute served as an instrument to coordinate the work of the international team of scholars that Kuttner had begun organizing to pursue his plan for a *Monumenta iuris canonici* (usually cited as MIC). The *Monumenta*, according to Kuttner's plan, would publish reliable critical editions of medieval canonistic texts and would also include modern studies of those texts. The

231

programme of the *Monumenta* called for three separate but related series of publications. The *Corpus collectionum* would publish editions of the medieval collections of canonical texts, the *Corpus glossatorum* would bring the glosses and other commentaries on those texts into print, while the *Subsidia* series would present scholarly studies and monographs on medieval canonical topics.

Realization of this ambitious project began in 1965 with the appearance of the first volume of the *Subsidia* and has continued ever since. The work of the Institute and the progress of the *Monumenta* are chronicled in the annual *Bulletin of Medieval Canon Law,* whose first ten issues appeared in the pages of *Traditio* between 1955 and 1970. Since 1970 the *Bulletin* (cited as BMCL) has appeared as an independent annual publication. Kuttner's *Repertorium,* together with the *Bulletin* and the *Monumenta,* are the indispensable foundations of current scholarship in this field.

The Institute and its publications have moved several times over the years since 1955. In 1964, when Kuttner accepted a chair at Yale, the Institute migrated with him from Washington to New Haven. Again in 1970, when Kuttner became director of the Robbins Collection at Boalt Hall, the University of California's law school in Berkeley, the Institute followed him there. In 1992 Kuttner stepped down as president of the Institute, which has since moved once more, this time to Munich, under the presidency of Peter Landau.

Although Stephan Kuttner has dominated this whole scholarly enterprise, and remains a forceful presence in it to this day, he was by no means alone. Fulfilment of his grand design required him to persuade dozens, and ultimately hundreds, of other scholars to pursue his twin goals of making the surviving evidence available and of producing scholarly studies of that evidence. Kuttner's success in realizing this goal has been quite astonishing. His Institute and its scholarly programme have attracted remarkable numbers of able young medievalists over the years. Many of them have come away from the experience convinced that the study of medieval canon law is so challenging and so vital to understanding medieval society and its history that they have made this work the central focus of their lives and their careers.

An international team of these scholars, led by Kenneth Pennington and Wilfried Hartmann, is now well advanced towards producing a multi-volume *History of medieval canon law* that aims to synthesize the scholarship in this field over the past two generations and point the way to further research. Until that project reaches fruition, however, students of the subject will continue to rely upon a battery of older publications for guidance.

For the period prior to Gratian, the *Histoire des collections canoniques en Occident depuis les fausses décrétales jusqu'au Décret de Gratien*, 2 vols (Paris, 1931–32; repr. Aalen, 1972) by Paul Fournier and Gabriel Le Bras remains fundamental. For the period after Gratian the standard reference work is Johann Friedrich von Schulte, *Geschichte der Quellen und Literatur des canonischen Rechts*, 3 vols (Stuttgart, 1875–89; repr. Graz, 1956). More than a century of vigorous research and publication has rendered a good many pages of Schulte's work obsolete. Serious scholars need to supplement what they find in Schulte's book by consulting more modern works. Among these the first volume of the *Handbuch der Quellen und Literatur der neueren Privatrechtsgeschichte*, edited by Helmut Coing (Munich, 1973) is particularly useful. The *Dictionnaire de droit canonique*, edited by R. Naz, 7 vols (Paris, 1935–65; usually cited as DDC) is an encyclopedia of modern, as well as medieval, canon law. While the quality of its articles varies considerably, it is a reference work of great value to anyone interested in this field. English-speaking students will often find a brief book by J. A. Clarence Smith, entitled *Medieval law teachers and writers, civilian and canonists* (Ottawa, 1975), very helpful as well.

Publication of the records of medieval church courts has lagged behind publication of the canonical collections and the commentaries of academic lawyers. Kuttner did not deal with record material in the *Repertorium* and until recently no guide to this body of evidence has been available. The Working Group on Church Court Records is attempting to fill in that gap and the first of its Reports has now appeared under the title *The records of the medieval ecclesiastical courts*, Part I: the Continent, edited by Charles Donahue, Jr, (Berlin, 1989). A companion volume on

English church court records has been promised, but has not yet appeared.

Among scholarly journals, in addition to BMCL, the annual volumes of the *kanonistische Abteilung* of the *Zeitschrift der Savigny-Stiftung für Rechtsgeschichte* regularly carry important articles, studies, and current bibliographical information. The bibliographies at the end of each volume of BMCL show the range of other journals that publish studies of the history of medieval canon law.

. . .

CHAPTER 1: LAW IN THE EARLY CHRISTIAN CHURCH

For an introduction to the canon law of the early church Jean Gaudemet, *L'église dans l'empire romain (IVe–Ve siècles)*, 2nd edn (Paris, 1989), provides a useful and reliable survey, while his *Sources du droit de l'église en Occident du IIe au VIIe siècles* (Paris, 1985) presents a good introduction to the source material for the period. For the law of the Christian church before Constantine, Charles Munier, *L'église dans l'empire romain (IIe–IIIe siècles): Église et cité* (Paris, 1979) is also highly recommended. Both the Gaudemet and the Munier volumes on the church in the Roman Empire form part of the series *Histoire du droit et des institutions de l'église en Occident.* Canon law in Christianity's first five centuries has not yet found its English-language historian. Although general histories of the early church usually give the topic some passing attention, writers on patristic literature are apt to be more informative. Johannes Quasten's *Patrology*, 4 vols (Westminster, MD, 1950–96) is particularly useful.

. . .

CHAPTER 2: CANON LAW IN THE EARLY MIDDLE AGES

The best current survey of canon law in the early medieval period is Antonio García y García, *Historia del derecho canonico*, vol. 1: *El primer milenio* (Salamanca, 1967). P. D. King's account of Spain under Germanic rule, *Law and society in the Visigothic kingdom*, Cambridge studies in medieval life and thought, 3rd ser., vol. 5 (Cambridge, 1972) also has much to say about the role of canon law in this period. A notable short introduction to the canonistic collections prior to Gratian is Gérard Fransen, *Collections canoniques* (Turnhout, 1973) in the series *Typologie des sources du moyen âge occidental,* fasc. 10. The standard guide to the penitential literature of the early Middle Ages is Cyrille Vogel and Allen J. Frantzen, *Les 'libri paenitentiales',* 2 pts (Turnhout, 1978–85) in the same series, fasc. 27. On the Pseudo-Isidorian forgeries the reigning authority is Horst Fuhrmann, *Einfluß und Verbreitung der pseudoisidorischen Fälschungen, von ihrem Auftractung bis in die neuere Zeit,* 3 vols, Monumenta Germaniae Historica, Schriften, vol. 24 (Stuttgart, 1972–74).

Other useful works for this period include: Rosamund McKitterick, *The Frankish church and the Carolingian reforms, 789–895* (London, 1977); Karl F. Morrison, *The two kingdoms: Ecclesiology in Carolingian political thought* (Princeton, 1964); Hubert Mordek, *Kirchenrecht und Reform in Frankreich: Die Collectio Vetus Gallica, die älteste systematische Kanonessamlung des fränkischen Gallien* (Berlin, 1975); Gerd Tellenbach, *Church, state and Christian society at the time of the investiture contest,* trans. R. F. Bennett (Oxford, 1959); and Uta-Renate Blumenthal, *The investiture controversy: Church and monarchy from the ninth to the twelfth century* (Philadelphia, 1988). Walter Ullmann, *The growth of papal government in the Middle Ages: A study in the ideological relation of clerical to lay power,* 2nd edn (London, 1962) is stimulating but controversial. So, too, is Carl Erdmann, *The origin of the idea of crusade,* ed. and trans. Marshall W. Baldwin and Walter Goffart (Princeton, 1977).

. . .

CHAPTER 3: GRATIAN AND THE SCHOOLS OF LAW IN THE CLASSICAL PERIOD (1140–1375)

Stephan Kuttner, *Harmony from dissonance: An interpretation of medieval canon law* (Latrobe, PA, 1960) furnishes an attractive introduction to Gratian's work. This short book – it was originally a lecture – has been reprinted with corrections in Kuttner's *History of ideas and doctrines of canon law in the Middle Ages* (London, 1992), pp.1–16. Kuttner has also surveyed current scholarship on Gratian's work in 'Research on Gratian: Acta and agenda', in *Proceedings of the seventh international congress of medieval canon law,* Monumenta iuris canonici, Subsidia, vol. 8 (Vatican City,

1988), reprinted with original pagination in his *Studies in the history of medieval canon law* (London, 1990). As for Gratian himself, the article 'Gratian slept here: The changing identity of the father of the systematic study of canon law', *Traditio* 35 (1979), 145–72, by John T. Noonan, Jr, is especially important. Noonan criticizes and corrects numerous legends and conjectures about Master Gratian that figure in the earlier literature. Stanley Chodorow, *Christian political theory and church politics in the mid-twelfth century: The ecclesiology of Gratian's Decretum*, Publications of the Center for Medieval and Renaissance Studies, UCLA, vol. 5 (Berkeley and Los Angeles, 1972) presents a useful analysis of an important aspect of Gratian's thought, although not all of his conclusions have found general acceptance. For an easily accessible sample both of Gratian's work itself and of the Ordinary Gloss see *The treatise on laws (Decretum DD. 1–20)*, trans. Augustine Thompson and James Gordley, Studies in medieval and early modern canon law, vol. 2 (Washington, D.C., 1993). For scholarly study of Gratian's text the recently-published concordance is indispensable: Timothy Reuter and Gabriel Silagi, *Wortkonkordanz zum Decretum Gratiani*, 5 vols, Monumenta Germaniae Historica, Hilfsmittel, vol. 10, pts 1–5 (Munich, 1990).

The best short introduction to decretals and decretal literature is Gérard Fransen, *Décrétales et les collections de décrétales* (Turnhout, 1972), in *Typologie des sources du moyen âge occidental*, fasc. 2. Charles Duggan, *Twelfth-century decretal collections and their importance in English history*, University of London historical studies, vol. 12 (London, 1963) presents a more detailed analysis of the extremely important English collections. I. S. Robinson, *The papacy, 1073–1198: Continuity and innovation*, Cambridge medieval textbooks (Cambridge, 1990) provides a particularly well-informed survey of the context within which canon law developed during the period between the investiture controversy and the beginning of Innocent III's pontificate.

. . .

CHAPTER 4: CANON LAW AND PRIVATE LIFE

Canon law's impact on medieval marriage and family has attracted the attention of numerous scholars in recent years. Two worthwhile guides to this literature are Michael M. Sheehan and Jacqueline Murray, *Domestic society in medieval Europe: A select bibliography* (Toronto, 1990) and Joyce E. Salisbury, *Medieval sexuality: A research guide* (New York and London, 1990).

Important studies of this aspect of medieval canon law include: Richard H. Helmholz, *Marriage litigation in medieval England*, Cambridge studies in English legal history (Cambridge, 1974); Charles Donahue, Jr, 'The case of the man who fell into the Tiber: The Roman law of marriage at the time of the glossators', *American journal of legal history* 22 (1978), 1–53; 'The canon law on the formation of marriage and social practice in the later middle ages', *Journal of family history* 8 (1983), 144–58; and 'What causes fundamental legal ideas? Marital property in England and France in the thirteenth century', *Michigan law review* 78 (1979), 59–88. Donahue has also edited, in collaboration with Norma Adams, a large collection of canonical court records from medieval England: *Select cases from the ecclesiastical courts of the province of Canterbury, c. 1200–1301*, Selden Society publications, vol. 95 (London, 1981). Other major studies of canon law and domestic relations include several by Michael M. Sheehan, 'The formation and stability of marriage in fourteenth-century England: Evidence of an Ely register', *Mediaeval studies* 33 (1971), 228–63; 'Choice of marriage partner in the Middle Ages: Development and mode of application of a theory of marriage', *Studies in medieval and renaissance history*, n.s. 1 (1978), 3–33; 'The influence of canon law on the property rights of married women in England', *Mediaeval studies* 25 (1963), 109–24; and 'Marriage theory and practice in the conciliar legislation and diocesan statutes of medieval England', *Mediaeval studies* 40 (1978), 408–60. John T. Noonan, Jr, has also written extensively on these matters: see especially *Contraception: A history of its treatment by the Catholic theologians and canonists* (Cambridge, MA, 1965), 'Marital affection in the canonists', *Studia Gratiana* 12 (1967), 479–509, and 'Power to choose', *Viator* 4 (1973), 419–34. Not to be overlooked are James A. Brundage, *Law, sex, and Christian society in medieval Europe* (Chicago, 1987) and *Sex, law and marriage in the Middle Ages* (London, 1993).

The economic theories and practices of the canonists

have also attracted considerable attention. See especially: John T. Gilchrist, *The church and economic activity in the Middle Ages* (New York, 1969); Brian Tierney, *Medieval poor law: A sketch of canonical theory and its application in England* (Berkeley and Los Angeles, 1956); John T. Noonan, Jr, *The scholastic analysis of usury* (Cambridge, MA, 1957); and John W. Baldwin, *Medieval theories of the just price: Romanists, canonists and theologians in the twelfth and thirteenth centuries*, Transactions of the American Philosophical Society, new ser., vol. 49, pt 4 (Philadelphia, 1959). John F. McGovern showed in several studies the critical influence of canon law in the formation of capitalist ideas and values in the Middle Ages; see especially 'The rise of new economic attitudes in canon and civil law, A.D. 1200–1550', *The Jurist* 32 (1972), 39–50 and 'Private property and individual rights in the commentaries of the jurists, A.D. 1200–1550', in *In iure veritas: Studies in canon law in memory of Schafer Williams*, eds Steven B. Bowman and Blanche E. Cody (Cincinnati, 1991), pp.131–58. A particularly important study for the impact of the canonists on testamentary practices in English common law is Michael M. Sheehan, *The will in medieval England: From the conversion of the Anglo-Saxons to the end of the thirteenth century*, Studies and texts, vol. 6 (Toronto, 1963).

. . .

CHAPTER 5: CANON LAW AND PUBLIC LIFE

Several chapters in the *Cambridge history of medieval political thought, c. 350–c. 1450*, ed. by J. H. Burns (Cambridge, 1988) provide helpful introductions to the influence of Roman and canon law on medieval government and politics. Other important studies that deal with these themes include two by Kenneth Pennington, *Pope and bishops: The papal monarchy in the twelfth and thirteenth centuries* (Philadelphia, 1984) and *The prince and the law, 1200–1600: Sovereignty and rights in western legal tradition* (Berkeley and Los Angeles, 1993). Among the older studies of these topics four merit special mention: Gaines Post, *Studies in medieval legal thought: Public law and the state, 1100–1322* (Princeton, 1964); Ernst H. Kantorowicz, *The king's two bodies: A study in mediaeval political theology* (Princeton, 1957; repr. 1970); Brian Tierney, *Foundations of the conciliar theory* (Cambridge, 1955; repr. 1968) and

Religion, law, and the growth of constitutional thought (Cambridge, 1982).

On canonical contributions to the laws of war and international relations see especially James A. Brundage, *Medieval canon law and the crusader* (Madison and Milwaukee, 1969); Maurice Keen, *The law of war in the late Middle Ages* (London, 1965); Frederick H. Russell, *The just war in the Middle Ages*, Cambridge studies in medieval life and thought, 3rd ser., vol. 8 (Cambridge, 1975); and Donald E. Queller, *The office of ambassador in the Middle Ages* (Princeton, 1967).

. . .

CHAPTER 6: CANONICAL COURTS AND PROCEDURE

In addition to the reports of the Working Group on Church Court Records mentioned earlier, Colin R. Chapman, *Ecclesiastical courts, their officials and their records* (Dursley, 1992) provides a brief introduction to the English Courts Christian. No short survey exists for the ecclesiastical courts of Continental Europe, although fine monographs are available for a few regions. Particularly notable are Paul Fournier's classic study of French bishops' officials, *Les officialités au moyen âge: Étude sur l'organisation, la compétence et la procédure des tribunaux ecclésiastiques ordinaires en France de 1180 à 1328* (Paris, 1880; repr. Aalen, 1984), and the more recent study by Anne Lefebvre-Teillard of the same courts during the early sixteenth century, *Les officialité à la veille du Concile de Trente*, Bibliothèque d'histoire du droit et droit romain, vol. 19 (Paris, 1973). Also of interest (at least to those who read Flemish) is a detailed study of the consistory court of Tournai: Monique Vleeschouwers-Van Melkebeek, *De officialiteit van Doornik: Oorsprong en vroege ontwikkeling (1192–1300)*, Verhandelingen van de Koninklije Academie voor Wettehschappen, Letteren en Schone Kunsten van België. Klasse der Letteren, vol. 47, no 17 (Brussels, 1985). Robert Brentano's *Two churches: England and Italy in the thirteenth century* (Princeton, 1968; revised repr. Berkeley and Los Angeles, 1988) presents an enlightening comparative study of church organization and structure in the two regions.

The leading collection of procedural sources was edited by Ludwig Wahrmund, *Quellen zur Geschichte des römisch-kanonischen Prozesses im Mittelalter,* 5 vols (Innsbruck, 1905–31; repr. Aalen, 1962). More recently Linda Fowler-Magerl has studied the development of procedural literature in *Ordo iudiciorum vel ordo iudiciarius: Begriff und Literaturgattung,* Sonderheft 19 of *Ius commune* (Frankfurt a/M, 1984). For a brief general survey of canonical procedures see Charles Lefebvre's article 'Procédure', in the *Dictionnaire de droit canonique* 7:281–309. On procedure in marriage cases see also Helmholz, *Marriage litigation,* pp.112–40. Richard M. Fraher has written several important studies of the history of canonical criminal procedure; see especially ' "Ut nullus describatur reus prius quam convincatur": Presumption of innocence in medieval canon law?' in *Proceedings of the sixth international congress of medieval canon law,* eds Stephan Kuttner and Kenneth Pennington, Monumenta iuris canonici, Subsidia, vol. 7 (Vatican City, 1985), pp.493–506; 'The theoretical justification for the new criminal law of the high Middle Ages: "Rei publicae interest, ne crimina remaneant impunita" ', *University of Illinois law review* (1984), 577–95; 'Conviction according to conscience: The medieval jurists' debate concerning judicial discretion and the law of proof', *Law and history review* 7 (1989) 23–88; and 'Preventing crime in the high Middle Ages: The medieval lawyers' search for deterrence', in *Popes, teachers, and canon law in the Middle Ages,* eds James R. Sweeney and Stanley Chodorow (Ithaca, NY, 1989), pp.212–33. For a rather different assessment of the evidence see Kenneth Pennington, *The prince and the law, 1200–1600: Sovereignty and rights in the Western legal tradition* (Berkeley and Los Angeles, 1993), chs 4 and 5. An older but still useful treatment of criminal procedure is Paul Hinschius, *System des katholischen Kirchenrechts mit besonderer Rücksicht auf Deutschland,* 6 vols (Berlin, 1869–97), v, pp.232–300, 337–60, 425–92.

Jane E. Sayers, *Papal judges-delegate in the province of Canterbury, 1198–1254: A study in ecclesiastical jurisdiction and administration,* Oxford historical monographs (Oxford, 1971) provides a lucid summary of the civil procedure in actions before judges-delegate. On the history of summary procedure see Charles Lefebvre, 'Les origines romaines de la procédure sommaire aux XIIe et XIIIe siècles', *Ephemerides iuris canonici* 12 (1956), 149–97.

Inquisitorial procedure has attracted greater interest than other varieties of canonical process. Many accounts are informed (and not a few are deformed) by sectarian interests or sensationalism, sometimes by both. Wilfried Trusen, 'Der inquisitionsprozeß: Seine historischen Grundlagen und frühen Formen', *Zeitschrift der Savigny-Stiftung für Rechtsgeschichte*, kanonistische Abteilung 74 (1988), 168–230, provides a recent and sensible account of the history and background of the procedure. *La parola all'accusato*, eds Jean-Claude Maire Vigueur and Agostino Paravicini Bagliani (Palermo, 1991) presents a collection of papers that deal with the use of the procedure, primarily in heresy cases.

On canonical punishments see: Elisabeth Vodola, *Excommunication in the Middle Ages* (Berkeley and Los Angeles, 1986); Peter Landau, *Die Entstehung des kanonischen Infamiebegriffs von Gratian bis zur Glossa ordinaria*, Forschungen zur kirchlichen Rechtsgeschichte und zum Kirchenrecht, no 5 (Cologne, 1966); and F. Donald Logan, *Excommunication and the secular arm in medieval England*, Studies and texts, vol. 15 (Toronto, 1968).

. . .

CHAPTER 7: CANONICAL JURISPRUDENCE

The best treatment of this topic is Gabriel Le Bras, Charles Lefebvre, and Jacqueline Rambaud, *L'âge classique, 1140–1378: Sources et théorie du droit*, Histoire du droit et des institutions de l'église en Occident, vol. 7 (Paris, 1965). Also helpful is Philippe Godding, *La jurisprudence*, Typologie des sources du moyen âge occidental, fasc. 6 (Turnhout, 1973).

. . .

CHAPTER 8: CANON LAW AND WESTERN SOCIETIES

Two older treatments of the place of the two learned laws in the society and culture of the high and later Middle Ages remain extremely valuable. They are Woldemar Engelmann, *Die Wiedergeburt der Rechtskultur in Italien durch die wissenschaftliche Lehre: Eine Darlegung der Entfaltung des gemeinen italienischen Rechts und seiner Justizkultur im Mittelalter* (Leipzig, 1938), and Paul Koschaker, *Europa und das römische Recht* (Munich, 1947). Also helpful on these themes are Manlio Bellomo, *Società ed istituzioni in Italia tra medioevo ed età moderna* (Catania, 1977) and *Storia del diritto comune* (Rome, 1989), as well as many of the conference papers collected in *Legge, giudici, giuristi* (Milan, 1982). Harold Berman's *Law and revolution: The formation of the Western legal tradition* (Cambridge, MA, 1983) stresses the key role that the two learned laws, and canon law in particular, have played in moulding the subsequent development of law and legal culture in the Western world. Berman's arguments are controversial. They do provide a useful corrective to the tendency, especially in the English-speaking world, to exaggerate the originality and importance of English common law in the history of Western legal systems. Still many scholars feel that Berman's interpretation is itself rather exaggerated.

John T. Noonan, Jr, *Power to dissolve: Lawyers and marriages in the courts of the Roman Curia* (Cambridge, MA, 1972) illustrates from modern case records the manifold ways in which medieval marriage law continued to inform Rotal jurisprudence even after the Council of Trent. The continuity between pre-Reformation and post-Reformation canon law in England was also quite remarkable, as Richard H. Helmholz has demonstrated in *Roman canon law in Reformation England* (Cambridge, 1990).

MAP

Western Europe in the Thirteenth Century

Index

Table of Scriptural Citations

Table of Legal Citations

Corpus iuris canonici

Decretum Gratiani
  D. 1 pr., 154, 157
  D. 1 c. 1, 154, 157
  D. 1 c. 5, 158
  D. 3 c. 3, 160
  D. 3 d.p.c. 3, 162
  D. 4 d.p.c. 3, 155
  D. 4 d.a.c. 4, 158
  D. 4 c. 4, 158
  D. 8 c. 7, 158, 159
  D. 11, 158
  D. 12, 158
  D. 19 c.1, 169
  D. 50 c. 25, 155
  D. 51 c. 1-3, 83
  D. 53 c. 1, 83
  D. 61 d.a.c. 9, 173
  C. 1 *per totum*, 94
  C. 1 q. 1 c. 41, 173
  C. 1 q. 7 d.a.c. 6, 161

Decretum Gratiani
  C. 1 q. 7 c. 7, 173
  C. 2 *per totum*, 94
  C. 2 q. 1 d.a.c. 15, 145
  C. 2 q. 2 d.p.c. 17, 145
  C. 2 q. 6 c. 40, 149
  C. 2 q. 7 d.p.c. 52, 47
  C. 3 q. 3 d.p.c. 3, 65
  C. 3 q. 6 c. 10, 149
  C. 11 q. 3 c. 71, 67
  C. 12 q. 2 c. 23, 26-31, 85
  C. 16 q. 1 c. 61, 47
  C. 16 q. 3 d.p.c. 15, 158
  C. 16 q. 7 c. 4, 170
  C. 22 q. 5 c. 11, 168
  C. 23 q. 1 c. 5, 69
  C. 25 q. 1 d.p.c. 16, 155, 168
  C. 25 q. 2 c. 16, 160
  C. 31 q. 2 d.p.c. 4, 166
  D. 3 de cons. c. 1, 83

Liber Extra
  1.2.2, 162
  1.2.8, 101-2
  1.2.13, 162
  1.3.21, 103
  1.4.8, 168
  1.4.11, 157, 158
  1.6.2, 172
  1.36.11, 171
  1.29.37, 169
  2.20.37, 132
  2.22.10, 133
  2.22.15, 133

Liber Extra
  2.24.26, 173
  2.25.1, 144
  2.26.15, 125
  3.28. *per totum* 90
  3.30.10, 170
  3.34.8, 163-4
  3.34.9, 69
  3.44.2, 83
  3.50.5, 92
  4.1.15, 166
  4.1.21, 167
  4.1.29, 167

Corpus iuris civilis

Codex Theodosianus

Beaumanoir

Bracton

Glanvill

United States Reports